RUSSIA UNDER KHRUSHCHEV

RUSSIA UNDER KHRUSHCHEV

BY ALEXANDER WERTH

> Comrades, we have entered a
> decisive decade—decisive socially,
> economically, internationally
> and—cosmically.
>
> N. S. KHRUSHCHEV

GREENWOOD PRESS, PUBLISHERS
WESTPORT, CONNECTICUT

.Library of Congress Cataloging in Publication Data

Werth, Alexander, 1901-
    Russia under Khrushchev.

    Reprint of the ed. published by Hill and Wang,
New York.
    Includes index.
    1. Russia--Politics and government--1953-
2. Russia--Foreign relations--1953-   3. Khrush-
chev, Nikita Sergeevich, 1894-   I. Title.
[DK274.W44 1975]   320.9'47'085   75-2704
ISBN 0-8371-8028-7

**Sections of the final chapter appeared in *The Nation*, and the author
would like to thank that magazine for permission to use them in this
volume.**

Originally published in 1962 by Hill and Wang, New York

Reprinted with the permission of Farrar, Straus & Giroux, Inc.

Reprinted in 1975 by Greenwood Press,
a division of Williamhouse-Regency Inc.

Library of Congress Catalog Card Number 75-2704

ISBN 0-8371-8028-7

Printed in the United States of America

CONTENTS

AUTHOR'S NOTE

This book concerns what I call the Khrushchev *phase,* rather than the Khrushchev *epoch.* An "epoch" suggests something complete, with clearly-defined limits and contours, and sharply-marked characteristics. A "phase," especially one still in progress, is something much more fluid. During these years, dominated by Khrushchev, the most changeable, most empirical and sometimes most unpredictable of Soviet leaders, Russia continues to be in a state of flux and transition.

The whole world today is torn between two fundamental forces: conservative or *status-quo* forces and more-or-less violently revolutionary forces. The Soviet Union, though a "have," and no longer a "have-not," nation, would, as a matter of principle, like to be on the side of "revolution." But would not her people, in reality, prefer genuine "peaceful coexistence" with America—if America were willing? The transition from the excessive Russion optimism surrounding Khrushchev's visit to the USA in 1959 to the disillusionment and truculence of 1960–61, and the accompanying succession of varying blends of the two fundamental Russian foreign policies (one loosely called "internationalist" or "Trotskyite," and the other "isolationist" or "Stalinite") are among the main themes of this book; another is "Soviet Man" in his numerous aspects and manifestations. Some deny his very existence; I do not agree with this. In this book, notably on pp. 133-36, I try to show why I don't.

Grateful acknowledgement is made here to *The Scotsman, The New Statesman* and *The Nation* (New York), in whose columns some of the material of this book was first used.

A.W.

RUSSIA
UNDER
KHRUSHCHEV

Chapter 1

THAT MAN KHRUSHCHEV

IT HAS OFTEN been said that the Russians are monarchists at heart, in the sense that they are used, throughout their history, to seeing one boss at the top, ostensibly taking care of everything—first the Tsars, then Lenin, then Stalin and then, after a brief confused interval, Khrushchev. When there is no real boss—as during the first years of the seventeenth century—then it's called *smutnoie vremia,* the "troubled times" or it's branded *Kerenshchina,* as it was during the eight months between the first and second 1917 revolutions. For Kerensky, who more or less ran the weak and disorganized Provisional Government of March-November, 1917, was only a bogus boss.

But Khrushchev is an entirely different boss from what the Russians had ever known before. Even the most disreputable of Tsars lived somewhere far, far above the people, wrapped in a mystical kind of cloud; Lenin, though kindly, approachable and profoundly human in present-day Lenin folklore, kept his distances, while Stalin became more and more the "genius," the "superman," hidden, except for rare appearances in the Red Square, from the eyes of the people; the great man, the oracle, who seldom spoke. But every word he spoke had been carefully weighed in advance, and it weighed a ton. He may have been hated by many, and dreaded by most, but he was respected by all; he was essentially the great State Builder, in the lineage of Ivan the Terrible and Peter the Great—a man with a vast Design, but to whom human life and human suffering were of no great importance. Occasionally, especially during meetings with for-

11

eign statesmen, Stalin could be witty and amusing in his own peculiar way; in 1944, for instance, he hugely enjoyed himself pulling de Gaulle's leg.[1] But, with his own people, no man was less of a back-slapper than he. Occasionally, too, he would summon to his office certain people not belonging to his immediate entourage; generals or top industrial executives, and even leading writers. And he would say to them caustic and unexpected things, sometimes curiously different from the official party line. Thus, in 1944, he called in a number of writers and said to them: "I don't know what's the matter with you people; when I read Dostoevsky, it makes me think about it at night; when I read the stuff you people write, it leaves absolutely no impression."

Especially during the war, Stalin became to the Russians the absolutely essential father figure, and if the "secret" Khrushchev Report denouncing the "cult of personality" at the Twentieth Congress in 1956 was resented by very many, it was because Khrushchev accused Stalin of having been an incompetent war leader. No doubt, grave mistakes had been made, especially at the beginning; the Germans had crashed into Russia with terrifying speed, overrunning vast territories within a few weeks; the three top commanders of 1941— Timoshenko, Budienny and Voroshilov—had proved absolutely incapable of coping with a war of this kind; and yet, collecting what first-class reserves he had, Stalin had saved Moscow and Leningrad in the nick of time. At the most critical moment, when all seemed lost, he had sent Zhukov to replace Voroshilov at Leningrad; and, in the end, it was the Red Army which, in Churchill's phrase, tore the guts out of the German Army. When things began to look desperate, Stalin appointed to the head of the Army all those brilliant generals—Zhukov, Rokossovsky, Vatutin, Malinovsky, Konev and the rest—who led the Red Army to victory. And he had nerves of steel: on October 16, 1941, when half the population of Moscow fled in a panic, Stalin had stayed on; when it was announced on the 17th that Stalin was there, people knew instinctively that Moscow would not be surrendered. And he had also cleverly handled Roosevelt and Churchill.

---

[1] "The truth is, he [Stalin] is a very likable person," James F. Byrnes wrote in *Speaking Frankly* (p. 45).

Although, with the "Jewish Doctors' plot" and the rest of it, the atmosphere was terribly unhealthy at the beginning of 1953, the news of Stalin's death nevertheless caused complete bewilderment. It was impossible to imagine who could replace Stalin. There was something like a panic during the days that followed Stalin's death, and several people were crushed to death in the wild stampede among the people anxious to have a last look at the dead leader. Memories of the war were still fresh, and many had gone into battle with the cry *"Za rodinu, za Stalina!"* (For country and Stalin). No doubt he had become strange, very strange in the last few years of his life. . . . Not that many things, worse than strange, had not happened before—in the days of collectivization and the Purge Trials of '36–'38.

Khrushchev did not succeed Stalin immediately; nor did his popularity come to him overnight. It was a long, arduous, tortuous uphill fight. After Stalin's death, Khrushchev was still relatively unknown, and was considered one of the least "probables"; the struggle for supreme power seemed at first to be between Molotov, Malenkov and Beria. For a time, Malenkov seemed to be the popular favourite; he was firmly believed to be the "consumer goods" man, the friend of the consumer and of the sorely-neglected peasant. After the liquidation of Beria only a few months after Stalin's death, the real struggle for supremacy began between Khrushchev and Malenkov. Right up to 1957, however, the semblance of the collective leadership was kept up. But Khrushchev, as First Secretary, was gaining an increasingly firm hold over the Central Committee which, with the help of men like Kirichenko (the boss of the Ukraine and for many years a close Khrushchev associate),[2] he gradually filled with as many "Khrushchev men" as possible. His technique in gaining supremacy was not all that different from the technique employed by Stalin during the years following Lenin's death. One of the greatest mysteries is the question why Malenkov, for years a Stalin man, did not realize that to be Premier in

[2] The complete elimination of Kirichenko in 1959–60 is one of the mysteries of "inner-circle" Kremlin politics which the man-in-the-street in Russia can explain no better than our "Soviet experts."

Russia was nothing, and to be Secretary-General of the Party was everything—in terms of power.

Always interested in agriculture, and realizing that this was the weakest point in Soviet economy, Khrushchev started on his famous maize campaign, earning in the process the contemptuous nickname of *kukuruznik* (the fellow gone crazy on maize), but also eliminating Malenkov from the premiership on the ground that Malenkov—as he himself was made to admit—was incompetent to deal with so vast and unfamiliar a problem. Khrushchev was determined to build up a new kind of peasant economy, in which the *kolkhozes* would be well paid, and would put all their energy into enormously increasing the country's livestock—so that there would, in Khrushchev's phrase, be more milk, butter and meat and other produce per head of population than in the most advanced of the capitalist countries, the United States. For years, as party boss of the Ukraine and before, Khrushchev had studied agriculture; no doubt he overdid his *kukuruza* campaign, making everybody plant maize, even in the most unsuitable climatic conditions. In some areas the cultivation of maize was subsequently abandoned; but where it had grown successfully, it continued to be cultivated in a big way; self-interest was proclaimed to be a principle essential for obtaining good results from agriculture; and already in 1958–59 a spectacular improvement in food production could be seen almost throughout the Soviet Union. The vast expanses of the Virgin Lands in Western Siberia and Kazakhstan were put under the plow by half-a-million young "volunteers"—boys and girls from the Komsomol, soldiers and others; there, as well as in Siberia, where "volunteers," but also some well-paid labor, had now replaced the slave labor of the NKVD, facilities were being created for a considerable number of people settling down permanently.

The decentralization of the Moscow bureaucracy through the creation of over a hundred *sovnarkhozy,* the Regional Economic Councils, was also largely Khrushchev's work.

He was a man of quite fantastic energy and vitality. He loved traveling about the country, talking endlessly to peasant meetings, and going, in the process, into no end of technical details on stock-breeding and the growing of various crops. Nor did it take long before, much to the annoyance of Molotov, he started on his globe-trotting career, first visiting

Yugoslavia where he made almost abject apologies to Tito, then going on to India, Burma and Afghanistan, together with the meek, polished and already slightly senile Bulganin (who had, by this time, replaced Malenkov at the head of the government). Then came the Twentieth Congress which ended with the "secret" Khrushchev Report on the "crimes of Stalin" and the evils of the "personality cult." The report was received in Russia with some dismay, and even resentment, if only because it made everybody feel a bit of a fool, and raised the inevitable question: "And what were *you* doing at that time?" For hadn't Khrushchev, too, as late as the Nineteenth Congress in October 1952, crawled on his belly before *veliki Stalin* like everybody else?

It was a dangerous game; and yet all this outrageous exhibitionism on Khrushchev's part gradually gave people the idea that here was the most forceful personality among all the leaders. Did they like him? Numerous groups no doubt felt that he was the man to back. He seemed to represent a new hope for the peasantry. The technocrats—who were largely Kaganovich's men—did not care for Khrushchev; he was encouraging "criticism from below," against which they had been well protected before. But, on the other hand, he symbolized *change*; something had clearly changed if anyone could speak of Stalin as he had done.

This was not without dangers; the repercussions of the Twentieth Congress and of "destalinization," though serious enough in Russia, were threatening, by the summer of 1956, to become catastrophic in Poland and Hungary. In Poland, largely thanks to the careful handling of a highly explosive situation by Khrushchev himself, an uneasy compromise was reached with Gomulka; in Hungary, the situation got out of hand in a much more threatening manner, and Khrushchev found there was no alternative to sending in the Army to "restore order."

Hungary was a serious setback to Khrushchev; already in April 1956, during his (not entirely satisfactory) visit to London, people around Khrushchev were openly saying that this visit to England was not very important *except as a first step to a visit to the United States.* In foreign policy, a *rapprochement* with the United States was Khrushchev's prime objective. Hungary stopped this process for a time.

Khrushchev's policy—or rather his *ensemble* of policies—

met with sharp opposition inside the Party Presidium. In June 1957 it came to a showdown; since Khrushchev appears to have had the majority of the Presidium against him, he demanded that the Central Committee as a whole be convened; and here the majority of the members were *his* men.

It was touch-and-go; if Malenkov, Molotov, Kaganovich and Shepilov had won, Khrushchev would have been destroyed, perhaps not only politically, but also physically. But luck and cunning were on his side. The Central Committee supported him against what soon came to be known as "the Anti-Party Group"; before long, others, too, were eliminated. First the immensely popular Marshal Zhukov, the victor of Moscow, Leningrad, Stalingrad and Berlin, was removed, ostensibly for merely having used a phrase to the effect that "the Army would not stand any nonsense from the Anti-Party Group"—against which he (Zhukov) had supported Khrushchev; but the phrase implied that the Army was an independent political force, and this was intolerable to the Central Committee, in fact the highest authority in the land. He was also accused of having started his own "personality cult" inside the Army. Later, too, Bulganin was first demoted and then finally pensioned off. Molotov—it was like a cruel practical joke—was appointed Ambassador to Outer Mongolia (of all places); Shepilov given a teaching job; Kaganovich and Malenkov put in charge of remote industrial enterprises. All except Malenkov, the most dangerous of Khrushchev's rivals, used to turn up in Moscow occasionally, and Kaganovich, too, was, like Bulganin, to be pensioned off before very long. Khrushchev added to his popularity by giving these people more or less ridiculous jobs, instead of having them shot, as they would have been in the old days.

On the face of it, Khrushchev had become supreme boss in the summer of 1957, after the liquidation of the Anti-Party Group. But he had not yet become *the* great popular leader he was to become soon afterwards.

Although there was perhaps no reason at all for personally crediting him with the tremendous technical victories of the Soviet Union during the next two years, there is no doubt that Khrushchev's great popularity began about the time of the Sputniks. He made enormous capital out of it, both for the Soviet Union and—for himself. He now became *the* spokesman of the technically mightiest and militarily most powerful country in the world. In popular imagination, the three Sputniks, the ICBMs (which were mightier than anything the USA could boast of), and, later, the "sun satellite," the rocket that hit the moon and the other one that went round the moon and photographed its unknown side, all became associated with the name of Khrushchev.

In the winter of 1959–60 Khrushchev was at the height of his glory. Gone were the days when in the villages people sang disrespectful and even ribald *chastushki* about Khrushchev, and when he was being referred to in derision as *"kukuruznik,"* when people, especially intellectuals, thought him garrulous, vulgar and undignified.

Khrushchev's visit to the USA in September 1959 seemed at the time the crowning achievement of his career. Not only was he no longer thought to be undignified; on the contrary, he had acquired a striking new dignity of his own; he had represented his country with immense skill and virtuosity during his by no means easy visit to the United States. In Russian eyes, he had now become the indefatigable fighter for peace and disarmament, the man who had spoken as a perfect equal to the President of the United States; who had made real friends of "peace-loving" Americans and had shown the others where they got off. He had said on every occasion that he was a Communist, and was proud of it, and the Americans had been made to realize that a Russian Communist leader was human, friendly and immensely intelligent and resourceful; he had done much to persuade them, despite years and years of Cold War and Dullesism, that peaceful coexistence and peaceful competition were the *only* way; perhaps he had even persuaded many that disarmament was in everybody's (except the "monopolies' ") interest. "And think," people were saying in Moscow, "how many houses *we* could build if we didn't have to spend 25 billion dollars a year on armaments." (This, according to Khrushchev, was the amount, calculated in dollars, that the USSR was spending on "defense," as against the USA's 42 billions.)

And now people in Moscow were referring to Khrushchev more and more frequently by name-and-patronymic. To all he had become "Nikita Sergeievich." The use of the name-and-patronymic is a sign of "acceptance." But although they used to talk in the past of "Vladimir Ilyich" (Lenin) and

"Joseph Vissarionovich" (Stalin), they never used these names with the same warm affection and familiarity with which they were speaking of "Nikita Sergeievich" now.

One could not but help wondering whether a new "personality cult" was not being built up.

For Khrushchev was now certainly receiving quite unprecedented publicity. Pages and pages of his speeches (often highly entertaining ones) were appearing day after day in the Soviet press—and this had now been going on for weeks; he had overshadowed completely all other Soviet leaders; everywhere a film was showing about his visit to the USA (the more unpleasant episodes had been cut out), and another film was also being shown—a documentary describing Khrushchev's progress, all the way from the "barefooted miner boy" to the two greatest leaders of the world shaking hands on the steps of the White House. (In this film all shots showing Malenkov or Bulganin had been cut out—history was being rewritten once more.) And in ideological articles Khrushchev was now being quoted much the way Stalin used to be quoted in the past.

Such fame and publicity could go to anybody's head. Nevertheless, there was still a great difference in the past approach to Stalin and this approach to Khrushchev. Stalin was the "genius," the "superman"; Khrushchev continued to be very much "one of us," a nice and simple man who was speaking so well to the outside world "on our behalf." And people were coming to the conclusion that Khrushchev must have a really first-class brain.

This gradual emergence of Khrushchev, the *kukuruznik,* as a great leader was, surely, one of the most curious episodes in the whole history of Russia. Nobody could *quite* figure out how much was policy and how much was personal pull which had eliminated all his rivals. But as long as the result was good, few really cared. And now many were already beginning to worry about his health. He was 65, and he had high blood-pressure, and wasn't taking care of himself.

He is said to have remarked to Harriman: "I am not making Stalin's mistake; *he* thought he would never die." And he· added: "I suppose if I die soon, Frol Kozlov will succeed me. However, that's for the Central Committee to decide. It doesn't matter very much. Russia is a machine whose wheels are turning beautifully; and they'll go on turning."

All the same, in that autumn of the Great Thaw, several Russians to whom I talked about it, said: "True, but the West had better hasten to improve and consolidate its relations with us while Khrushchev is still here. If he were to die, one never can tell who and what would take his place." And one even added: "And if you are too slow about it Khrushchev himself may throw up the sponge. And perhaps adopt a different policy. He may seem to be the supreme, unchallenged boss now, but conditions may change. If his 'Western' policy of 'Peaceful Coexistence' is sabotaged by the West, he may—or somebody else may—switch over to a *different* policy. After all, we have to consider China, and China is not enchanted with the present policy. And if this policy were to fail, the Chinese would speak up. And, believe it or not, but *we also* have what you might call a 'China Lobby.' "

"And what," I asked a Russian friend, "do you make of Khrushchev taking Nina Petrovna and the daughters and the son and the son-in-law with him all over the place?"

"Looks a bit unusual to us," he said. "In Stalin's days wives and families of the high-ups were kept in the background; there was no virtue in being the wife or son or daughter of a leader. It was his private business, and nobody else's. But I suppose Americans like to see a man surrounded by his family. Makes him look even *more* human. That's one way, I suppose, of putting across the idea that the top Communist leader is human, since he has a wife, and children and grandchildren. Perhaps Nikita Sergeievich overdoes it a bit. You know the Russian proverb: 'Don't have a hundred rubles, but have a hundred friends.' This has now been changed to: 'Don't have a hundred friends, but get married like Adjubei.'

"Adjubei is the editor of *Izvestia,* and Khrushchev's son-in-law. He took him to America, and he takes him all over the place. He's good publicity for Khrushchev in more ways than one. These cracks about Adjubei are, of course, hard to avoid. No doubt, a little touch of envy comes into it." (More recently, of course, Adjubei returned to America—to interview President Kennedy at Hyannisport.)

This, however, belonged to the "anecdotic" side of Khrushchev. In the following narrative other Khrushchevs will appear, among them an angry and embittered Khrushchev, whose "optimistic" policy had been wrecked by the Pentagon, and by the he-men around "my friend Ike," as well as a threatening Khrushchev, the "African Missionary" and Fidel Castro's dearest friend.

Apart perhaps from Mikoyan, Voroshilov and one or two other fairly familiar figures, all the other top Soviet leaders were "blanks," compared with Khrushchev. Who, to the man-in-the-street, were Aristov, Beliayev or even Brezhnev—who was later to become "President" of the USSR? In short, since the elimination of the "Anti-Party Group," the "one-man" tendency seemed as strong as ever.

Chapter 2

END OF AN OPTIMISTIC ERA?—OR
"WAITING FOR KENNEDY?"

THIS CONVERSATION took place in the Café Kléber, opposite the Palais Chaillot, in Paris, soon after Khrushchev's press conference in May 1960, which finally put the lid on that abortive Summit for which the pudgy little man had worked, and argued and agitated for three years or more. He now seemed to be in an exasperated, almost hysterical state in which I had never seen him before. Was he losing his grip?

"It's a tragedy, a real tragedy," Comrade N, one of the younger Soviet diplomats, was saying. He was a man of 29 or 30, a Soviet Russian of the "Khrushchev period."

"Khrushchev," he said, "is just as angry, just as upset as every man, woman and child in the Soviet Union. I was in Moscow only a few days ago. Everybody was rushing to the Gorki Park to see the new 'American Exhibition,' the remnants of that U-2 spy plane. People were furious, and rather worried. Ever since his visit to the United States in the summer of 1959, Khrushchev had been telling them that there were warmongers and cold-war maniacs in America, but that he trusted Eisenhower. A few, I don't mind telling you, whispered that this was 'un-Marxist'; that Eisenhower was a class enemy like the rest of them; but Khrushchev kept on stretching points. Now everything has changed. He has come to the conclusion that Eisenhower may be a good man for all he knows, but hopelessly weak and helpless—and dominated by the CIA, by the people who sent their spy plane over the Soviet Union a fortnight before the opening of the Summit Conference. Once, twice, three times he gave Eisenhower a chance to disavow the saboteurs of peace, to say

21

that he was sorry it had happened, and that it wouldn't happen again."

"But Eisenhower *did* say the flights would now be suspended. Wasn't that enough?" I said.

"No, it came too late, it came too half-heartedly; and he did not squarely, as he should have done, condemn the *principle* of the U-2 flights over the Soviet Union; worse still, he did nothing to invalidate all the earlier American statements to the effect that, since the Soviet Union was a 'totalitarian' country, capable of aggression, the normal rules of international behavior just did not apply to her. Khrushchev insisted on an apology from Ike, not because he's a stickler for etiquette, but because this was *fundamental.* Such apologies are the recognized practice amongst all civilized, and even uncivilized, nations when sovereignty is violated; not so long ago the United States even apologized to Cuba. Of course, we all have spies; Khrushchev knows it as well as Eisenhower; Khrushchev has known for the last four years about these Lockheed U-2 planes."

"What then is he so upset about?"

"I'll tell you—if you haven't understood yet. The real point is that by behaving the way he did, Eisenhower destroyed (temporarily, I hope) that system of peaceful coexistence and international negotiations *which is the very basis of Khrushchev's policy.* For what the Americans proclaimed by refusing to make even the most routine apologies to us was that the Soviet Union was a totalitarian country, *whose sovereignty it was not necessary to respect.* It was a terrible blow to Khrushchev's doctrine of coexistence. For this doctrine consists of two elements: first of all, the personal negotiations he was conducting with Eisenhower, Macmillan, de Gaulle, and so on; secondly, a continuous reinforcement of *international legality,* to us an essential corollary of *socialist legality* inside the Soviet Union. This international legality is constantly reinforced by trade agreements, attempts at controlled disarmament, which would enable the world to devote itself to its peaceful tasks, in short, the recognition by every possible means of the sovereignty of the Soviet Union as a Great Power. Under this system, the West must give up any attempts to 'liberate' our East-European allies; as against this, we have implicitly agreed not to encourage communist insurrections and revolts in Asia and

Africa (for instance, no Chinese penetration of India—as you know, we've done our very best to stop it)."

"There's Hungary," I remarked.

"Yes," said N, "there's Hungary, on which a good deal could be said one way or the other. And there's also Suez. Let's not flog dead horses. The fact remains that the prime object of Khrushchev's whole foreign policy has been completely equal treatment, in diplomatic matters, of the so-called Free World and of the Socialist Camp. (The recognition of China is, of course, only a matter of time, in Khrushchev's view.) And our diplomats have been very insistent that international law must be applied absolutely equally to all parts of the world, whatever the ideological differences; and that these need not prevent a decent minimum of confidence, collaboration, and genuinely peaceful competition. Only all these considerations are, from our Soviet point of view, subordinated to the acceptance of the axiom of the inviolability of all countries' sovereignty; and Eisenhower's refusal to recognize the absolute sovereignty of the Soviet Union—which meant that we were *not* an 'equal partner'—knocked the bottom out of the Summit Conference, even before it had started."

"You mean then," I said, "that Khrushchev really stands for the *status quo* in the world?"

"*Status quo*—well, no, not exactly. We don't want to prevent the Belgian Congo from declaring its independence—that's *its* business. But apart from the German treaty and Berlin (and even here Khrushchev is not all that insistent) he wants the *status quo* to be observed in East-West relations; for this alone can enable our country to go on evolving and consolidating itself peacefully for years and years to come. Peaceful competition—yes. And if Khrushchev is so bitter about Eisenhower, it's because Ike, in his eyes, betrayed the Camp David spirit, and struck a terrible blow at the policy he (Khrushchev) has now been trying to pursue for years. For doesn't Ike realize that, by acting as he did, he was playing into the hands of Khrushchev's critics both inside Russia and—outside?"

"China, you mean?"

"Yes, China, and other places, too. It's an open secret that there are ideological differences between us and the Chinese, who have tended to pooh-pooh Khrushchev's American trip and all that; he may now be forced, despite his very strong personal preferences, to make concessions to the *other* policy. . . ."

"You won't have a separate peace treaty with Eastern Germany?"

"Doesn't look like it," N replied, perhaps unprophetically.

"And the American bases in Turkey and Pakistan and Japan?"

"Well, we warned these countries. If there are any more spy planes, we *may* have to do something."

"Wouldn't that mean war?"

"It might, and it mightn't . . ." said N.

"That sounds dangerous talk," I said. "And didn't Khrushchev treat Ike in an insulting manner which would be difficult for any President of the United States to swallow—calling him a liar, canceling his invitation to Moscow, and so on. Won't it be difficult for Khrushchev to go to America again after that, whoever is elected President in November?"

"Now, after what has happened, you can't really expect us to treat Eisenhower as a dear and welcome guest. And to think that only a fortnight ago, they were preparing to give Eisenhower a more tremendous reception—and a perfectly genuine one—than our country had ever given to *any* foreign statesman, from either West or East. It was *that* which those Pentagon and Allen Dulles bastards were afraid of. The write-up in the American press would have been tremendous, and think what TV would have done with 'Ike in Moscow!' "

"So didn't Khrushchev cut off his nose . . . ?"

"No, he had no alternative. He wanted this conference desperately, he wanted Ike's visit to Moscow; but he couldn't have the conference on *any* terms. Already, in his talks with de Gaulle last month, he wasn't too pleased about the complete deadlock over Berlin, but he was still prepared to swallow this. But the U-2 was the last straw."

"But are you sure that, after the insulting way he treated Ike, world opinion is going to be on your side?"

"We are not sure of anything," said N dismally. "You saw what Walter Lippmann said about the insanity of American policy. No doubt, the well-orchestrated press in the West will go on screaming that Khrushchev has 'sabotaged' the Summit. Nobody in the Soviet Union is going to believe a word of it."

"You suggested Khrushchev had no great illusions in coming to Paris; then why did he come at all?"

"Well, he still wanted to give Eisenhower one more chance to disavow Allen Dulles and the rest of them."

"Why did Malinovsky have to follow him about like a shadow?"

"Oh, just as a reminder. And don't you worry about the Army dictating its will to our government. If there's a country where this does *not* happen, it's the Soviet Union."

"Is it true, as the papers now say, that American tourists are being ill-treated in Moscow?"

"I shouldn't think so; just another fabrication. But our people are angry, frustrated, and anxious once again. . . . They fear the bad Cold War days may start again—with internal repercussions—perhaps greater austerity and . . ."

"More police supervision?" I ventured.

"Well, yes—that too," N said reluctantly.

"But won't people be angry with Khrushchev for having allowed himself to be bamboozled by the Americans?"

"No, I don't think so. Possible, all the same, that some people in the Party will now argue that he has gone as far in his 'Western' policy as possible, and that he has received no thanks for it. Mind you, Khrushchev never trusted the United States 100 per cent. But now he's been let down with a bang. He has an alternative policy which is to turn his back on the West and go 'Asiatic.' I don't think he'll do it. He wants to give *his* policy one more chance—after the American election."

"What makes you think Kennedy or Nixon would be any better than Eisenhower?"

"They couldn't be worse, so there's a chance they might be better—Kennedy at least. If he's just as bad, Khrushchev won't have much choice. He may even have to go. Remember, he has been right on top for less than three years, and he is *not* as invulnerable as Stalin was. . . ."

"That," I said, "is what Nehru told de Gaulle recently. He said Khrushchev was being criticized by some of the Party high-ups, who were advocating a more pro-Chinese policy, a more active policy for scrapping those bases in Turkey, Pakistan and Japan, etc., a more 'revolutionary' policy in the underdeveloped countries. Is that true?"

"I don't know," said N, "I'm not on the Central Committee

Presidium to know. But we had a private conference with Khrushchev yesterday and he sounded very fed-up; said the whole West was under the thumb of Adenauer and the 'Pirates.' "

"Isn't there a certain coincidence between Khrushchev's present stand and all the funny things that are going on in Africa, in Turkey, and South Korea and Japan?" For the first time N grinned.

"Getting cold feet, are you?"

And then, very earnestly:

"No, we are in no desperate hurry. South Korea will join the rest of Korea some time, and Turkey and Japan will go neutral, you'll see. And Vietnam *must* unite before long."

"Yes, but how? By Soviet or Chinese intervention in a 'just war?' "

"Direct intervention—no. But in countries like South Korea and South Vietnam big internal uprisings are sure to mature in time. If it's sufficiently safe, we shall support them; if not, we shan't. But to return to Khrushchev . . ."

"Yes, there was," I said, "as many people here will tell you, one easy way out of it, if Khrushchev was as desperately anxious, as you say, to have the Summit meeting; and that was to say nothing about the U-2—or at least not to make a big public issue of it."

"That's complete nonsense; since it was absolutely impossible to disregard this deliberate act of provocation. And the line Eisenhower took made it impossible for us to go on talking in such conditions. It's a piece of the most fantastic dishonesty to say that Khrushchev is to blame for the breakdown of the Summit. Eisenhower could have ended his presidential career in a blaze of glory—as the Man of Peace; now, thanks to what he did these last few days, he will go down in history as one of the most absurd and feeble Presidents the United States has ever had. A general with no guts. One who allowed himself to be engineered into this mess by Allen Dulles, his CIA with its 30,000 agents, the Pentagon and all that."

"And what are you going to do now?"

"Nothing much. Just wait. Wait till more favorable conditions develop. Wait till there are other top people in America who will realize that there is no alternative to peaceful coexistence and peaceful competition, and till there's a

President who *can* and *will* refuse to be the prisoner of the warmongers."

"Is that all?"

"Perhaps not. Events are moving fast in the world these days. Africa is about to blow up in your faces. Things are stirring in Turkey, Iran, Japan, South Korea. If the Camp David spirit had been kept going, we would have been as untroublesome to you people as possible. Now I won't guarantee anything. Remember, after all, that Khrushchev is a Communist, and not a 'Rooseveltian liberal,' as some of your people like to call him. The phrase is just silly. We are hard-headed people; we offered the West a sound *modus vivendi;* if it doesn't want it, it can blame itself if things start going wrong."

"Are you suggesting then there might be a war?"

"*That*—no. With H-bombs on both sides, nobody can afford to be trigger-happy. But——"

During those anxious days in May 1960 the Western press kept plugging the idea that Khrushchev had been *forced* from *inside* Russia to change his policy. Against those who wanted a return to the hard line, there was no valid argument that Khrushchev could use, all the more so as he had lost faith in the American leaders. His Baku speech had already made *that* clear. He still tried to cling to Eisenhower as the last straw; but with the U-2 incident the straw broke. Now he was in an awkward dilemma. Was he going to "go Chinese" or— as Comrade N had suggested—"wait for Kennedy?" Or, as he was to say later, "if not Kennedy, then the fellow *after* Kennedy."

What, I began to reflect seriously that day, was that Soviet Union in whose name Khrushchev had gone to America and in whose name again he had now refused to pursue his talks with the West? And I went through my memories and notes on that Khrushchev Russia which I had only recently re-visited, in the winter of 1959–60, after an absence of eleven years. And it soon became clear to me that the apparent contradictions of Khrushchev's policy were a reflection of the numerous, and often contradictory trends, existing in the country itself. Russia wanted to live in peace with the West; but again: on what terms? The economy, the civilization it was building up were different from Western economy and Western civilization. Could it be said that the West was pessimistic and declining, and Russia optimistic and constantly rising? Nothing was quite so simple. . . .

Chapter 3

KHRUSHCHEV IN SIBERIA

THE TIMING of my arrival in Moscow was almost as lucky as that of my arrival in the USA two years before in the fall of 1957. I got to the USA just in time to see the great upheaval caused by Sputnik. In Moscow I was to see the sequel of the process that had started with Sputnik. The globetrotting Khrushchev was just about to return to Moscow after two important journeys—the first of which had really been, at least to the Russians, a world-shaking one—his journey to the USA. For the past fortnight Moscow had been talking about nothing else; it was going to go on talking about it for months. The second journey, which Khrushchev had just completed, was to China, and there was a good deal of talk about that one, too, and also some slightly anxious whispering about the Chinese brothers not being sufficiently enthusiastic about Nikita Sergeievich's triumphal visit to the United States. . . . It was even said that after his visit to China, he had stopped at Vladivostok and Bratsk (the tremendous new power-station on the Angara, still in process of being built) and Krasnoyarsk and Novosibirsk partly in order to reassure the "Siberians" that all was well, that there was nothing to fear from China, now or ever. . . .

Be that as it may, everybody was reading, and commenting on, during those first few days I was back in Moscow, Khrushchev's "Siberian" speeches. In these, he was speaking to his own people. He had (if one may use so unsuitable an image) let his hair down; he was not watching his step as carefully as in America, nor was he reading his speeches; they

29

were improvisations, exuberant, and often brilliant and amusing. He talked to the Russians as "an ordinary chap," very
much as "one of us"; and people like this particular Khrushchev style better than any other. He loved boasting, and pulling people's legs, and making cracks at the Americans' expense, and even satirizing certain aspects of "Soviet reality."

Needless to say, there were columns and columns of
Khrushchev in every paper in the country; and it had been
like that for weeks now. He had, clearly, eclipsed all the
other Soviet leaders. Was a new "personality cult" developing? Perhaps not, but Khrushchev was undoubtedly popular
during that period, more popular than he had ever been. *He*
was the first Soviet leader to be photographed with the President of the United States on the steps of the White House. It
was symbolic of all sorts of things. . . . He had, clearly, become one of the Big Two leaders of the world. And now it
was nice to have him back in Russia, talking informally
and amusingly to the people of Vladivostok, Krasnoyarsk, etc.

These improvised speeches he delivered in Siberia were
amongst the most illuminating he had ever made. They explained, better perhaps than anything else, the secret of his
personal appeal.

Thus, in Vladivostok:

> Things are going well in our country. However much the de-
> fenders of capitalism may try to embellish that decaying old
> system, they won't succeed. A young horse runs about like mad
> with its tail in the air; but an old nag can't put up its tail, no
> matter how hard it tries.

Loud laughter and cheers, said the press reports. And it
was part of Khrushchev's technique to slip playful little
"sexy" innuendoes into his speeches.

And then came cracks about America—good-natured on
the face of it, but still cracks. Of course, it was an impressive
and rich country; but that wasn't enough to impress him
(Khrushchev) or make him change his mind about the rightness of the Soviet system. The Americans were, indeed, being
a bit shamefaced about their capitalism, calling it "people's
capitalism" or "humanistic capitalism," but really they couldn't
get away with that. And then, the Americans had had 150
years in which to get rich; the Soviet Union had achieved

what she had achieved in 42 years, including the years of economic collapse, civil war and the years of World War II. "I don't want to hurt the Americans by saying so; most of them are good people, but they still haven't understood that their capitalist system is bad." And he said that they had made a big mistake in thinking that they would convert him (Khrushchev) to capitalism by taking him round the USA. He made most of the fact, of course, that the Soviet Union had sent a rocket to the moon and another round the moon, while the American moon rockets had so far all "dropped to the bottom of the sea."

And the American way of life? Having failed to send a rocket to the moon, the Americans, Khrushchev said, were now boasting of having more passenger cars than the Soviet Union.

That's true; but we have no intention of competing with them in this field; we shall develop our automobile industry, but not in the American way. We don't believe in encouraging the American system under which people say: "It's a lousy car, but it's mine." We shall have a very large number of taxis; but we don't want people to bust themselves trying to discover where they can park their own car. . . .

So far, he said, the USA was still producing more than the Soviet Union, and had a higher standard of living, but the time was not far off when the Soviet Union would equal and surpass the USA.

Having got that one off his chest, Khrushchev spoke with some warmth of President Eisenhower.

I liked talking to him. He is an intelligent man, and fully aware of the gravity of the international situation. When I said that it was absurd and dangerous for our two countries to go on trying to frighten each other, he agreed, and said: "Yes, as a military man I can tell you candidly that I am very much afraid of war." "You are quite right," I said to him, "only a very stupid man can not be afraid of war these days."

In short, Eisenhower's heart was in the right place, but the question of disarmament and control was not an easy one to settle; there were still strong influences in the USA in favor of the Cold War, and these influences were hampering the acceptance of the total disarmament plan he (Khrushchev) had put before UN.

If these people wanted to inflict the Cold War on the Soviet Union, well then, it couldn't be helped; she would have to go on strengthening her defenses and keep her rockets in a state of readiness, to smash any aggressive attempts. . . .

Such, comrades, is the position. But the fact that President Eisenhower had the wisdom to invite me to the United States and has agreed to come on a visit to the Soviet Union points to his farsightedness and to the American people's desire for peace.

He hoped these fruitful exchanges could continue at the Summit Conference.

He emphasized the fact that if the Soviet Union was being treated with so much consideration, it was because it was strong and powerful and formed part of the mighty Socialist Camp.

And he went on to describe the visit he had just paid to China:

We celebrated there the tenth anniversary of the Chinese People's Republic. It was a grandiose celebration. Under the leadership of its Communist Party, the Chinese people are successfully developing the economy of their country. Things are going well in People's China. We had friendly and cordial meetings with Mao Tse-Tung and the other Chinese leaders. Our talks showed that we were standing on the same Marxist-Leninist positions, and that both our countries were going towards the same aim—Socialism and Communism.

And then this typical Khrushchevism:

We are being respected and hailed because we are strong. While I was standing on the airfield in Washington—and it is a tremendous honor for a man to represent a country like ours—and saying good-bye to America, the band played the Soviet Anthem, and then the guns fired 21 salutes. So I said to myself: "That first salute is for Karl Marx, and the second salute for Friedrich Engels, and the third salute for Vladimir Ilyich Lenin, and the fourth salute for His Majesty the working class, and so on—salutes for our country, for its various peoples. Not bad, comrades, really not bad at all!" (*Loud prolonged cheers.*)

And then he added:

But you can be sure that if our country, our heroic working class, our peasantry and intellectuals hadn't achieved all that we have achieved, there wouldn't be any such salutes for us. You can be sure of that. . . .

But then came a Khrushchevism of another kind; of course, he said, things were going well in the Soviet Union, but it was no use pretending that all was perfect.

Here in Vladivostok we met a woman in the street; she was walking along with her kiddies. "Well, how are things going?" I asked. "Not bad," she said, and then added: "We are very glad you have come to visit us, and that I am having a chance to talk to you." And then, after a short silence she added: "In connection with your visit, they've chucked a lot of shoes and boots and textiles and milk into our shops. Come to see us more often; the shops will be full of stuff then." So I said: "So they've 'chucked in' the stuff, have they?" "Yes," she said, "they chucked it in." "And," I said, "since you live on the coast, do you get enough fresh fish in the shops?" "Well," she said, "there's plenty of salt herring; as for fresh fish, sometimes we get it, and sometimes we don't." No doubt, salt herring is very nice with potatoes and onions, or *tsibulka,* as we call it in Ukrainian; but all this is not good enough. We talked about it to the local leaders. I told them it was no good "chucking in" goods to mark the arrival of top leaders; "and when I'll have left, you'll no doubt begin to 'chuck out' the stuff?"

And then Khrushchev said that, since arriving in Vladivostok, he had received a very large number of letters from local inhabitants, and nearly all of them were concerned with housing; he said the housing situation was, obviously, very unsatisfactory, despite the considerable effort that had been made; but the fact was that a large number of people were now coming to work in the Soviet Far East; only, unless they were given decent housing conditions, they wouldn't stay on. He was going to raise all these problems in detail when he returned to Moscow.

The whole "style" was radically different from Stalin's.

At Bratsk, where a gigantic power station was being built, at Novosibirsk and Krasnoyarsk, he spoke along similar lines, but raising a number of other topical points. Thus, at Krasnoyarsk he said that tremendous progress was being made in Siberia, particularly in the Krasnoyarsk, Novosibirsk and Irkutsk areas. People from abroad, however malevolent, were amazed at what was being done in Siberia. Harriman had come here, and so had Nixon, and Nixon had expressed amazement, after talking to young people in Siberia, that all of them were getting trained at an Institute or a *technicum,* or were attending evening classes while still continuing to work on production.

Some of our enemies abroad are kidding themselves with the thought that the more educated people we have, the more readily will our country want to return to capitalism. . . . In reality, the more educated our people are, the more readily will they tell the capitalists to go and flog themselves.[1] (*Loud cheers and laughter.*)

And, as at Vladivostok, he dwelt on the immense importance of the Sputniks and rockets. The whole world had now seen how the Soviet Union had won first prize in what he called "technical maturity." But in all fields further efforts would have to be made to achieve the best results—in industry, in agriculture, etc. And not least in the chemical industry, which was developing at a spectacular rate in Siberia. He advocated the mass production of paper diapers, "a tremendous saving of labor." And then:

During the war we used to laugh at German uniforms being "made of wood"; yet the principle of the thing was right; for chemistry is already providing us with immensely useful and cheap synthetic materials. . . . No doubt, people are looking better dressed than before, but some clothes are still on the dismal side. We are producing an ever-growing quantity of all kinds of consumer goods; all the same, we must not force the pace unreasonably as regards the lowering of prices. We don't want to lower prices to such an extent that there will be queues and a black market.

[1] This, I should say, is the nearest equivalent of the euphemism that Khrushchev used. Such camouflaged "vulgarisms" are very much part of his rhetorical technique. The above "a lousy car but my own" is also a variant of the Russian "proverb"— "Sh—t, but my own."

In short, be patient, and don't expect too much all at once. And he switched on to foreign aid. "We don't need foreign aid, and, in any case, one never gets anything for nothing." And then came his domestic-consumption "line" on aid to underdeveloped countries—a line which was much blunter than what he used to say in the West:

As you know, the imperialists are making a great fuss over the help they are supposed to be giving to the underdeveloped countries. In reality all that happens is that they give them left-overs which nobody wants, on the principle of "God can take what I don't want." (Laughter.) They robbed these countries, and they go on robbing them, and now, with grand gestures, they give them a few crumbs from all this loot. What's more, they'll give them a kopek and want a ruble in return. There was a time when they robbed our country, too. But that's finished for all time. (Loud cheers.)

After referring to the *genuine* aid that the Soviet Union was giving underdeveloped countries like India, Burma, etc., Khrushchev turned to another highly topical question which was often to be discussed in Moscow in the next few months, and that was the question of cultural exchanges:

While I was in the USA several American representatives kept pestering me with their so-called free exchange of ideas. They told me they wanted to distribute in our country the books and films of their own choice, and flood us with their broadcasts. They want to inflict all kinds of rubbish on us, which would poison the minds of Soviet people. We just cannot agree to this. . . . So I told these Americans: Let's build up our relations on the following principle: we shall buy from you what we want, and you shall buy from us what you want. In this way we shall exchange only the best things; as for any de-cayed food, you can eat the damned stuff yourselves. (Loud cheers and laughter.)

Then he talked about disarmament and international trade.

I talked to Mr. Dillon in the USA. I said to him: Go ahead and convert your war industries. If you give us credits, we shall buy an awful lot of your stuff. And you needn't worry; we'll pay you back all your money. Even if we borrowed money from

the Devil himself, we'd pay him back. (*Laughter and cheers.*)
But the trouble is that the monopolists want to go on with their
Cold War. . . .

And again he returned to the theme of the more rapid
progress made by the Soviet Union than by America:

> What amazes Americans is that, last year alone, 94,000 engi-
> neers should have graduated in our country, and only 35,000
> in the United States. So we turn out nearly three times as many
> engineers as the USA. Comrades, this is a very big achievement!
> (*Loud cheers.*)

What Khrushchev said when he was in America is sufficiently familiar. What is less well known is what he said
on his return from America and, above all, the way he said
it. No doubt whatsoever about his desire for peaceful coexistence; but this did not exclude the constant demonstration of a Soviet superiority urge, expressing itself in a good
deal of understandable boasting and flattery, but combined
with warnings against complacency or excessive optimism.

I have quoted at some length some of these "Siberian"
speeches of Khrushchev, because, better than anything else,
they set the tone, as it were, of most of the official pronounce-
ments to be made in the months to come, and also because,
to a large extent, they colored much of the informal talk
one could hear in Moscow about the same time. And, better
even than his rather carefully-calculated speeches in the
United States (or other foreign countries) they throw a light
on the personality of Khrushchev, and on the secret of his
extraordinary success in the Soviet Union, especially since
Stalin's death.

Chapter 4

THE STALIN "PERSONALITY CULT"

THE PRESENT RUSSIAN ATTITUDE to Stalin, as we have seen, and as we shall see again in later chapters, is an extremely mixed one. On June 30, 1956, only a few months after Khrushchev's "secret" report, the Central Committee issued a long Statement explaining the evils of the "personality cult."

Why was this necessary? The truth is that the Khrushchev Report in particular was beginning to have important consequences in the outside world; the Statement dwelt on the fact that "the enemies of the Soviet Union" were trying to make enormous capital out of certain things said at the Twentieth Congress and, significantly, it ended with a reference to the Polish "anti-people demonstrations" at Poznan which had been "provoked by American agents," who were now taking advantage of the Russian attack on the "personality cult."

Moscow was getting worried, and there is good reason for saying that men like Molotov and Kaganovich were already blaming Khrushchev for what was only just *beginning* to happen in Poland; they were, clearly, expecting further trouble after Poznan, and insisted on a proper explanation being given for the line adopted by the Twentieth Congress.

The Statement—which is something in the nature of a compromise between "Stalinites" and "anti-Stalinites"—dwelt on the fact that the abolition of the "personality cult" could in no way be regarded as denoting a fundamental change in the structure of Soviet society, or as the abandonment of the basic aims of the Soviet Union's progress towards Com-

37

munism. It said that all foreign Communist Parties had fully understood the significance of the Twentieth Congress resolutions, though a few Communist leaders had gone wrong. It noted, in particular, that while Togliatti had correctly understood that "the substance of the Socialist order had not been changed, since none of the former conquests, such as the full support of the Socialist order by the peasants, workers and intellectuals forming Soviet society had been lost," he nevertheless had wondered whether Soviet society would not "undergo certain forms of regeneration."

The Statement protested against any such suggestion, vague though it was, and proceeded to show just why exactly the "personality cult" had had to be denounced. It claimed (not very convincingly, it must be said, since right up to the Twentieth Congress, the attitude to Stalin had remained ambiguous) that "for the last three years [1953–56] the Party had conducted a consistent struggle against the cult of Stalin's personality."

It was natural that this question should have taken an important place in the deliberations of the Congress; this noted that the Central Committee had correctly pointed out that the personality cult had minimized the role of the Party and the mass of the people, had greatly reduced the role of collective leadership, and had led to numerous mistakes and to gross violations of Socialist Legality.

The Statement further recalled that Lenin had described as anti-Marxist the juxtaposition of "the hero" and "the crowd."

Further:

The publicity given by the Party to the violations of Socialist legality arising from the "personality cult" inevitably arouses feelings of bitterness and regret. But Soviet people realize that this condemnation of the personality cult was essential to the further building of Communism . . . and that the Party has recently been successfully eliminating all the evils that had arisen as a result of the personality cult.

The bulk of the Statement, was in a sense, a defense of Stalin.

"While Lenin was alive, there had been a sharp class struggle inside the Soviet Union; after Lenin's death hostile tendencies became even more active: Trotzkyites, Right Opportunists, and bourgeois nationalists were, in fact, aiming at the restoration of capitalism in the USSR. . . . In the circumstances, for the Party to follow a strict Leninist line, iron discipline was required, as well as the utmost vigilance; this could not but have a negative effect on the development of certain democratic forms." The capitalist encirclement in which the Soviet Union then found itself made this even more inevitable.

In this immense struggle against enemies at home and abroad, and in this tremendous transformation of the Soviet Union into a highly developed modern state, with new scientific and technical cadres, Stalin held an outstandingly important place. As General Secretary of the Party, Stalin acquired immense authority during those years, and also enormous popularity. But the fact that the tremendous successes of the Party and the country were largely associated with his name went to his head.

The Statement then recalled the criticism made of Stalin by Lenin, first in 1922 and then in 1923. In this 1923 letter Lenin actually recommended that Stalin, "who was too rough," be replaced by somebody else as Secretary-General of the Party. When, after Lenin's death, the Thirteenth Congress met, these Lenin letters were communicated to the delegates; but they agreed to maintain Stalin at his post, recommending, however, that he draw the necessary conclusions from Lenin's "testament." For some years Stalin took full account of Lenin's criticism, but later began to believe in his own infallibility.

Certain limitations of Party and Soviet democracy, which were inevitable during the intense class struggle of the early years of the Revolution, as well as during the war against Nazi Germany, Stalin began to elevate to the rank of permanent rules of the State and Party Life. The plenary meetings of the Party became more and more infrequent, and, finally, there were no plenary meetings or Congresses for many years. Stalin thus remained wholly outside criticism. . . . He also made the grave mistake of asserting that, as Socialism progressed in the Soviet Union, so the class struggle would become increasingly acute. This statement, first made in 1937, when the whole economic basis of the exploiting classes had already been liquidated, became the basis for the crudest violations of Socialist Legality and for mass repressions.

Thus the Party now implicitly condemned the 1936–38 Purges. Stretching an historical point (for Beria was appointed *after* the main Purges carried out by Yagoda and Yezhov) the Statement went on to say that things went from bad to worse after "the imperialist agent Beria" had been placed in charge of the Security Organs.

But it is significant that, with a few exceptions, none of the main accused in the Purge Trials were rehabilitated, while nothing very explicit was ever said about the *magnitude* of the camp "system."

The Statement then tried to make out that even when Stalin was at the height of his glory, there was

some resistance at certain periods against the negative phenomena arising from the "personality cult," phenomena which were retarding the progress of Socialism. . . . Notably during the war, members of the Central Committee and outstanding military leaders took over certain sectors at the front and in the rear, and acted independently in their political, organizational, economic and military work, together with the local party and Soviet organizations, thus working for victory. But after victory the negative consequences of the "personality cult" became very apparent again.

This again was stretching a point: Stalin's authority had never been so high as during the war, though for a number of reasons—expediency, the *rapprochement* with the West, etc.—the NKVD had not been quite as much in evidence during the war as before or after. That the Generals resented excessive police interference is well-known; whether Khrushchev, Molotov or Malenkov had done much to "democratize" life during the war is exceedingly doubtful.

The Statement then dealt with the awkward question why no one had rebelled against Stalin if he was all that he was said to be.

Why was Stalin not removed from the leadership? In the given conditions this was impossible. Stalin, as the facts show, was guilty of many illegal acts, especially during the last years of his life. But it cannot be denied that the Soviet people looked upon Stalin as a man who was always defending the USSR against its enemies, and was fighting for the cause of Socialism. The fact that he often used unworthy methods was his tragedy. . . . Yet in such conditions any attack on Stalin would not have been understood by the people, and this was not a matter of lack of courage (!). Simply, nobody attacking Stalin in such conditions would have been supported by the people. Such an attack would, indeed, have been considered as an attack on Socialism, as an attempt to undermine the unity of the Party and the security of the State. . . . It should also be noted that many facts and many wrong actions by Stalin, especially his violations of Socialist Legality, did not become known until later, after Stalin's death, and in connection with the showing-up of the Beria gang and the establishment of a strict control by the Party over the Organs of State Security.

And all this, this section of the Statement concluded, explained, though it did not justify, the "personality cult." This had done great harm, but it could not, and did not, change the social structure of the Soviet Union.

It did, however, for a time, interfere with the development of Socialist democratism and with the creative initiative of millions.

What this, and many other documents published later, stressed was that, so long as Stalin was following strictly in the footsteps of Lenin, all went well; it was after he had distorted Leninism that things began to go wrong. All of which was oversimplifying things a bit.

A curious phenomenon, especially in the last few years, has been the development of a kind of super-cult of Lenin. It was made out that the Party and Khrushchev in particular had returned to "Leninist purity." In countless articles Lenin was exalted as a particularly human, humane, charming and warmhearted man, a man of extreme modesty. But this somewhat artificial "Lenin Cult" is a very different story.

Chapter 5

BACK IN MOSCOW

TO TELL THE TRUTH, I don't like Intourist. No doubt, it exists in order to be helpful to visitors from abroad; but it also robs them mercilessly, and, worse still, it's a kind of weapon of psychological warfare: one of its jobs is to remind every visitor that he *is* an outsider. You can talk perfect Russian to them, but they'll still make a point of addressing you as *gospodin*. And anyone in Russia who's addressed as *gospodin* belongs to a sort of more-or-less untouchable caste.

At the same time, there is, at least on the purely material side, no means of evading Intourist if you go to the Soviet Union at least on a short visit. In view of the housing shortage, you can't very well expect to stay with friends; so you've got to live in an Intourist hotel, whether you like it or not. Not that I dislike the Intourist personnel as such; the men tend to be on the formal side; but the female staff—waitresses, and maid and floor clerks (whom so many visitors always think to be police spies, who are there to watch all your movements)—are as chatty as any other Russian females, and love telling you about their domestic problems, their husbands, and children, their war experiences, and all that. . . . And some are poor miserable old women, still very poorly paid. Quite unlike spies. All the same, you don't feel quite free in Moscow except when you get away from Intourist tutelage, with their *gospodins* and their luxury cars.

Travel is so much simpler now than it was during the war. What a difference between my present trip and the PQ16 Convoy in May 1942, which took 28 days to sail from Middles-

brough to Murmansk, was dive-bombed for six days, and lost
eight out of its 35 ships! And then six days and nights in a
"hard" carriage to get from Murmansk to Moscow. Or else
that flight in one 16-hour hop on the Catalina flying boat
from the Shetlands to Archangel, on July 2, 1941, a few days
after the war had begun in Russia. . . . My first contact
with "Russia 1959" was a contact with the super-modern
Russia of Khrushchev. Three and one-half hours from Paris
to Moscow. TU-104—the famous Tupolev. At the beginning
of the journey the air hostess announced: "Our route takes us
over Brussels, Amsterdam, Copenhagen, Riga. We shall be
flying at an altitude of 30,000 feet and at a speed of 520 miles
an hour. The outside temperature will be 40 to 58 degrees
below zero. The captain is called Mendelberg, and my name
is Tamara. . . ." Less than an hour after taking off from Orly,
we were flying across the North Sea, between Holland and
Denmark. Then the whole of green Denmark, islands and all,
was down below, looking like a relief map, with bits of Sweden
and Norway included. Gadgets the same as on any modern
Western plane—little eating-tables, napkins wrapped in cello-
phane, and the wrappers saying "AEROFLOT" and "Made in
Liepaja, Latvian SSR, Order No. 6220, Printing 20,000,000
copies." Meal—a bit of rather dull cooked veal with peas and
carrots: a triangle of processed cheese made somewhere near
Smolensk (grim memories of 1941!); a sticky cake and an
apple, thermos-flask tea, but no wine—all well below Air-
France standard. A certain "English" sloppiness about it, if
you like. (Funny, by the way, about the pilot being called
Mendelberg, as much as to say "Remember once and for all:
in the Soviet Union we don't discriminate against Jews, if we
allow a chap called Mendelberg to fly a TU-104.")

A paper was passed round: flying over Amsterdam 17.21;
Copenhagen, 18.13; Riga, 19.03; landing Moscow 20.02. By
the time we crossed the Latvian coast, it had grown dark and,
except for an occasional light, nothing could be seen of Russia.
But exactly at 20.02 the plane landed at Vnukovo. Long wait
at the customs until all the passengers were cleared—among
them half a dozen African students from Guinea. Sign of
the times, too. Then an Intourist car drove me into Moscow.
The miles and miles of brand-new blocks in the southwest,
the spire of the University and of the other Stalin–Gothic
skyscrapers were all new to me; but the center of Moscow

looked much the same as before. I was taken this time not to the Metropole but to the equally old-fashioned Savoy, recently re-christened "Berlin." The driver made a point of commenting on the enormous amount of building that had been done in the southwest, and also talked about the weather. There were some patches of snow on the ground; the remnants of an unusually early snowfall a few days before.

I had come as a *de luxe* tourist, paying about $28 a day, on a ten-day visa; but the Soviet Embassy in Paris had received word that once I got to Moscow, I could get myself temporarily accredited as a correspondent, and live a cheaper and more normal life thereafter. I found there was no difficulty about that; within a few days I was given a blue press-card as *The Scotsman* correspondent, had my visa extended; was also able to collect some of my ruble royalties on the Russian translation of *France 1940–55;* whereupon I promptly gave up the *de luxe* suite (sitting-room, bedroom, private bath) and moved into a simple single room, costing 22 rubles a day, or about $2.25. So it's wrong to say that officials are *always* obstructive in Moscow. In this case everything went off perfectly nicely, and with the minimum delays. . . .

The Savoy—or rather, the Berlin—is, together with the Metropole and the National, one of the most old-fashioned hotels. On the stair leading down to the restaurant, there was a gigantic stuffed bear, holding out his paw, who must date back to the reign of Alexander III; on the staircase, there were oil paintings: copies of Shishkin's forest scenes, and of good old Socialist-Realist paintings of Stalin inspecting a battleship, or of Stalin and Voroshilov walking along the Kremlin battlements. The "floor clerk" on the third floor was a motherly, elderly widow, called Polina Afanasievna; a nice woman full of quiet dignity and a whimsical sense of humour, though belonging to one of the least fortunate groups of Soviet citizens; she had only a very small room to herself, and her wages were 500 rubles a month; small wonder she liked to do little odd jobs for hotel visitors, such as running errands for them like getting medicines at the *apteka,* and so on. She was a real godsend to me during the few days I was laid up with a bad spell of flu. And Liza, one of the maids, with dark hair, perfect white teeth and a beautiful Madonna-like face, a woman of about thirty-five, had, as a young girl, been under the German occupation; and she had a lot to say about that; but more about that later.

And the lift man, who brought up my papers while I was ill, was an elderly man and quite a character. He said he took part in the storming of the Winter Palace in Petrograd, back in November 1917; and then, in the early 1920s in Moscow, he worked in the *Ugrozysk*—the criminal investigation department—and "the banditism in Moscow was really something terrible in those days. . . . And then there were the stray children, the *bezprizornyie*—what a problem!" He was wounded in the last war, was now getting an old-age pension, but was allowed to earn a little extra by working the hotel lift a few hours every day. . . .

And there were lots of other characters in the hotel, and even more so among the customers of the downstairs restaurant. But more about them later, too.

The $2.25 room wasn't bad at all, though rather on the old-fashioned side: a lampshade with tassels over the heavy lamp standing on the large mahogany desk; a ghastly old inkstand with oily purple ink and with a bronze eagle attached, and weighing four or five pounds—sort of damned thing Smerdiakov must have used for battering in the skull of old man Karamazov. Also, an old-fashioned sofa, and tassels on the table-cloth, too. A nondescript "Crimean" landscape on the wall; but the wardrobe was new and modern, in light wood, made in Leningrad. . . . Outside, in the corridor, there was a constant coming and going and something of a babel of tongues; a lot of the customers here were members of Bulgarian, Czech and East German delegations. When I first moved into that room, it was still quite light; after a fortnight it had grown much darker; across the street they were building an annex to the *Detski Mir,* the children's department store, and in a fortnight they had put up two big new floors. The clanging of the huge crane on top of the new building and the motor horns went on from morning till night.

A short digression on being ill in Moscow. Sure enough, I had caught a very bad cold and, four or five days after arriving, I spent a miserable night. Temperature 39.9 or *anglice,* about 103. So, in the morning, I called for Polina

Afanasievna; she went down to the "service bureau," and, an hour later, the doctor came. Also an elderly woman, cheerful, neat, efficient-looking. Stethoscope and the thing for taking blood-pressure, and all that. "Acute catarrh of upper respiratory organs," she diagnosed. "Bad bronchitis. I'll send a nurse in an hour. You'll have to get six shots of penicillin. Also *banki*—cupping—tonight. You people from abroad," she added, "always seem to get ill when you come to Moscow in autumn. . . . Anyway, you ought to be all right in a few days. Only heaven help you if you go out too early—it'll be pneumonia and hospital." "Rather interesting to go to a hospital," I feebly ventured. Her manner suddenly changed. "I'm not joking. You've got to do as you are told." She wrote out a prescription for a cough mixture, and penicillin ampules, and codeine tablets. Whereupon Polina Afanasievna was sent off to the *apteka*. "How much do I owe you, doctor?" I said. "You owe me nothing," she grinned. "You're in the Soviet Union, and you don't pay doctors. We are paid by the State. However," she added, "since you aren't a registered patient, and there's no time to fill up the necessary forms, you'll have to pay for the medicines." Actually, the medicines came to next to nothing; the penicillin, which would have cost six dollars came to seventy or eighty-five cents and the rest only to a few kopeks—70 kopeks for the cough mixture, 60 kopeks for each little packet of codeine tablets. All of which shows what huge profits must be made by capitalist drug manufacturers.

The nurse came an hour later; a pretty, shy little thing who blushed as she stuck her syringe needle into my behind. However, she sat down for a moment, told me she was a medical student, but was doing a *stage* as a nurse; after that, I had several more visits from the motherly woman-doctor and from the nurse. The doctor was very insistent that I stop smoking; whereupon we compromised on four cigarettes a day; but when I said I'd probably cheat anyway, she said resignedly: "You men are all the same. Only, mind you, Soviet science has proved very definitely that smoking is very, *very* bad—bad for lungs, heart, digestion and everything—not to mention even more serious things like cancer which is often stimulated by excessive smoking. . . ."

Was she a good doctor? It was hard to say. Probably just a routine G.P. There are hundreds of thousands of them

(350,000 I'm told) in the Soviet Union; they have to work damnably hard (my doctor said she had 15 to 20 visits a day to pay); but there are so many doctors that there isn't enough money to pay them a lot. Such a "routine" doctor gets 900 rubles a month, slightly less than an average worker's wage.

Why so many visits? Well, anyone with a temperature of 99.1 can call a doctor to the house, free of charge; lately even this rule has been relaxed; there are, indeed, some types of flu, for instance, which you get without showing a high temperature. When a G.P. can't cope with a patient, he (or she) calls in a specialist, or else gets the patient sent to a hospital.

While I was in Moscow, I checked, as far as possible, on how the system worked; and it worked all right; several people I asked about it said that every Soviet citizen considered it his sacred right to get the doctor to come to the house at very short notice. "It's become part of our *mores,* of our way of life; some anxious mothers are even a bit irresponsible the way they get the doctor in for any little complaint—upset stomach or sore throat. . . . Our doctors are wonderful people; but they are overworked and underpaid." When I described my experiences—and within four days I *was* up and about—I was told: "Don't worry, we haven't doctors for Intourists only—we all have precisely the same facilities."

Apart from this unfortunate four days' interlude in bed, I spent the first few days in Moscow looking up old friends, dealing with various formalities, and just taking a look at the city. There were 5,000 taxis in Moscow now; this was new. The first night I was in Moscow I took a taxi to see my old friends Ralph Parker and Valentina Mikhailovna. They were living in Khokhlovski Lane, in the same old flat where I had lived through the bitterly anxious summer and autumn months of 1941. Now the shabby old flat had been beautifully modernized. How time flies! Valya's daughters were both married, the little one, who was a mere infant when I first knew her, being married to an Indian, and living in India, and the other one now a high-ranking dancer at the Bolshoi Theatre. Ralph had now lived in Moscow since 1942, and loved it. He was now playing an important part in organizing theatrical and musical ex-

changes between the USSR and the West. Other friends I
saw were Henry Shapiro and Ludmilla; Henry was now
very much the *doyen* of the press corps; he was the best-
informed correspondent on Russia, and was now being
treated by the Soviet authorities with all the respect he
deserved. He had done a supremely good newspaper job
even in the most difficult conditions; his comments had always been fair and moderate; his 1953 series of articles
—later published in book-form—were the best assessment
to be made by anyone on the immediate post-Stalin situation.
Ludmilla—the perfect buxom Russian blonde—was as charming and beautiful as ever. Also, I looked up my old friends Ed
Stevens and Nina; they were again living—after a longish
interval abroad—in their "Americanized izba" in Zatsepa, in
the wilds of Zamoskvorechie—on the other side of the river,
in what is still one of the most wooden and tumble-down
parts of Moscow, with its Ostrovsky associations and its
jungle of one- and two-story wooden houses. Nina's mother
—*Mamasha* to everybody—was there, looking as old and as
full of life as ever, and with the usual woolen scarf round her
head which she wore even indoors.

The same old streetcars were rattling along Zatsepa and
past the Paveletski Station; the crowds in and around the
Zatsepa market were, as before, on the rough side, and it
is scarcely surprising that the *vytrezvitel*—the "sobering-up
point"—attached to the local militia station, was still going
strong.

But what was most striking, of course, in a rough, rowdy
street like Zatsepa was the enormous amount of food that
was now around everywhere—enormous meat shops and
fish shops, full of goods, and what have you; a kind of Soviet
version of the "juicy potbellied Moscow" of Boborykin's
novel, *Kitai-Gorod,* describing Moscow in the 1880s. How
miserable Zatsepa used to look during the war, or during the
first post-war years. . . .

Parker, Shapiro, Stevens—theirs were, for all their differences, *the* three houses in Moscow where, thanks to the
hospitable Russian hostess in each case, you came nearest
to the idea of a most attractive East-West home.

What then were the great outward changes in Moscow,
where I hadn't been since 1948?

As I said before, a huge number of new houses and 5,000 taxis. A good number of private cars—27,000 in Moscow, I was told—besides many thousand "office" cars, but no major traffic problems, as we get in London or Paris. Many of the streetcar lines had disappeared, to be replaced by buses and trolleybuses, and, except at rush-hours, these were seldom overcrowded, and the familiar wartime sight of human "bunches of grapes" hanging from every platform had disappeared completely. Some of the buses were run without a conductor. The honest citizen dropped his 35 or 40 kopeks in a glass case and tore off a ticket; since there was nearly always somebody around, it was unlikely that he would cheat; even if, not having enough change, he paid 5 kopeks less than he should, there was a good chance that he would pay an extra 5 kopeks next time. The Mossoviet had been a little doubtful at first about the venture; after some months' experience it was found that the amount dropped into the glass box almost exactly corresponded to the number of passengers.

Several new lines had been built on the Metro; this was no longer called the Kaganovich Metro, but the Lenin Metro; the new stations were only slightly less sumptuous than those built in Stalin's days. In these old ones, the various Stalin effigies were still the same as before. In short, urban transport had enormously improved in the last eleven years.

Railway stations, too, looked much tidier and more orderly than before; a peculiarity about railway stations was that you couldn't get a drink there for love or money. It was part of the fairly strong anti-alcohol drive. Many of the railways had been electrified, and there were spick-and-span streamlined carriages on both suburban and long-distance lines.

A novelty to one who hadn't been in Moscow since 1948 was, of course, the skyscrapers, the *vysotnyie zdania;* they were absurd in many ways, yet had, somehow, become familiar and cherished landmarks of the Moscow scene. Khrushchev had severely condemned them as wasteful and totally unsuitable for family dwellings—though some of them *were* just blocks of flats and had remained so; others were hotels like the "Leningrad" and the "Ukraine;" a few were government buildings, such as the Foreign Ministry. A forbidding sort of place to which you weren't admitted without a pass, or without the uniformed guards first phoning a secretary to come down to the cathedral-like hall to escort you up to the tenth or twentieth floor. It made me miss the easy-going old establishment in the Lubianka, where you gained admittance, without much difficulty, to the office of my old friend Nikolai Grigorievich Palgunov, the head of the press department during the early stages of the war (and who had been *Pravda* correspondent in Paris in the late 1930s). I liked Palgunov—who later became head of TASS—and never quite understood the pathological hatred he aroused in so many correspondents; many Soviet officials I had got to know, then or later, were much more difficult and disagreeable.

Shops, shops, and more shops. Many of them simply labeled RYBA (Fish) or MIASO (Meat). Lots of new department stores, too, not only the GUM and TSUM and the various shops in Gorki Street, but in the outlying districts, too. I spent a couple of hours one morning in the *Detski Mir*, the Children's World, just across the street from my hotel; it has elevators, escalators and it really doesn't look very different from a similar shop in the West; what strikes one is not so much the difference as the similarity. Same old celluloid dolls, plush teddy-bears and other animals; more animals made of wood or *papier mâché;* greater perhaps than in the West is the emphasis on "science" toys— vast collections of "make-it-yourself" boxes for assembling wireless sets, car models, submarine models, etc. The wooden toys and teddy-bears cost 10 or 12 rubles,[1] some even less; all toys are relatively cheap. Also, there's a clothing department; a reasonable-looking boy's suit—jacket and trousers—100 to 150 rubles. Some of the toys are made in East Germany. Altogether, there's a lot of stuff of one kind or another imported from the "satellites." The *Detski Mir* is, of course, always crowded, but especially so on Sunday mornings. Typical of its "modernity" are the various automats which, for a mere 15 kopeks, throw out a flimsy notebook or a pencil.

---

[1] Although the official ruble rate is four to the dollar, this is largely theoretical; the "tourist" rate is 10 to the dollar; in terms of purchasing power the rate should be around 16 or 20. Thus an average wage (in terms of purchasing power) is about $57 a month, but allowances must be made for very low rents, and a large number of free services. (I am not taking account here of the subsequent—and largely nominal one-to-10 revaluation of the ruble.)

There are also self-service buffets in the shop, where they sell sandwiches and sausages, and applejuice for one ruble a glass.

There are also a lot of various "Russian handiwork" objects—wooden boxes and little vases and spoons; all these gold-and-red-and-black objects are now mass-produced, and cost next to nothing: 2 rubles for a "hand-painted" spoon, 7 rubles for a vase, etc.

I shan't describe the GUM in the Red Square or the TSUM near the Bolshoi Theatre (the old Muir and Merrilees); the point, I think, is that the stuff isn't uniformly good; and when it's good, it's expensive; but the stuff is *there* for anyone to buy according to his means. If you can't buy a high-quality to-measure suit for 1,500 rubles (more than an average month's wage) you can buy a suit of more or less "synthetic" stuff for 350 or 400 rubles; it won't look wonderful, but it'll wear, longer perhaps than the "pure-wool." High-quality shoes for men are between 300 and 400 rubles, but fairly presentable shoes can be bought for 150 rubles, while some women's shoes, made of "synthetic" material, cost 60 or 70 rubles.

There's a battle going on between the women's scarves and hats and the men's caps and hats; the "proletariat" is still wearing caps mostly, but hats are even invading the world of the manual worker. As for winter wear, fairly presentable men's fur hats can be bought for 70 to 100 rubles. No doubt, in the case of women, apart from the unlimited choice of inexpensive cotton fabrics, there are also plenty of expensive silk dresses and fine woolen costumes, and these cost a great deal. But certain articles can now be bought on a hire-purchase basis—men's suits, watches, jewelry, fur coats, expensive women's furs, also TV sets, washing machines, cars, etc. Only you have to be "regularly resident and regularly employed in Moscow." The TV sets cost, on the average, about 2,000 rubles or say, $200. A small car still costs some 20,000 rubles; and there's no eagerness on the part of the authorities to bring the price down; if it cost half that, there'd be too many people ready to buy a car.

Apart from cars, the purchase of which on a large scale is just *not* encouraged, there's plenty of stuff in the shops; some of it on the tawdry side, but it's *there*. If you want fancy stuff from abroad, you can even get some of that: in the big Gift Shop in Gorki Street, apart from some rather hideous and horrible pieces of domestic statuary (inkstands with bronze eagles and bears, etc.) there is a fine choice of glass, crockery, cutlery, etc., some of the stuff coming from Eastern Germany or Czechoslovakia, but most of it Russian-made. Some of the nicer enameled metal vases come from China (fairly expensive—120 to 150 rubles), and some beautiful handmade vases in different metals come from India.

Is there a craze about Western consumer goods? Among some Soviet citizens apparently there still is; there was an article in *Sovietskaya Rossiya* one day ridiculing the craze among certain Soviet girls for French perfumery; and the article went on to say that certain Soviet perfumes were every bit as good as French perfumes, and, indeed, better. There was an Englishwoman at the Brussels Exhibition, the paper related, a Mrs. Fry, who bought a bottle of *Red Moscow*, and now she keeps on ordering more bottles of the stuff, and "she says she won't touch French perfume with a bargepole." And Soviet perfumes are now being exported to 24 countries, including Canada and the United States.

This is one of the more extreme cases of Soviet chauvinism, or rather, of the desire to persuade the public that almost *everything* is as good as abroad, and even better. This, people don't quite believe; but the reactions to the American Exhibition at Moscow's Sokolniki Park last summer were significant, all the same: most of them thought that the consumer goods *were* better than Russian consumer goods; but that this was only a matter of time; in five years from now Russian goods would probably be every bit as good. All the same, what did impress young people tremendously were American *cars!*

I can see the objection: Well yes, this is Moscow, but what about the rest of the country? Large cities like Kiev, Leningrad, Tbilisi, Odessa, etc., are just as well supplied as Moscow; a few places like Riga (for obvious political reasons) are even *better* supplied; in other parts of the country, on the other hand, conditions vary considerably, as we have seen from the caustic remarks Khrushchev made at Vladivostok.

But I don't like to generalize; I shall later deal with a few concrete cases of how people live. . . .

Chapter 6

SOCIALIST LEGALITY

ONE OF THE GREATEST CHANGES between 1948 and 1959–60 was to be observed in the changed attitude to the police. People were no longer afraid of arbitrary arrest by the MGB or MVD (or NKVD or GPU or Cheka, as it was called before—*ein schönes Kind hat viele Namen*) and of that proverbial 3 A.M. knock on the door.

In this respect immense changes had taken place since the death of Stalin. The worst of the Cold War years—1948 to 1952—were, in their own way, just as terrifying as 1936–38, which were marked by the famous "purge" trials.

Everybody knows that there was a great deal of forced labor in Russia, and that there was a whole great "NKVD Empire" where millions of prisoners were made to work. How many? It is impossible to tell; but in any case, the prisoners did not run to 20, 30 or 35 millions, as some anti-Soviet propagandists used to claim at the height of the Cold War; these figures made absolutely no sense in the light of the population figures generally, or in the light of the number of adult males serving in the armed forces during the war, or running industry, transport, and everything else.

Broadly speaking, it may be reckoned that a few million people were in camps at the beginning of the war, and that perhaps half of them were, for one reason or another, released in 1941–42. A number, but not a large number, of people were sent to camps during the war, and a much larger number after the war, including deserters, "Vlassovites" (Members of an all-Russian Nazi brigade) recuperated in Germany, collaborationists, especially in the Western Ukraine and the

53

Baltic republics, etc. Moreover, a number of *nationalities* were resettled in the East, among them the Volga Germans (in 1941), and later, the Crimean Tartars, the Kalmuks, the Chechens and Ingushi and a few other minor Moslem nationalities in the Caucasus, all of whom had shown their "disloyalty" to the Soviet fatherland.

Thousands more—though not tens or hundreds of thousands—were deported between 1948 and 1952 as a result of various lurid affairs, of which the most famous was the "Leningrad Affair" of 1949, in which Voznesensky, a member of the Politburo, Popkov, "mayor" of Leningrad, and others lost their lives, while the whole Leningrad Party organization underwent a heavy purge at the hands of Beria and (as was later alleged by Khrushchev) Malenkov.

Similarly, there was, about the same time, a purge among Jewish intellectuals (some of whom, like the famous actor Michoels, were mysteriously murdered, others, like the poet Feffer, executed, and others deported).

But these were "political" operations, unconnected with any need for forced labor, the whole economic absurdity of which was becoming more and more apparent to many top members of the Party even in those days.

As we know, one of the first things the Party and the government did after Stalin's death was to disband the "NKVD's Forced Labor Empire." Under the various amnesty laws, as far as can be ascertained, all prisoners, other than the worst of the common criminals, were released in fairly rapid succession—though some such deportees actually did not get back till 1955 or 1956. Apart from a vast number of people who were amnestied (among them Vlassovites, collaborators, etc.) many were specifically "rehabilitated"; these rehabilitations were also extended to many people who had died or been executed a long time before.

My own view—which I put forward in the *New Statesman* at the height of the Cold War in 1948–49, and much to the indignation of those who talked of "twenty or thirty million slaves"—was that (not counting the resettled nationalities) there were somewhere between three and four million people in NKVD camps—which, heaven knows, was quite horrible enough.

In Moscow this time, I had a long talk on the subject with Henry Shapiro, in my opinion one of the very best

Western experts on Soviet affairs. How many people, I asked, did he think were still in camps at the time of Stalin's death? "About three or four million," he said.

"How about all those Dallin-Kravchenko-Nikolaevsky figures of twenty, thirty or even more millions?"

He shrugged his shoulders. "That was part of the Cold War gone completely crazy," he said. "You were here during the war, and you know what things were like. The simplest arithmetic made nonsense of these figures. When I was in the States in 1950 I was up against the same kind of thing as you in England. It was easy enough to disprove the Dallin-Kravchenko kind of stories; but in those days even the simplest two-and-two-make-four commonsense made you suspect of Communist sympathies!

"But you don't need much imagination," he went on, "to realize that if it was 'only' three or four million people in NKVD camps it was quite a monstrous enough business. And I can tell you this: if, as you say, 1948 was bad enough here, 1949 to 1952 was very, very much worse. Quite terrifying at times. First the Leningrad business, then the Jews. . . . But what happened since then—I mean the liquidation of Beria and his NKVD Empire, the amnesties and the rehabilitations, and the enforcement of Socialist Legality—is by far the most important thing that has happened in this country. *It is really the Third Russian Revolution.* Socialist Legality is *not* an empty phrase; it has utterly transformed the mood and temper of this country; morally and psychologically, it's more important than the Russian discovery of the H-bomb; it's more important than the enormous growth in prosperity in the last five or six years. People are no longer scared of the police; this is no longer, as it was in the Stalin days, a state within the state. Briefly, the main points of the present position are these: the sinister Troika, the Committee of Three,—which had a vast bureaucratic machinery at its disposal, and had the power to hold secret trials, to convict people secretly, after they had been arbitrarily arrested— exists no longer. The 'secret police' (the State Security police) is no longer an independent body, and there is no Ministry representing it in the Government. There is, instead, a Committee of State Security attached to the Council of Ministers; its head is a comparatively young man of about

40 called Shelepin,[1] a former head of the Komsomol—in other words, a man not associated in any way with the sinister old NKVD gang. The secret police can no longer arrest anybody without an order from a Court or from the *prokuratura* (a government department, roughly the equivalent of our Attorney-General's department). The head of this is the Procurator-General, General Rudenko—who, it is true, was active under Stalin, but who is now said to be completely converted to the concept of 'Socialist Legality.' But the most important point, of course, is that there can be not only no arbitrary arrests, but that all arrests must be followed by an open trial—except that, in some cases—but this is true in other countries, too—the Court may decide to try a person *in camera,* either for security reasons (spies, etc.) or for moral reasons (certain sexual crimes, for instance). And, of course, as in other countries, arrests can be made without a warrant only in cases of *flagrante delicto,* but, even then, a formal charge must be made within a strictly specified time. As far as can be ascertained, there are (except for a few actual spies, no doubt) no political prisoners in Russia any more; in jails and 'labor colonies' all you find now is ordinary offenders and criminals.

"It is, of course, openly admitted now, not only by Khrushchev in his secret report, and on other occasions, but by the texts of the new laws themselves, that confessions were extracted by intimidation, threats and tortures; the law now specifically states that none of these methods may be resorted to any longer and the NKVD Empire, with its slave labor, has gone; anyway, even during the last years of Stalin, it was being generally recognized that the whole system was not only inhuman, but also wasteful and thoroughly uneconomical. So the gold mining in Siberia, and all that, is now being done by well-paid labor, and the production per head is much higher than it used to be. . . . Further, the secret police is now under the authority of the Ministry of the Interior, and the green-capped frontier guards—with their rather sinister reputation—chiefly under the authority of the Ministry of Defense. I might also add that the Shelepin Committee works under the close supervision of the Central Committee, which is, in reality, the highest power in the land.

---

[1] Now promoted to the Party Presidium.

And the Central Committee is very hot on Socialist Legality."

"The question arises, of course," I said, "of who keeps custody over the custodians."

"Well," said Henry, "this, I daresay, is *the* 64-dollar question. But public opinion in this country *does* count for a great deal; the Party knows that Socialist Legality is immensely popular, and that there would be bitter resentment if an independent secret police were allowed to operate in the Soviet Union again.

"I daresay, if there were a serious threat of war from somewhere, and there were something of a super-vigilance campaign and a new kind of spy mania, people might get more easily arrested than now. Besides, the various constitutional guarantees that Soviet citizens now genuinely enjoy are not, strictly speaking, extended to foreigners in the Soviet Union."

"You mean," I said, "things like the secrecy of postal mail? Well, yes, there must be some reason why, occasionally, an air-mail letter from London or Paris takes 10 or 12 days to be delivered to me!"

"Sure, they continue to check on foreigners, and also inevitably keep a check on Russians who have anything to do with Western embassies."

"Yes," I said, "in this particular respect things haven't changed very much, have they? The other day I went to the British Embassy, and since it was cold and snowing, I was wearing the particularly grubby old fur hat I had bought here back in '47. The two cops outside were sure I was Russian, especially after I had greeted them with a breezy *dobryi den,* whereupon they sternly asked me who I was, and what I wanted. When I explained, they were all smiles and apologies. . . ."

A sort of codification of "Socialist Legality" is to be found in twelve texts, dated December 25, 1958, including the "Bases of Criminal Legislation of the USSR and the Union republics, adopted by the Second Session of the Supreme Soviet of the USSR," the "Law on Responsibility for State Crimes," the "Bases of Legislation on Legal Procedure in the USSR, the Union Republics and Autonomous Republics," the "Statement of Principles concerning Military Tribunals," etc., etc.

It is impossible to summarize briefly this enormous mass of legislation; but, throughout, "Socialist Legality" is stressed. Thus:

No person can be arrested other than by a Court order or on the instructions of the Procurator. The Procurator must immediately release any person illegally arrested, or detained beyond the term specified in his sentence.

Judges are independent and submit only to the law. They must try every case only on the strength of the law, in accordance with their legal Socialist conscience, and in conditions excluding any kind of outside pressure.

Preliminary investigations are public, except in cases when state secrets are involved. A "closed" investigation is also allowed in the cases of crimes committed by minors, in the case of sexual crimes or other cases involving the intimate lives of the persons concerned.

The Court, the procurator and inquiring magistrate must deal with every case from every angle, and aim at a complete and objective inquiry, and weigh up all the favorable and unfavorable elements. . . . The *onus probandi* must not be shifted on to the accused.

It is forbidden to extract evidence from the accused by means of violence, threats and other illegal means. [In other words, no more torture as was, admittedly, practiced in the Purge Trials of 1936–37.]

In assessing the evidence, the Court [etc.] must weigh this evidence on the strength of their inner conviction, based on the all-round, complete and objective examination of all the circumstances of the case. . . . No evidence can be given *a priori* value.

The particularly dangerous state crimes are the following:

Treason (anything up to death penalty); Espionage (ditto); Terroristic Acts (8 to 15 years); Terroristic Acts against the representative of a Foreign Power (ditto); Diversionist Acts (anything up to death penalty); Wrecking (8 to 15 years); Anti-Soviet Agitation and Propaganda (3 to 10 years); War propaganda (ditto); The Organization of Activities aiming at Specially Dangerous State Crimes and Participation in Anti-Soviet Organizations (anything up to death penalty).

Other "State Crimes" include:

Violation of national or racial equality (6 months to 3 years' imprisonment [2] or exile from 2 to 5 years) [3] ;

The Revelation of State Secrets (5 to 8 years);

The loss of documents containing State Secrets (ditto);

Banditism (anything up to death penalty);

Smuggling (3 to 10 years, and confiscation of property);

Mass disorders (2 to 15 years);

Evasion of Military Service (1 to 5 years);

Evasion of Mobilization Order (anything up to death penalty);

Evasion in wartime of fulfilling orders or paying taxes (1 to 5 years);

Illegal departure abroad, or illegal entry into Soviet Union (1 to 3 years);

Violation of currency regulations (3 to 8 years and confiscation of property).

The definition of "anti-Soviet agitation and propaganda" is as follows:

Agitation and propaganda the aim of which is to undermine or weaken the Soviet State or to encourage dangerous state crimes, or the spreading of slanderous fabrications injurious to the political and social structure of the Soviet Union, and the fabrication, storing or distribution of literature aiming at this are punished by terms of imprisonment ["deprivation of freedom"] from 6 months to 7 years, or by deportation from 2 to 5 years.

In wartime, or in the case of old offenders, the penalty can go up to 10 years' imprisonment.

Punishment is defined as being not only "a penalty for the crime committed," but also as something "the purpose of which is to improve and re-educate the prisoner, so that he develops an honest attitude to work, a respect for the rules of Socialist society, a strict respect of the law"; and also as a warning to others.

[2] The exact term for imprisonment (here as elsewhere) is *"lishenie svobody,"* i.e. "deprivation of freedom," which does not necessarily mean being locked up in a *prison*.

[3] This is defined as follows: "Propaganda and agitation which aims at arousing racial or national hatred or animosity, as well as the direct or indirect limitation of a citizen's rights on the strength of his race or nationality, or the granting of privileges to citizens on the same basis is punishable by terms of imprisonment from six months to three years or by exile from two to five years."

The death penalty is defined as exceptional and existing only "pending its complete abolition."

> The death penalty—by shooting—may be applied in cases of treason, espionage, diversionism, terrorist acts, banditism and premeditated murder with aggravating circumstances, as defined by the relevant laws. . . . Persons under 18 cannot be sentenced to death nor women pregnant at the time of the crime, the sentence or the execution of the sentence.

At the Twenty-first Congress, on February 4, 1959, an important speech was made by A. N. Shelepin, the head of the State Security Committee. This speech was interesting in several respects; it pointed to a wholehearted devotion to Khrushchev personally; it stressed the absolute importance of Socialist Legality (or "revolutionary legality," as Shelepin called it); and it dwelt on the vital need to strengthen the "security organs" of the USSR in view of the tremendous efforts made by foreign, and especially American espionage, to cause damage to the USSR.

> The point of our proletarian sword—our security organs—is directed against the agents who are sent here from abroad. The capitalists and revisionists would, of course, like us to fold up the work of our security organs—but this is an idle hope. . . . Sabotage against the USSR and the other Socialist countries and the blunt interference in their internal affairs have been raised to the level of a state policy by the USA.
>
> Over 20,000 people are working in the central American intelligence agency, which alone costs the USA one and one-half billion dollars a year; American counter-espionage is now twelve times more extensive than just after the war. In Western Germany alone there are over forty American espionage organizations, while in West Berlin, there are sixty spy organizations belonging to the various capitalist countries, and engaged in actively disruptive work in the Soviet Union and the Peoples' Democracies. . . . A similar feverish activity is shown by the USA in the Near and Middle East. The enemy is looking desperately for every little chink in our armor.

Then Shelepin came to "Socialist Legality":

> The organs of State Security are given the daily care of the Communist Party and the support from the whole of the Soviet people. Inside these organs the consequences of the nefarious

activities of Beria and his henchmen have been completely liquidated. Under the immediate guidance of the Central Committee
of the CPSU, its Presidium and Comrade N. S. Khrushchev
personally, revolutionary legality has been wholly and completely
restored in the last few years, and those guilty of breaches of
this legality have been punished. And every Soviet citizen can
be absolutely sure that this shameful business—the violation of
revolutionary legality—will never happen again. The Party and
its Central Committee, inspired by the example of Lenin, will
never allow it. (*Loud cheers.*)

When Soviet officials start on historical reminiscences, they
sometimes become a little puzzling—even to their own audi-
ences. Thus Shelepin rather unexpectedly declared that the
present State Security organs should follow "in the glorious
traditions of the Cheka (the original name for the Soviet secret police) and Comrade Dzerjinski."

For although Comrade Dzerjinski was merciless to the enemies
of the Socialist State and the working class, the Cheka, at the
same time, carefully distinguished between real enemies and
those who were committing crimes out of stupidity, or because
they had temporarily fallen under the influence of the enemy.
. . . He instructed the Cheka to arrest only those whose criminal
activity had been proved, and not on the strength of suspicions.

To show that State Security was returning to the "purity"
of the Cheka in the days of Lenin and Dzerjinski, Shelepin
was stretching historical points mercilessly, such as the suggestion that the Cheka never arrested mere "suspects."
Then Shelepin quoted a prophecy by Lenin, according to
which, as Soviet society progressed and revolutionary legality
grew stronger and stronger, "the sphere of activity of the security organs would become increasingly narrow."

"And it is, indeed, true," Shelepin said, "that the punitive
functions of the security organs have been greatly reduced, and
will continue to be reduced. But the reduction in the number of
persons engaged in state security and the reduction of their
punitive role do not mean that we have less to do, or that the
enemy has become less active. . . . The point is that whereas
foreign espionage is more active than ever, there are no longer,
inside the country, any more social reasons for mass-criminality.
Several generations of new men have been born since the Revolu-

tion, men 100 per cent devoted to the Party and the Soviet people. But there are still some outsiders, irresponsible babblers, degenerates and drunks who may easily be caught on the enemy's fishing hook."

On the whole, however, he thought a new attitude should be adopted towards offenders, especially young offenders. There were still too many people who liked to make criminal charges against young people, even for minor offenses. The important things were prophylactic educational measures and persuasion. Minor offenses should not be dealt with by criminal courts, but by the Komsomol, the trade unions, factory and *kolkhoz* collectives, etc. They should take under their tutelage people who have committed minor crimes, and give them a chance to mend their ways as members of the collective, rather than let them serve a court sentence.

An increasingly important role in this should be played by things like "Comrade Courts." [4]

This tendency to give short, rather than long sentences, and to let "Comrade Courts," aided by volunteer militia forces, deal with minor offenses and even crimes was one of the things that I found actively discussed in Moscow. The "collective," the "pressure of public opinion" replacing court action in cases other than major crimes seemed one of the most interesting developments in Russia. As Shelepin said, such methods were also "more charitable to the guilty man's family and friends"; in other words, better to be temporarily disgraced by the "collective" with a small fine or demand for apology than to go to jail.

"Comrade Courts," it seems, dealt particularly effectively with cases of drunkenness, hooliganism, and sexual immorality—though, in this case, there was a tendency to interfere with a person's "private affairs," and this was being resented by some, who also claimed that "Comrade Courts"

[4] Comrade Courts are "elective social organs called upon to help actively in the education of citizens in a Communist spirit. . . ." The main task of such Courts was to prevent lawbreaking "by means of persuasion and public pressure." Such Courts could be created in enterprises, offices, senior schools, on collective farms, among tenants of a house or block of houses, etc. Members of the Court were elected by the "collective," for a period of two years.

had a somewhat subjective way of assessing "anti-social behavior."

A few curious examples of how the system worked could be quoted. I shall tell later the story of how a Komsomol cell dealt with an example of "swinish behavior"; here the punishment took the form of a personal boycott by the offender's fellow-workers. Another case was that of a student of a technical college who had been guilty of a "gross act of hooliganism." In the past, he might have got five years. Now he was sentenced to 15 *days* "compulsory labour"—he was made to sweep the street outside the institute, and do other menial jobs all day under the supervision of a cop, while his comrades would talk past and laugh at him. "Young hooligans are much more scared of this kind of punishment than of a more dramatic five-year sentence." I was told.

Another story I liked (and which is apparently true) was that of a young student in Georgia, a Stalin devotee. One day he thought of nothing better than to tear down a picture of Khrushchev and spit on it. He was arrested and charged with anti-Soviet activity, and given eight years. His mother rushed to Moscow, wrote frantic letters to Khrushchev, whereupon Khrushchev got the case revised; the young man was sentenced instead to three months' imprisonment for "hooliganism"; since he had already served this term, he was let out at once.

All this gradual (if only partial) transfer of "judicial" authority from the Courts to the various "collectives" is treated as being a very important contribution towards the building of an increasingly Communist society.[5]

[5] Whereas all this marks, in respect of "Socialist legality," a great advance on the state of affairs under Stalin, there remains, as we have already said, *an element of unpredictability in the Khrushchev régime.* Under a number of decrees approved by the Supreme Soviet of the RSFSR on May 4, 1961, not only was the death penalty extended to crimes such as the looting of State property, the forging of bank notes, certain types of organized banditism, and also to certain "particularly dangerous old offenders"—which seemed a serious departure from the "re-education" principles governing the criminal code, but a new form of labor camps was devised for "idlers" and "parasites."

As regards the first point, Khrushchev, during his long journey through Asiatic Russia, sharply denounced various cases of "large-scale looting of State property"; these crimes had been committed by the very people whose job it had been to enforce the law; instead, to hide their misdeeds, they had forged the statistics. Soon afterwards, indeed, it was announced that the First Secretary of the CP of Tajikistan, the Prime Minister of Tajikistan and a large number of high officials in the same Republic had been summarily dismissed. Would these now be shot?

As for the camps for "loafers, parasites and other anti-social elements," this raised a number of very tricky points. Who *was* a "parasite" who could be sent to a camp for anything from two to five years, and also have that part of his property confiscated which had been acquired by means other than work? And who could condemn the "parasite" to such deportation and confiscation?

The charges of "parasitism" could be brought against a person not only by the legal authorities, but also by trade unions and other "mass organizations" (such as "Comrade Courts"), and even by individuals. No doubt, a camp sentence passed by a "collective" was subject to the ratification by the local soviet; but even so, it was only too obvious that this system could give rise to personal vendettas and other abuses.

This is all the truer as the offenses in question do not come under any definite criminal category, and can only be assessed "subjectively." Those liable to be deported, in terms of the decree, are:

persons dodging useful work, and living on incomes not derived from work, but from practices such as the exploitation of plots of land, automobiles, or houses, or guilty of other anti-social activities allowing them to lead a parasitical form of life.

The decree also applies to illicit distillers of alcohol, particularly numerous in the countryside.

Only what do "parasite" incomes mean in practice? They can, at a stretch, cover a multitude of sins. In fact, any kind of speculation may be regarded as "parasitical": if, for example, a man buys a dilapidated hovel, repairs it, and sells it at ten times the price he paid for it, it is a case of "speculation." Similarly, a peasant who is little more than nominally a member of a *kolkhoz,* and makes his money from selling vegetables grown on his own plot, may also rank as an "idler." But the truth is that there are perhaps millions of people in Russia whose incomes may rank as "parasitical" in the sense that they, in fact, fulfill functions which should be, but aren't, fulfilled by such-and-such ministries or industries. Where there are short-ages, there is bound to be "speculation," and shortages are still numerous; thus, agricultural implements which cannot be got in a village through "normal" channels, are often bought for a higher price from some private individual who has taken the trouble to obtain them from a factory. In fact, there is a kind of black market caused by the deficiencies in Soviet distribution. Numerous cases are known of factories, anxious to fulfill their plans, but hampered by red-tape delays, which resort to "speculators" who supply them more quickly than official organizations do, with spare parts, raw materials, etc.

So the root of the trouble is economic, rather than moral. Even though "speculation" may be morally unworthy of a Soviet citizen, the temptation to go in for it has often been created by certain economic flaws in the system itself. The revival of the "camp" system with a view to discouraging or stamping out "speculation" and "irregular incomes" does not appear to have made a good impression in Russia; it has reminded people of the bad old days, and the very loose criteria by which "parasitism" is defined are apt to lead to dangerous abuses and miscarriages of justice.

Chapter 7

THE DEPORTEES' RETURN

IN HIS SPEECH on February 4, 1959, Shelepin recalled Khrushchev's phrase: "Today nobody in the Soviet Union is imprisoned for political motives any longer." This showed, Shelepin said, that the Party had "forged an unprecedented unity of political convictions amongst the Soviet people, and a monolithic unity around the Communist Party and the Soviet regime." Was the Khrushchev phrase quoted to be taken literally; or did it contain a slight quibble? If there were no political prisoners in prisons, were there perhaps some in camps? It seems fairly, though not absolutely, certain that there was no such quibble. It is extremely difficult to be positive about a matter like this. But I can say with certainty that *all* the people who, to my personal knowledge, had been deported between 1948 and 1952, were back in Moscow now.

The only exception was one man who, being too ill to travel, was still in hospital at Karaganda. I was shown some letters he had sent to his family in Moscow.

During the seven years I spent in Russia from 1941 to 1948 I had not had, I am glad to say, much personal experience of the NKVD, except that one took it, of course, for granted that people like Jack Margoulis, the nasty little London-born sub-manager of the Metropole, was there to keep an eye on you, and that the correspondents' secretaries —I didn't have any secretary—had to report to "the authorities" all the correspondents' doings and indiscretions—and *what* indiscretions? But one did hear, of course, of certain deportations—particularly from Poland and the Baltic Republics in 1940–41. In Moscow, during the war, such deportations were not numerous; but one incident does stick in my memory.

That is the case of Elizaveta Feodorovna. A strange case altogether. Her husband was a mysterious Greek, as ugly as sin. I first met him in 1941; he used to hang round correspondents and act as a sort of secretary and (curiously defeatist) tipster. His behavior was altogether odd. He used to go to the Japanese Embassy, where he had friends. And, during the evacuation of Moscow in 1941, he stayed on, and took his possessions to the Japanese Embassy.

Then, in October 1942, he was picked up, which was understandable perhaps. But a year later his wife was picked up, too. She was about 30, handsome, rather than pretty; with a kind of old-time "upper-class" dignity. She belonged to an old family of the Moscow gentry; and she lived in a wretched tumble-down wooden house, full of icons and family photographs (gentlemen in Tsarist uniforms, ladies dressed up in the sumptuous style of the 1800s) together with her aged mother, a religious old lady in a high-necked black dress, and also full of old-time dignity and a deep grievance. Elizaveta had, clearly, received an oldtime education, and spoke good French and English, and *madame mère* also spoke a refined French of the former upper classes. She had grievances galore; the old house was falling to pieces, the roof was leaking; her only son had been in trouble during the 1936 purge, and was, I gathered, still in Siberia; and then there was this appalling *mésalliance* with the Greek— "horrible creature," she would say, "an adventurer. He's going to get Liza into trouble yet. How he got round her, heaven only knows;—*lubov slepà, polubish i kozlà* (Love is blind, you can even fall in love with a goat.);—there were so many really *fine* people who were in love with her, and wanted to marry her; but no, she fell for this monster. . . ."

So the Greek vanished in October 1942, and then, a year later Elizaveta was also picked up, and (as I learned much later from her mother) was sent in a cattle-truck, together with dozens of other "suspect" women and children, and almost at the height of winter, to Novosibirsk. The journey lasted a fortnight, and nearly all suffered from frostbite when they finally reached their destination. They were all dumped in wooden barracks; and Elizaveta would probably have died (as some of the others did) out of sheer neglect, had not her sister-in-law—the wife of the "purged" brother—discovered her, and got her out of the Novosibirsk barracks, and been allowed to take her to her home in a Siberian town about 200 miles away, where she had a teaching job. After nursing Elizaveta for several weeks, she managed to get her a job in the same school. . . . Meantime, the Greek husband had been declared a spy and a *vrag naroda,*—an enemy of the people—and shot. A notification was sent to that effect to *madame mère.*

I tried to argue about this case with a high official of the Soviet Foreign Office, but he went all green with fear at the very mention of it. "I would strongly advise you," he finally said, "to say nothing more about it." "But," I said, "is a wife responsible for what her husband does—even if he *did* something?" "The NKVD," he said, "has discretionary rights in these matters, and, anyway, they must have known something about her. In any case, a wife-husband relationship covers a multitude of things, at least an indirect sort of complicity." "I don't quite see it." "I know you don't," he said, "but I don't wish to discuss the matter any longer, and would advise you to forget about it." Well, that was that.

Now I heard, at second hand, that Elizaveta was back in Moscow, married to a Soviet engineer, and very happy. Her mother had died long ago, and the old house had been pulled down. . . .

I made no attempt to see her; I thought it might embarrass her. That was *one* of my experiences of the NKVD during the war; as said before, many others were to follow, particularly after 1947.

The number of people whom I knew and who had been "in trouble" between 1948 and 1952 was quite substantial. As already said, all of them were back in Moscow now.

I met a few of them; but the one thing they would *not* talk about was their years of exile. All I could gather was that, although the journey *there* was often terrible, most of them, being "intellectuals," were given some sort of "intellectual" job, like teaching in a local school, or working as a clerk at some factory. . . .

A few, however, had had a much worse time; and these, while now fully rehabilitated, and working in good jobs in Moscow, were positively scared of meeting any foreigners;

they had had, as a result of being friends with foreigners, quite enough trouble, and they weren't going to tempt providence, Socialist Legality or no Socialist Legality. One never could tell; there might be another "vigilance campaign" or something. . . .

But the most astonishing phenomenon was this; I met several persons (some I had known before, others not) in important and highly responsible positions, who never breathed a word about *also* having been in trouble; it was from others that I learned that so-and-so had been picked up in 1950 or 1952, and had been "away" for a few months or even a few years. . . .

The attitude to these people on the part of their friends and relations was, as a rule, particularly warm, affectionate and considerate; the only amnestied people to whom the attitude of others was a good deal more reserved, and sometimes downright hostile, were the "collaborationists" and Vlassovites. But, in their case, too, there were different shades, and their case was frequently discussed in recent Soviet fiction.

Was Socialist Legality now firmly entrenched, and would arbitrary arrests never start up again? That this would be so was the deep conviction of most people and yet, where foreigners were concerned, they were still a little chary; for the easiest way of getting into trouble was still to have been, in some way, associated with a foreigner who, for all one knew, might some day turn out to have been a spy. . . .

However, by and large, the whole beastly NKVD "system" seemed to have gone forever. It had caused terrible misery to millions; it wasn't sadistic like the Gestapo, but it had often shown terrible callousness; on the whole, people weren't tortured or beaten to death; but many had been allowed to die of neglect.

This was also true of the "disloyal" nationalities who had been transplanted to Siberia and Central Asia. Apart from a substantial number of Poles and Balts (many of the latter, in particular, were suspected—some with good reason—of Fascist leanings and pro-Nazi sympathies), whole nationalities had been "resettled" in the East. The first to go were the Volga Germans who were living in a strategically important area on the Volga through which several railway lines ran (and some had committed railway sabotage in the early days of the war). All these Volga Germans—whose ancestors had settled there in the reign of Catherine, but who had remained extremely particularist—were sent off to Siberia in the summer and autumn of 1941, in conditions very similar to those Elizaveta had known. General conditions in 1941 were terribly hard, and many were allowed to die of hunger and neglect.

Others who were later deported *en masse* were the Kalmuks (who, egged on by Kalmuk *émigrés* living in Nazi Germany, such as the notorious "Prince" Tundutov, had fraternized with the Germans in a big way), and certain predominantly Moslem nationalities like the Crimean Tartars as well as the Chechens, Ingushi and Karachaii in the Caucasus. The Crimean Tartars were being collectively punished for the active collaborationism of many of their men; when I was in the Crimea in 1944, people still talked of the auxiliary police, working hand-in-hand with the Gestapo, and entirely composed of Tartars, which did much to track down loyal Soviet citizens. And it was recalled that during the Crimean War, the Tartars had also worked for the French and English! The small Moslem nationalities in the Caucasus also proved thoroughly disloyal, remembered their long guerrilla war against the Russians throughout most of the nineteenth century, and declared themselves "for Hitler." When I was in the Northern Caucasus in 1946, the Russians there spoke, almost with a touch of admiration, of the "tremendously efficient job" the NKVD had done in deporting the entire Chechen and Ingush population in two or three days. A considerable number of arrests were also made among the Kabardinians. But these were, on the whole, "let off with slight injuries"—even though there was a Kabardinian Prince who had presented a splendid white charger to Hitler personally.

Whatever losses in human lives they had suffered during their exile, the Kalmuks and the Caucasian Moslems had now all been allowed to return to their homes;[1] as for the Volga Germans and the Crimean Tartars, whose "disloyalty" had been even more blatant, there was no evidence that they had been permitted to return. Many of the Germans had settled

---

[1] To show, as it were, that bygones were bygones the Kalmuk Autonomous SSR was awarded in 1959 the Order of Lenin to mark . . . the 350th anniversary of the Kalmuks joining Russia!

round Barnaul, where even a German paper was now being published. But the rest? Here was still one of those little mysteries which one still finds in Russia, even under Khrushchev. All that could be said with any certainty was that both the Crimean Tartars and the Volga Germans were not wanted back. The Crimea had become part of the Ukraine, and a famous holiday playground for the whole of Russia; the Tartars would be a foreign body there. And the Volga Germans?—well, they were Germans, and now probably more anti-Russian than ever. Whether they would ever be allowed to return to their once "autonomous" territory, with its capital called Engels, was hard to say.

The whole thing was, of course, an anomaly. Estonians, Latvians and even the Catholic Lithuanians were more or less adapting themselves to being good Soviet citizens. In their case, the process was being hastened by very special privileges that were being heaped on the Baltic Republics— notably an intensive development of industry, especially in Estonia and Latvia, a higher standard of living than in the rest of the USSR, and a great deal of flattery in the form of prizes for Baltic writers, composers, etc. This went together with a considerable amount of assimilation and intermarriage with Russians who had been moved in large numbers to cities like Tallinn and Riga.

Chapter 8

THE ANTONOVS

I HAD GOT to know Anna Ivanovna Antonov during the war;
she was working as a clerk in a government office, and I had
met her at a friend's house. I had got to know her and both
her sons. The elder one, called Vanya, was an uncouth youth
of about 20, whom I met when he came to Moscow on leave
from the Front. Her husband, Peter Ivanovich, was also in the
Army and I met him only once; her younger son, Kolya, was
only 11 then. Anna Ivanovna, who was in her forties then,
had one of those round, amusing, typically Russian faces,
with a turned-up nose and a large mouth, with several
teeth crowned in steel. She was of peasant stock, and she,
little Kolya and her mother, Pelageya Matveievna, lived in
an old wooden izba, which had been built by her father
around 1890 in what was then still a village, miles from the
center of Moscow. In 1943, however, it was only about ten
minutes' walk from the Metro terminus. *Babushka* was an
old peasant woman, almost illiterate and deeply religious;
and I remember going to her funeral in 1944; it was a church
funeral, with choir, priests and all. Anna Ivanovna herself
was very religious in those days. She had a miserable enough
time, and, though always sounding and looking cheerful, she
was, deep-down, constantly worried about her husband and
her elder boy (the oldest of all had been killed at the beginning of the war), and, perhaps even more so, about Kolya.
Kolya was a tall slim fair-haired boy, with delicate features
and delicate hands; he was doing remarkably well at school;
but he was always hungry. In 1944 or 1945 I used to visit
them fairly frequently, and bring Kolya from NAAFI a

couple of tins of Nestlé's which he adored. The izba was terribly bare; all the same, every time I turned up, Anna Ivanovna insisted on producing a glass of tea with a bit of sugar and a small slice of black bread.

Now, eleven years later, I found the old izba still there, though nestling now in the shadow of an enormous new eight-story block of flats. It was snowing. I was greeted by the loud bark of a huge Newfoundland kind of dog, who kept jumping threateningly at the garden gate. And then Anna Ivanovna came scurrying out of the izba. She chased away Polkan, there were shrieks of joy, hugs and embraces, and she then took me into the crowded main room of the izba.

All the Antonovs were there: the husband, Peter Ivanovich, now a foreman at a biscuit factory, and Vanya, the elder boy, now 35, looking as awkward and uncouth as ever, and my old friend Kolya, now a tall handsome lad of 26. Here also was a dark pretty girl, a little on the plump side, called Valya, and I was at once told that they were going to get married next week, and I must come to the wedding party.

Peter Ivanovich promptly brought out a bottle of vodka, and, after a lot of fussing in the kitchen, Anna Ivanovna produced a huge meal—consisting of soup, sliced ham, three different kinds of sliced sausage, hot dogs, a huge tube of processed cheese, a mountain of white bread, tea and a two-pound tin of Bulgarian strawberry jam.

She was looking distinctly fat now, and I had never seen her so happy before. "Look at the amount of food we get these days!" she exclaimed. And she seemed particularly pleased about the tube of processed cheese: "That's the kind of stuff we Soviet people are now producing!" The huge slobbering dog was also admitted to the feast, and joyfully swallowed a couple of hot dogs. Dogs being fed on sausages—this was quite a symbol! I remembered the days of the glass of tea and the bit of black bread.

Anna Ivanovna was pleased with life. She was 58 now, and, for three years, she had now been on an old-age pension of 520 rubles (about $51) a month, quite a handsome contribution to the family income. She was entitled to this pension after 25 years' service.

Peter Ivanovich talked about his biscuit factory, and about how much better people were living now; many of his fellow-workers had already got new flats, and he was hoping that next year he and Anna Ivanovna would also get a flat in the new block that was being built a short distance away. Vanya was not living in Moscow, but in a provincial town about a hundred miles away. He had his wife and two children there, and he worked as a mason on the blocks of flats that were being built there; but he had come to Moscow for a three-months' course to "improve his qualifications" as a crane operator. After fighting all his way to Berlin, he had stayed on in the Army, and had spent a couple of years in the Western Ukraine fighting Ukrainian nationalist bands who were still active under the command of German SS officers. "A rotten lot," he said, "and we had to be pretty tough with them. But we, too, lost quite a few men." He had also done some service in Poland after that, fighting the AK underground. "Funny people, the Poles," he said, "as false and doublefaced as you make them." And after completing his military service, he was induced to spend a couple of years on the Virgin Lands in Kazakhstan. "It was hard work, but we got some pretty wonderful results in the end."

Kolya was a different type. He had worked hard for four years at a Technical Institute, and was now a fully-qualified chemist, with a good job at a chemical laboratory; his fiancée also worked in the same lab. And now they were going to get married.

Anna Ivanovna talked about how wonderful life had become in the Soviet Union, and said she was particularly happy to have her TV set. Whereupon this was duly demonstrated, while Kolya showed me a very modern camera and the numerous pictures he had taken while vacationing in the Caucasus last summer and climbing Mount Elbrus. Peter Ivanovich showed off his Soviet electric razor. "We are getting on pretty well," said Anna Ivanovna, and remarked on what a wonderful man Khrushchev was. "And he was pretty good in America, too, wiping the noses of some of the cheekier Americans! I tell you," she said, "things are much, much better than they used to be under the old man."

At this point Vanya intervened and remarked that, after all, Stalin had done his stuff during the war. "Without him, we might never have won." "Quite true, quite true," said Anna Ivanovna, "but he wasn't the nice, human sort of chap Nikita Sergeievich is. He can be *so* funny! And *papa* Stalin did become a bit strange towards the end." And then she asked no end of questions about the West of which she, obviously, didn't think much. What was bread like in France, for instance? she asked. When I described the *baguette*, and said it was delicious when fresh, but that in a few hours it got stale, she said: *"Ach!* must be maize bread; only maize bread goes stale so quickly." When I assured her it was made of good wheat flour, she said: *"Ach!* that's what *they* tell you." And again she got on to Khrushchev's visit to the USA, and although she thought Eisenhower "probably all right" ("though if we weren't as strong as we are, they wouldn't have invited Khrushchev to America"), some of the things they did were really indecent. "That awful *cancan*—can you imagine! Pretty depraved lot, aren't they? . . ."

The main room of the izba was crammed with old icons. "They were *babushka*'s," Anna Ivanovna explained. "And they do look pretty, don't you think? However, when we move into a new flat next year, I shall put them away, or maybe sell them to tourists." "Oh no, she won't," Kolya laughed. "Mother has still a soft spot for religion, and she'll stick to her icons all right." "Nonsense," said Anna Ivanovna, "I never go to church now!" "Yes," said Kolya, "but you still hanker for it, hard as we have been trying to educate you!" He took down from a shelf a large bundle of *Science and Religion* magazines, with some snappy articles about the Pope, and "The Racket of Lourdes," the "anti-Soviet" activities of the Baptists in Russia, and the great harm done to *kolkhoz* harvests by religious holidays, such as St. Peter's Day in June, when whole villages went on the binge for days on end. . . .

But it was now eight o'clock, and Anna Ivanovna turned on the television. There was a long newsreel about Khrushchev, and they again commented on what a nice, simple man he was. And then there was a long program of "Extracts from Classical Viennese Operetta." When it was over, Kolya said: "We don't often get this sort of stuff on TV, but it's great fun once in a while. . . . But, on the whole, I am not altogether in favour of TV. It's all right for people like Mother and Dad, but it has a bad effect on young people, stops them reading books. . . ."

I saw the Antonovs again a few days later. Anna Ivanovna

was alone in the house when I arrived. She told me with great delight that, after the wedding, Kolya and his wife would stay with her in the little annex of the izba, until they got a flat of their own.

Kolya was, obviously, her great favourite. "I just can't tell you how proud I am of him," she said. "He's such a hard worker, so terribly conscientious; you should have seen how he got top marks every time at his Institute. You know what a hard time I had with him when he was a child; I was absolutely terrified he might get TB, or something. And his father wasn't much help, as you know. First he was in the Army; and then, when he got back—with his Warsaw medal and his Berlin medal—he was so damned pleased with himself, he didn't take much interest in us. Now he's settling down, but for a time, he had a girl on the side, and used to drink a lot, too. So it was I—with the help of the Soviet State, of course—who had to bring Kolya up. And I can tell you, the way he has been getting on with his work, he is going to be a very great scientist. His chief thinks the world of him. . . . And the girl he chose—they work together in the lab—is a very good, earnest girl. He's turned out ever so much better than Vanya. I am not too happy about him. First he spent all that time in the Army, and then on the Virgin Lands, and now he's just a stone mason. No culture at all. No doubt, after he has done his course here, he'll work a crane, and make a little more money; but what kind of job is that, operating a crane?. . . . And he married an awfully silly woman; picked her up somewhere in the Western Ukraine just after the war, she speaks a ridiculous kind of Russian, and has no idea about bringing up the children; now that our government has started these *internats*, these boarding schools, I'll see if I can't get them admitted to one of those. . . . They'll never become responsible Soviet citizens with a mother like that. . . ."

Kolya and Valya came in, and told me about the wedding arrangements; at 5 P.M. on Saturday they would go to the ZAGS, the registry office—"Oh no! no church wedding!"— and then at 6.30 the wedding party would start at her mother's and stepfather's house; and they gave me instructions of how to get there by streetcar—a good three-quarters of an hour from the Paveletsky Station. Again we had supper,

and then Kolya said he couldn't be bothered looking at the
TV, and we went for a long walk towards town.

"Your mother," I said, "thinks you are going to become a
very important person in the Soviet State."

Kolya laughed. "That's just like Mother; she thinks I am
the great masterpiece of her life. But really, I assure you, I
am a very ordinary man. And there are millions like me. I
am just a young Soviet technician, and there's nothing unusual about me. Of course, I had to work damned hard at
the Institute, and now I can earn about as much as my
father, and twice as much as my brother Vanya. I and all my
comrades—or nearly all—look at it this way: we make a good
life for ourselves, but at the same time, we are very conscious
of doing our part to serve the Soviet State. And we are not
ashamed of being well-paid; I earn 1,200 rubles, which is
very good at my age. But to be a Communist you don't have
to be miserably poor!"

"Are you a Party member, Kolya?"

"No, but I hope to be next year. I've been very active in
the Komsomol, and there should be no difficulty. Mind you,
we aren't all goody-goody; we Soviet boys like work, but also
we like to enjoy ourselves. We are not like the Chinese. They
really work like maniacs. We had a few Chinese students at
the Institute; they'd form their own study groups, and grind
all night long—anything to come out on top. They never
relax at all. I suppose the Revolution is new to them, and
they are at the stage our Komsomols had reached by the beginning of the first Five-Year Plan. They're a bit adolescent
in their enthusiasm. We take things more calmly. We know
our machine is working; and I suppose Khrushchev is right
when he says that, in the end, we'll 'bury capitalism.' We've
got practically the whole world on our side; look at Africa
and Asia. *We* turn out more engineers and technicians than
anybody else; and of course they'll go to India and other
underdeveloped countries; one of the men working in my
chemical lab is going off to Bhilai, in India, next month. I
have never been abroad myself; I'd like to go. Only I'd be
more interested in going to China, India or Indonesia than to
Western Europe or America."

"When you say you relax, what do you mean?"

"Well, last summer, for instance. Valya and I went for a
whole month to the Caucasus. I showed you some of the

photos I took. We lived for a fortnight in a 'Young Scientists' Camp' at the foot of Mount Elbrus; we climbed nearly up to the top of Mount Elbrus; later we went to Vladikavkaz; there we took a taxi (there were six of us) and drove in it all down the Georgian Military Highway—which is really quite marvelous. It cost a hundred rubles a head, but was worth it. We sang songs, and recited Lermontov. It was great fun. Then we stayed a few days at Tbilisi and then took the train back to Moscow. It was a wonderful holiday. And when you say 'relax,' well, people like me also read a lot (that's why I am a bit against TV)—I've read most of the Russian classics, and and also some foreign authors, Dickens, Stendhal, and, of course, some modern Soviet books; but, of course, with specialization like mine, one hasn't really time to read everything. Altogether an encyclopedic kind of culture they used to have in the past is quite impossible now; technicians like me are, first and foremost, interested in science and technology; so we haven't really much time to read fine literature and go to the theatre; but, of course, we are all crazy about things like Sputniks and moon rockets. Some time ago I even thought of volunteering as a passenger in the next moon rocket; but that's childish, of course—but I bet you there'll be thousands of volunteers, all the same!"

"In fact," I said, "you intend to belong to a sort of technological élite, to what they call in the West the New Class?"

He screwed up his face. "Oh," he said, "that's probably what my mother thinks; she imagines I'll be President of the Academy of Sciences, or Minister of something-or-other. There is no such thing as a New Class. As I said before, you don't have to be miserably poor to be a Communist. But certainly a very large number of people in the Union today are earning good money, and why not? That doesn't make them bourgeois. No doubt, there's some wirepulling here and there, and some nepotism; but you don't belong to what you call the New Class for more than one generation; doesn't matter whether you leave your children a million rubles, or a car or a datcha—for unless they also work very hard, it won't get them very far. . . ."

"There's been a lot in the papers lately," I said, "and especially in *Komsomolskaya Pravda*, about Socialist morality, and all that. Also about the pressure of public opinion, about not getting drunk, about not being dissolute in your love life, and all that. What do you think of that?"

"I suppose," he said a little squeamishly, "you are interested in our sex life? How Western you are! Aren't people in the West just obsessed with sex? Here, honestly, we don't attach all that much importance to it. Of course, we are no saints, but we believe in observing certain minimum rules of what's called Socialist morality. The important thing to most young people of my generation is the comradeship existing between boys and girls—complete equality, and ordinary human respect. Not everybody observes these rules. Not long ago, we had to deal with a case of swinish behavior. My Komsomol cell had to take up the matter. There was one chap who really behaved swinishly to a girl; got her in the family way, then tried to deny that it was he—altogether a disgusting business. We did not press him to marry her; it would have been worse than useless. But we expelled him from the Komsomol for uncomradely behavior, and, although he's a good worker, we scarcely ever talk to him now. I am not saying that this kind of 'public opinion' pressure is general; in a city like Moscow, some pretty funny things must be going on; and in the country, too, where there are far more women than men, some pretty lurid things still happen in a big way; but among young students and technicians and engineers this cult of comradeship is very widespread. And it really does make life easier and simpler not to have constant emotional complications. It's much better to get married young, and take it all in your stride. And also," he grinned, "if you are respectably married, it's much easier to get a new flat!"

"That's not why you are marrying Valya?" I said.

"Of course not," he laughed. "Valya and I have been very, very good comrades for nearly a year. . . ."

"You sound optimistic about the future, Kolya," I said.

"Optimistic—of course I am optimistic. Young people of my generation have every reason to be optimistic about our own future, and about the future of our country."

Here, I reflected, was the model young Soviet citizen, that real Soviet Man they like to talk about in ideological journals. This healthy, handsome, self-assured, but not arrogant, youth —how different he was from the half-starved kid I had known twelve or thirteen years before! Was he really, I wondered, the perfectly-balanced human individual he seemed to be; was he not, perhaps a little deliberately, oversimplifying himself and oversimplifying life itself? Deep-down, he knew life was not quite so simple; he only had to look at his elder brother; compared with him, his brother, so awkward, so uncertain, with that wretched and absurd wife of his, with his grievances and his lack of enthusiasm, was *also* a Soviet citizen—but one who had missed the bus.

No, they couldn't all be the same; and yet, as I was soon to discover, Kolya was merely an unusually good specimen of a new type of man, who was developing in Russia today. This was not the Komsomol type of 1920—the romantic, violent, ignorant, scarcely literate and somewhat anarchistic individual; or the equally violent, self-sacrificing Stalinist Komsomol of 1930, or the patriotic youth of World War II, or even the puzzled and bewildered youth of 1950, when the Cold War was at its height and the glamour of Stalin was wearing off. This was a boy of the Khrushchev period, with its cult of science, science, and still more science. To be a successful analytical chemist made him feel that he was not only rising in the world (his grandmother had been an illiterate peasant woman), but that he was a person of weight in the new society; whether "complete Communism" was thirty or fifty or a hundred years ahead, whether America was going to be Communist in our lifetime or in a hundred or two hundred years didn't seem to matter much; but everything, he felt, was moving in the right direction. In *that* scheme of things, personal happiness was easy to achieve.

And perhaps it was not even the most important thing of all, or rather, it was part of something bigger.

That wedding was really something! I did not go to the registry office—the ZAGS—but was later told that Valya and Kolya and their respective parents and a few friends had had to wait quite a long time till their turn came. It was a Saturday afternoon, a great wedding day in Moscow. It wasn't like the ZAGS in the old days—just a bare office; at the ZAGS now there were flowers and evergreen plants, and a crest of the Soviet Union and a portrait of Lenin; and there was a side room, also with flowers, where, if desired, champagne could be served. The wedding feast that followed was taking place in the new three-room flat of Kolya's in-laws, and they had managed to cram long tables and chairs into the three rooms—enough to accommodate nearly seventy people! Apart from the parents and a few elderly relatives and the "boss" and his wife, all of them were young people, at least half of them colleagues from the chemical lab, where both Kolya and Valya worked.

The amount of food and drink was terrifying—countless zakuski, including red caviar, then borsch and pirozhki, followed by chicken and two enormous joints of roast beef, and then three big mountains of *plombir*—ice-cream with crystallized fruit—accompanied by biscuits and *Mishki* chocolates. Later I learned that 30 half-bottles of vodka had been consumed, besides a dozen bottles of Georgian white wine and another dozen of Soviet champagne.

Except for a certain self-control (for nobody got *really* drunk but merely, as they say in Russia, "infinitely merry") it wasn't all that different from a pre-revolutionary wedding. Same old cries of *"gorko,"* and loud cheers whenever, following a demand from the guests, the bridegroom kissed the bride, and a lot of short improvised toasts and speeches, the most solemn of which was from the "boss," the director of the lab, who exalted the qualities and virtues of bride and bridegroom, and said that they were the kind of young people who were working for the greatness of the Soviet father-land, and for the rapid transition from Socialism to Communism. The Chemical Industry, he said, was one of the great new industries of the USSR, and the enormous increase in the production of synthetic fibers, for instance, as Nikita Sergeievich had recently said, would . . . and so on, and so on.

They then drank more toasts—to the lab, to the bride's and bridegroom's parents, and Anna Ivanovna was moved to tears, while Valya's mother couldn't help remembering her first husband, Valya's father, who had been killed in the battle of Kursk back in 1943, and also shed a tear.

In the corner of one room there was a mountain of presents—mostly table linen, crockery, glass, cutlery and so on: but also a sumptuous modern camera—this was a collective gift from Kolya's and Valya's colleagues.

I suppose a Western expert would have sneered at some of the clothes—some of the more extravagant men's ties, and

the cut of their ready-made suits, and some of the girls'
color schemes. But to me, they looked all very neatly and
conscientiously dressed, and everybody had, obviously, been
to the hairdresser before coming to the wedding, except perhaps the completely bald-headed chief of the lab. Three of
the boys were in army uniform.

Nearly all these young people, Kolya's and Valya's colleagues, were either married or engaged. Several talked, in
passing, about their new flats, or the flats they were hoping
to get shortly.

Weddings, with all their noise and toasts, are not the best
occasion at which to have serious conversations with people,
but I got to know a young cousin of Valya's, a student at
Moscow University, where he was studying literature; amongst
all these young scientists, he seemed slightly out of his element; I also talked to a young man who was on the staff of
Komsomolskaya Pravda; I was to meet both of them later.
Vanya, of course, was there too, and also feeling slightly
out of his element amongst all this young "élite."

He was, obviously, a little envious of Kolya; when I asked
him what his wedding had been like, somewhere in the Western Ukraine, he screwed up his face, and said, "It was very
different; there was very little to eat, but the men got very
drunk on *samogon*."

By about midnight, not feeling too steady on my feet, I
slunk away; but the party was still going strong. The young
people were mostly reminiscing now about their summer
vacations; one young man was saying he was going to China
as member of a delegation; Peter Ivanovich was looking very
much the *paterfamilias,* and Anna Ivanovna was in a mixed
sentimental and slightly aggressive mood. Her last words to
me were: "You didn't expect people in the Soviet Union to
have such a good time, did you? Thought we were still scared
to death of the Gaypayoo?" And kissing me on both cheeks,
she said: "You come and live in Moscow. Here people are
genuine."

Chapter 9

BRIEF ENCOUNTERS—SOME OF THEM GRUBBY

I JUST DON'T understand people who say that Moscow has no charm. Of course, it is architecturally a mess, with some streets with two-story stucco houses still looking like backdrops to some 1850 Ostrovsky comedy. Also, if you take a trolleybus to the Agricultural Exhibition (now called the Exhibition of Economic Achievements) you can travel almost for miles without seeing anything but rather tumble-down wooden houses. The buildings at the Exhibition itself (you'd need days to go all over it) are, in many cases, still survivals of the "grandiose" Stalin style, vaguely modeled on things like the St. Petersburg Admiralty, etc. Lots of old Moscow streets like the Kuznetski Mosst look shabby and down-at-heel, and the "grand sweep" of Gorki Street is a bit questionable, too. I can't even say I like the Red Square; it has on me the effect of Rachmaninov's TUM-TUM-TUM *Prelude*—heard too often. But I at once feel the charm of Moscow if I sit down, for instance, in the little square off the Neglinnaya, and just watch the people sitting on benches (usually young people reading books—either novels or, more often than not, some textbook on physics or chemistry) or watch the people walking along the streets or getting in or out of trolleybuses. The Moscow crowds—whom so many outsiders find so dismal and "gray" and objectionable, always remind me of the Pasternak lines:

> Skvoz proshlovo peripetii,
> I gody voin i nishchety,
> Ya molcha uznaval Rossii
> Nepovtorimyie cherty—

83

Through the ups and downs of the past, and the years of war and hunger, I was silently recognizing once again Russia's inimitable features;

and then—

In adoration I watched these simple Russian people; and there was no sign of that slavishness with which people are marked by hunger and poverty; bad news and so many troubles they carried like masters. . . .

Soviet Russians have, indeed, an enormous dignity of their own. I noticed it during the war, when they were really poor and hungry. Not that this necessarily excludes a good deal of more or less jocular rudeness in streetcars and buses, or even that *podkhalimstvo,* the cringing to the boss, which is one of the stock jokes of *Krokodil.*

Anyway, life in Moscow is full of little comedies and tragedies—sometimes quite unexpected ones. In a booth off Neglinnaya Street I bought a pair of shoelaces from an elderly woman; and she spontaneously started telling me the terrible tragedy that had befallen her; her young son, a 22-year-old painter, who "adored Levitan," was out in the country painting a landscape, when he was killed by lightning. And she couldn't stop weeping, as she was telling that story for probably the thousandth time. "On the first of August," she kept on repeating. . . .

Another day, in the square opposite the Mossoviet in Gorki Street, I got into conversation with a very, very old man with a walrus mustache. He started telling me something of his life story. He was an old Bolshevik; had been a member of the Party since 1911, had been deported to Siberia by the Tsarist police; and now he was 79. Whereupon—what an anticlimax—he got up, bought for a ruble a paper bag of maize, and proceeded to feed the pigeons—who have become about as numerous in Moscow as they are in London or Venice.

Partly to save money, and partly to get away from the Intourist atmosphere of the "Berlin," I liked to go to those cafés or self-service places in the Neglinnaya or in Stoleshnikov Lane; if you are willing to rough it, and not to smoke, or drink beer, wine or vodka, you get quite a reasonable meal in these cafés (with waitresses) or self-service buffets—*zakusochnyie*—for 6 or 7 rubles, which is, after all, only 56 or 70 cents.

Here one met usually some small officials, working in some close-by ministry, or soldiers on leave, or some minor officials who had come to Moscow from the provinces, often with wife and children. Not that they were particularly impressed by these modest surroundings; but they were happy to be in Moscow; and many talked of the war years and the immediate postwar years, and of the terribly hard time they had had; but now everything was getting better and better every day. And practically all of them spoke with a sort of affection about Nikita Sergeievich. Of course, Stalin was "a bigger man, but——."

For more extravagant characters, there was, of course, little to equal a place like the restaurant of the "Berlin," with its dance band. Here one got all kinds of types—highly respectable Party members, feeling a little wicked about celebrating some special occasion in such a degenerate den, but also real *stilyagi* and others living near some vaguely criminal fringe. . . . Or else, plain drunks. Not to mention various "exotic" visitors to Moscow, some coming from the depths of China, Kazakhstan or Uzbekistan, others from Czechoslovakia or Eastern Germany.

The young man I mistook one night for a Chinese—for he spoke with what seemed to me a Chinese accent—turned out to be an apparently eminent Kazakh poet, who had been given a scholarship by the Soviet Writers' Union to spend several weeks in Moscow. He was eating ice cream and drinking sweet Crimean wine.

"No, I'm not Chinese," he said. "I'm a Kazakh." And he related how the Writers' Union had brought him here. "We Kazakhs are very unlike the Chinese," he said, "and also we're very unlike the Uzbeks. The Uzbeks are still very particularist; there's a lot of religion in Uzbekistan, too. Of all the Central-Asiatic peoples we are by far the most assimilated, the most Russified. As distinct from the Uzbeks, who fancy themselves a rather superior people with a civilization of their own, about 98 per cent of young Kazakhs speak Russian; and there are so many Russians in the main Kazakh cities like Alma-Ata and Karaganda that we are becoming rapidly assimilated. We take to the Soviet way of life like a duck to water—don't give a damn about religion, and all that. And the Russians remember that we had a very fine war record—better than the Uzbeks, Turkmens or Tajiks."

"Yes, I know," I said, "I also remember how the Germans were scared of you 'Mongols.' "

He grinned. "Never mind," he said, "it helped to knock the racialist ideas out of their heads. There must be quite a few little Kazakhs running about Germany now!" Then, earnestly: "My father was killed in Germany."

Then he suddenly said: "We Kazakhs have a great regard for Stalin. It was his nationalities policy that made us what we are. The *usatyi* [the one with the mustache], he was really somebody. History won't be able to step over him. As I told you, we are becoming more and more Russified; all the same, thanks to Stalin, we have a national culture of our own, and a literature of our own; when, in Tsarist days, did one ever hear of Kazakh poetry?"

"And Khrushchev?" I said.

"He's all right, but he belongs to a new phase of development. Twenty or thirty years ago, Khrushchev would have been no good. Stalin had a great historic mission, and he fulfilled it. Khrushchev made that 'secret' report on Stalin. Well, that was *policy*; I bet you Khrushchev didn't believe half of it himself."

"What do you think of the Chinese?" I said.

"We have an immense respect for the Chinese," he said. "But I can tell you; they're uneasy neighbours to have. Too many of them. And they work like mad. Here in the Union, thanks to mechanization and automation, we are beginning to take things easy. Seven-hour day, six-hour day, soon it'll be a five or four-hour day. The Chinese are the kind of people who will still work 12 or 14 hours a day with pick and shovel. And they take their work so damned seriously! You should see their students. There are Chinese students everywhere—here, in Moscow, and in Leningrad, and in Kharkov, and a terrible lot of them at Alma-Ata. They are fanatical about their work; they are fanatical about everything. A friend of mine went to Peking last summer. The driver of the bus that was taking him from the airport, suddenly stopped in the middle of the road, and started chasing a fly inside the bus. He didn't drive on again until he had killed the fly. And at the University of Alma-Ata, where I studied myself, and where I now lecture on Kazakh civilization, there was a group of forty Chinese students who were getting a State subsidy of 300 rubles ($30) a month; well, believe it or not, they got together one day, and sent a petition to the Rector saying that they could manage to live on 200 rubles a month, so why should the State give them more than they needed, and would he please cut them down to 200. Mad sort of thing no Russian—or Kazakh—would ever do!"

Suddenly he said: "Will you excuse me; there's a *devushka* there I've been keeping an eye on for the last hour; I must go and dance with her and perhaps——" However, a few minutes later he came back, looking a little sheepish. "No good, she's got that devil of an army lieutenant with her. . . ."

Then he asked me about myself. "Oh," he said, "I know about you. At the University I've been following a course in contemporary history, and your book on France was very strongly recommended by the professor. Haven't had time to read it, though. . . ."

Another night, I had an even odder brief encounter. This one was some sort of official who had something to do with foreign trade. He had been to France recently. His impressions of the Western world were a little rudimentary. "I was in Paris, and then in Marseilles, from where I sailed on a Soviet ship. French women are terribly immoral. Prostitutes everywhere. Marseilles full of bordels. Later we called at Naples. Also full of bordels. And we were taken on a trip to Pompeii. And then, for a tip to the guide, we were shown . . . Oh dear, to think that people did *that* sort of thing 2,000 years ago! Then we called at Piraeus; also heaps of bordels; they do a lot of business, especially thanks to the American naval base there. It's what they call Free World Solidarity, I suppose. Makes the Greeks feel safe to have a couple of American warships there. Just window-dressing! At Istanbul, where we then called, there were also plenty of bordels. At last we got back to Odessa. Nothing like that in our country. That first night a comrade of mine and I were having dinner at the hotel, and there were two girls who latched onto us. Mine was a pretty good-looking *devushka*. I asked her if I could see her home, and she said I could. It was good fun, and I stayed till two in the morning. 'Time you went home,' she said, 'and the tariff is 75 rubles.' I was really furious. 'The tariff, what tariff? You lousy bitch, you're not behaving like a Soviet citizen. I would have given you 100 rubles, perhaps 200—but, since it's the "tariff," here's 75, and not a kopek more.' And she lived at the far end of the town, and it was a hell of a job getting a taxi, and I had to pay the taximan twice the normal fare to take me back. Terrible city Odessa," he summed up, "must be that Greek and Turkish influence. . . ."

The next, rather longer encounter was with a bunch of what has come to be known as *stilyagi*. Well, not perhaps real *stilyagi*, but people somewhere near the hooligan fringe. There were four of them at the table next to mine; a man of about 30, a much younger man and two girls, both of them very crudely painted-up. They were very noisy and pretty far gone. I heard the young man call the waiter and order two quarts of vodka. A moment later, the waiter came up to me. "I say," I remarked, "surely these people have had enough to drink; and isn't vodka limited to one pint a person?" The waiter—a good youn̄ man, to whom I had talked before, and who told me how he was following evening classes three times a week at the Catering Institute, which would qualify him for becoming a director of a restaurant—grinned, and said: "Of course, they are allowed only a pint of vodka each; but up till now they've been drinking cognac—at 25 rubles a pint—and cognac is *not* rationed. So if you have enough money, you can get round the 'one pint' restriction. . . . And what would you like to order, *gospodin?*"

The *gospodin* did the trick. The two men heard the magic word. And the younger of the two came up to me and asked if he could sit down. "You're a foreigner, I take it," he said, "English, American?" Then, in a whisper: "Can you sell me some pounds or, better still, dollars? You see, my friend over there is a merchant seaman; often goes abroad, and I am dying to get some decent clothes. Can't wear this rubbish they make in the Soviet Union." He pointed at the rather snappy blue-and-white sweater with a zip he was wearing; said his friend had brought it to him from Finland. "They don't make such nice things here." "I'm an engineer," he said. "I earn 800 rubles a month." "This binge of yours," I said, "must make a pretty big hole in your budget." "Oh, it doesn't matter," he said, "my friend there —the merchant seaman—has a lot of money; and then I've got four brothers, all in good jobs; and they help me out when necessary. We are Jews, and always help each other out. Mind you, not orthodox Jews. I'm a member of the Komsomol. Don't know a word of Yiddish, of course, though my mother and dad still talk it occasionally." "Is there any disadvantage in being a Jew in the Soviet Union?" I asked. "No, of course not. As I told you, I and all my four brothers have good jobs." "Have you got 'Jew' written in your passport?" "Yes." "Wouldn't you like to have it changed to 'Russian?' " "It really hasn't occurred to me; doesn't make much difference. If I got it changed, I suppose it would hurt my mother and dad. It's not a bad country," he added, "but, my God, the Soviet clothes stink. Are you sure you can't sell me some pounds or dollars?" I said No.

He went back to his party and, after he had whispered something to the merchant seaman, the latter came over to my table. This one talked to me in English, in the broadest Brooklyn—heaven knows where he had learned it. He repeated that he was a merchant seaman, and had been all over the world—New York, San Francisco, Singapore, and so on. Again, he started on the pounds or dollars. Said he'd pay me a very good price for them—a hundred rubles for a pound, and fifty rubles for a dollar. Then he looked at his friends' table. "I think those two goils," he said, "are hoors." And again he talked about Singapore and San Francisco, and again asked whether I was sure I hadn't any pounds or dollars. When I said I hadn't any, he said: "Well, sorry, if you'll excuse me, I must get back to my wife." "But you just said she was a prostitute?" "Well, a wife, a wife," he laughed, "a wife for one night. We in Russia like a piece of tail, too."

Another brief encounter—this one on the night of November 6, the eve of Revolution Day. I had just come back from the great meeting at Luzhniki, with Khrushchev and the rest of them there. From this encounter I concluded that if Russians got drunk, it was often because they didn't know how to drink. This being the eve of Revolution Day, the place was terribly crowded, and I managed to get a seat at a small table where two people were already sitting. A girl of about

30, with a real Russian pudding-face, and a rather handsome and timid-looking young man of about 25. They had
started with drinking liqueurs, then sweet Crimean wine, and
now they had reached the champagne stage. The girl was
taking it in her stride, but the boy was becoming more and
more bleary-eyed. He was silent, and obviously unhappy.
"This is a very great day for us," pudding-face said. "It's
the eve of Revolution Day, and my friend here has just
been made a member of the Party, and my son (from my
former husband) has just been made a Pioneer. So this is a
triple celebration. It's the first time we've come to a place like ·
this. . . ." And she went on babbling about her son, and
her partner—to whom she now indiscriminately referred as
"friend," "comrade" and "husband." Then she said: "Volodya,
come and dance with me." But Volodya had, by this time, his
face buried in his hands. "Ah, well, if that's the way he feels,
you come and dance with me." So we shuffled two or three
times round the thronged dance floor, and then went back to
her "husband." This one was hastily paying the waiter. He
was looking terribly miserable and ashamed of himself.
"Poidyom skoreye, k chortu (Hurry up, and to hell with all
this)," he muttered angrily. "Terribly sorry," said pudding-
face to me. "Perhaps we'll meet some other time." I was
quite sure we never would. The young Party member had,
obviously, hated every moment of this "triple celebration" in
a fishy Intourist restaurant.

Chapter 10

FIFTY-YEAR-OLD INTELLECTUAL

THERE IS A big difference between the various generations of Soviet citizens. Men in their fifties are different from those in their twenties; they even think that life comes too easily to the young people, and that they are apt to be smug, without fully realizing what a struggle it all was for their fathers.

In a small flat at the top of Pushkin Street I looked up an old acquaintance, Vasili Petrovich, who was a lecturer in modern history at the —— Institute. He was in his fifties, and had a distinguished war record. He was living in the small flat where I had already visited him in 1947, with his wife and two sons. One was still at school, the other was an engineering student. They had gone to the *datcha* for the week end, and he was alone in the book-infested flat.

"Well," said Vasili Petrovich, "things have changed a lot since I last saw you. There are an awful lot of people now who are very comfortably off. I don't mean a New Class. There's no such thing, really. You can't be rich and important for more than one generation— Stalin's daughter has a humble teaching job, and that's all—unless the next generation has very great ability, too. No doubt the son of an important father has a *slightly* better opportunity to make a good start— if he's got the will and the capacity—than the son of obscure parents, but there's not much in it. But I can tell you this: the intellectuals are being well looked after. As you know, I am fairly small fry; but I've got this flat in Moscow, and I've got a *datcha,* and my elder son is hoping to get a car once he has got a job. No, we are *not* being Americanized, but is there any reason why we should live poorly? This country is making staggering economic progress and—if there isn't a war—we will, by 1970, be as well-off as the Americans."

"Are you sure?"

"There's a good chance, anyway. Or shall we say 1980?"

"But aren't there, and won't there be, great inequalities?"

"Well, there is already greater equality now than there used to be. The top academicians who used to get fantastic salaries of 30,000 or 20,000 rubles a month are now getting nearer 10,000 ($1020). Authors and playwrights don't get the stupendous incomes they used to get in the past—just because their books sell in hundreds of thousands of copies, or because their plays are shown in a hundred theatres. Complete equality—well no. Perhaps not even under complete Communism."

"I keep hearing about complete Communism; well, when is the present transition to be completed?"

"That's hard to say; but it should be possible, by degrees, to achieve something like complete Communism in 25 or 30 years. Already much is being done in that direction. Very low rents. Free education. Free medical services. Soon certain things will be completely free: bread, and urban transport, and telephone calls. And then more and more and more things. No doubt, the Chinese are *already* trying to be more Communist than we with their Peoples' Communes; but it won't work: you *can't* skip the Socialist stage, as Khrushchev pointed out at the Twenty-first Congress. And the Chinese have now realized it, and are watering down their Communes. *We're* using the right tempo in the transition to Communism.

"There's another thing; in the West, they are scared of automation; it'll mean unemployment. Here we are not scared. It merely means that our working days will be shorter and shorter, and there'll be more and more time for leisure, for sport, for various kinds of 'self-perfection' as we say. All people will become more and more educated. *Everybody* will have read all the best books of Russian and foreign literature; everybody will have some artistic and musical culture."

"Isn't that looking a bit far ahead? What you are having meantime, it seems to me," I said, "is a somewhat more advanced form of what we call the 'welfare state.' "

"That isn't quite correct. In what we are doing, there is, of course, a 'welfare state' element, and we are quite conscious of the fact that in England they have, even in capitalist conditions, gone a good deal further in that direction than in most other countries. But the 'welfare state' isn't everything. We are also developing a new type of man—Soviet man, as he's called. I know you people don't much believe in his existence; you say that the old individualism is still strong, and that, as we get richer, the more individualist are we going to become."

"I didn't say so. But I *have* heard such arguments."

"Just because you meet a few drunks and hooligans, or a few people who go crazy for American jazz records, or about some foreign film, you think we'd all *like* to be like Americans!"

"I am not saying anything of the kind. I have met people of the young Soviet intelligentsia who completely contradict this theory. But you will admit that there still is a good deal of inequality."

"Of course, there's inequality. Some people live in nice new flats. I still live in a rather grubby old flat. Some people still live in 'communal flats,' where they have to share the kitchen and bathroom and toilet with the others; there are stinking rows. It's still Zoshchenko stuff.[1] But, in fact, the better of the new flats and the less good of the new flats are becoming more and more like each other. That's to say, the big and small new flats that are now being built will be succeeded by medium flats, with pretty much the same facilities and comforts, and, in proportion to the number of people, the same size. It's a sign of progress. But, of course, it's a long, a very long business; it'll take another ten or perhaps fifteen years before the *whole* of Moscow is going to live in approximately identical conditions; but it's coming, I can tell you. In the last three years alone they've resettled about a million people into new flats."

"But then, you said that some were still living in Zoshchenko-like conditions, and aren't some people still earning only 300 rubles a month?"

---

[1] A Russian author who wrote short stories satarizing Soviet life and was denounced during the postwar Stalin years for making too much fun of the Soviet Man. Lately, Zoshchenko's works have been returning to favor.

"Three hundred—no. The minimum will now be 500. As for Zoshchenko—well, yes; some people still live the way they did in the 1920s. But they are becoming much fewer. And when you say Zoshchenko, do you know that I gave my younger son a volume of Zoshchenko stories the other day, and he just didn't see the point. Didn't think them funny. I mean all those stories about drunken brawls in 'communal' kitchens, and chaotic bathhouses, and about people going to the theatre dressed in a tattered old overcoat with nothing but a dirty nightshirt underneath. It just didn't ring a bell. Didn't mean anything to him.

"Anyway, our housing difficulties, which are still far from settled, though Khrushchev is doing his best, are an inevitable outcome of two things. The immense increase in our urban population and the war. You know as well as I do how many towns and villages and large cities were destroyed during the war. Hundreds and hundreds of our cities were partly or completely destroyed. It's one of the damned miracles of our reconstruction—and of our endurance—that, with only a few exceptions, like Kerch and Novorossisk and a few towns in Belorussia, which were just obliterated, the population in these 'destroyed' towns should now be larger, often *much* larger, than it was before the war!

"You people in the West—and I have seen quite a few lately—keep bothering about little things that don't matter; but you don't seem to realize the quite incredible reconstruction effort that was made during the years following the war."

"I know," I said, "I saw some of the destroyed cities. Voronezh, Sebastopol—not a house left; Rostov, scarcely a house left; Kiev and Kharkov and Minsk—half or three-quarters destroyed. Not to mention Stalingrad."

"Well, there you are. You should see Kiev, and Minsk and Voronezh and Rostov and Stalingrad and all the other hundreds of cities, and thousands of villages which have been *completely* rebuilt. It took some doing, I can tell you, and all that in the midst of the Cold War, and with resources severely limited, and with no help coming from anywhere. . . . You may think we Russian people are nice, easy-going, pleasure-loving people. But once we put our backs into a job, we get it done. Anyway, you saw us during the war."

"Yes," I said, "I saw Russia during the war. And I shall

never forget it. And I know that any other people would probably have broken down out of sheer despair and fatigue."

"And how do you explain it? A combination of two things: genuine patriotic devotion and self-sacrifice, and discipline imposed by the Army and the Party."

"I was in Leningrad during the blockade," I said.

"Yes—Leningrad," said Vasili Petrovich. "They probably then told you that 200,000 or 300,000 people died of starvation. That was the figure they used to put out during those days. I can tell you now: the number of people who died in Leningrad during the blockade was—900,000. Can you *imagine* 900,000 people dying of hunger, because they were determined not to surrender the city to the Germans? I know, they weren't consulted. But they would have been ready to die all the same, even if they had been consulted. . . ."

"Leningrad," I said, "was an unforgettable experience. But it's disturbing, all the same, when I think that, in September 1943, I spent an evening with Popkov, head of the *Lensoviet,* at the Smolny Institute; and in 1949 this very fine, patriotic man was shot like a common traitor."

Vasili Petrovich made a face. "That was a bad period, and we try to forget about it. They now say it was Beria's fault; also Malenkov was said to have been mixed up in it. Popkov was a Leningrad particularist; Leningrad was very isolated from the rest of Russia during the war; in Leningrad they did *not* like Stalin; and they started playing about with the idea that Leningrad should become the capital of the RSFSR. . . . Beyond that, nobody knows anything definite. . . ."

"Voznesensky also was shot. Didn't it all rather shock you?"

"Of course it shocked us. But they were mad times. The Cold War was in full swing. Old man Stalin started seeing ghosts everywhere. The thing to do in those days was to keep your trap shut. Khrushchev knew it as well as anybody. We had to put up with these things. They still did not affect the main aim, which was to rebuild Russia, and make Russia invulnerable. It was in 1949, the year of the rotten Leningrad affair, that we exploded our first A-bomb. It made a big difference to morale. . . ."

"Then other things happened—the 'Jewish Doctors' plot' . . ."

"That," said Vasili Petrovich, "was a very dirty business.

And that was really Beria's doing. Stalin had become odd by this time—thoroughly odd. And he was morbidly suspicious. It shook Moscow. A great friend of mine, who's a Hero of the Soviet Union and a Jew, was in a streetcar the day they announced the Doctors' Plot. There was an old drunk there, who started saying things about the 'damned *zhidy* (yids)'; not only did he meet with no response; but when my friend protested, and pointed to his gold star, and to his artificial leg—for he had lost a leg in the war—and said he was a Jew, all the people started not only shouting down the drunk, but demanded that the streetcar stop and that he be thrown out. And the conductress did stop the streetcar, and they did throw him out. . . . Yes, it was a nightmarish kind of winter, and yet, when Stalin died, people got kind of hysterical. . . . They just didn't know who would take over, and they were scared of a Beria dictatorship. The death of Beria was popular, I can tell you that. . . ."

"Are you quite sure that Beria was all the things that you now say he was? I recently read pages and pages of eulogy in the Big Soviet Encyclopedia in honor of Beria—those pages which were later replaced by something else—a picture of whales in the Bering Straits, I believe—so that there was no article about Beria at all. . . . Do you really believe that Beria had been in the pay of the British for twenty years or more?"

"I know all these old arguments," said Vasili Petrovich. "You want what you call 'objective history.'[2] You see, it's like this. Where the history of the Party is concerned, we have to think of the immediate needs of education; we can't always pursue purely academic objectives. Things have to be presented in a certain way; there are *more* important things than the purely objective enumeration of the facts. History has got to be interpreted in a certain way. We historians know perfectly well that Trotsky played a positive role at certain moments of his career; but, *on the whole,* his role was thoroughly negative; so that's the thing that has to be stressed,

[2] In the view of I. Kairov, President of the Academy of Paedagogical Sciences of the RSFSR, *"history is a party science.* No routine or formalism (?) in its teaching can be tolerated. A teacher of the History or Constitution of the USSR must be a passionate propagandist of the ideas of Communism, an ideological guide of the young." (*Pravda,* November 15, 1959.)

and not the fact that he may have been all right at such-and-such a particular moment of the Revolution or the civil war. Maybe Beria, too, was valuable to the country at some stage; but the final assessment of Beria is negative."

"Final?" I said.

"Well, 'final' may be putting it too strongly. In 20 or 30 years from now we may be able to afford the luxury of writing a wholly 'objective' account of Trotsky or Beria. Just now it doesn't suit us to do it. But don't underrate historical science in the Soviet Union; the documents are all there; senior students of history know exactly what's what. And, in the long run, there won't be any discrepancies between 'factual' history and 'official' history. Already the Stalin *History of the Party* has been rewritten; in the original history they overplayed Stalin's role in the October Revolution. You should be grateful," he said ironically, "we haven't made Khrushchev Lenin's right-hand man!"

"Maybe you would have if only Khrushchev were ten years older!"

"Maybe," he said, and grinned.

"Isn't your young generation of students critical about this kind of approach to history?" I asked.

"Our young generation know exactly what's what. They study foreign history with immense eagerness and here, I can tell you, there's little or no monkeying with the facts. Or we wouldn't have published your *France 1940–1955* book. As regards Soviet history, they know better and better every year what the facts are, but they also know why certain facts should be played down, and others played up. We know that the Purge Trials of 1936–38 were largely a fake, but it is also obvious that there were some *very* strong *raisons d' état* behind them. Not a good excuse but—there was Hitler ready to jump on us. Also, we know about the war years today infinitely more than we knew about them a few years ago. Not only the official history of the war, but also novels, now openly talk about the chaotic condition our army was in during the first months of the German invasion. You were here at the time, so maybe you remember. . . ."

"Of course I remember. I remember Yelnia and Dorogobuzh, those two miserable towns, which at a heavy loss, Konev reconquered from the Germans in September 1941. It was the first territory in Europe to be reconquered from Hitler since 1939. It was a pretty deadly business, but what a symbol, all the same! And I remember Surkov who was on the trip, and how bitterly anxious he was about the general situation."

"All that is well known today," said Vasili Petrovich. "In a novel like Simonov's latest, *The Living and the Dead,* he speaks about the chaos of those early days of the war. But at the time, one didn't write about such things—one hinted at them at most, as Simonov did in his 1941 poems. . . . Some day, we shall probably also tell the full story of what happened in March 1953, just before and after Stalin's death. But it's too early now."

"What happened?"

"Honestly, I don't know. But even if I knew, I probably wouldn't tell you!"

"Khrushchev is very popular today," said Vasili Petrovich. "And long may it last. His American trip made him more popular than anything else. Our people have suffered far too much in the past. They are optimistic; they are confident about the future—but they are still not absolutely sure that there won't be a war. The United States or Bonn may start a war, because they know that, with peaceful coexistence, time is on our side. The fact that Khrushchev has done his utmost to come to terms with the Americans gives people the hope that they may go on living peacefully, with conditions improving year by year. Of course, we have no illusions about our being loved for our own sakes. We are feared and respected because of the Sputniks, and the ICBMs—a field in which, we are told, we are far ahead of the Americans. We think—or rather, we hope—that Dulles's death marked the end of an epoch. We are not absolutely sure. We still don't know whether Khrushchev's disarmament proposals at the UN will be followed up even in a limited sense. We know the power of the arms monopolies in America; they won't easily convert their industries to peaceful needs. Yet our people would be immensely relieved if at least part of the 25 billion dollars we are spending on armaments yearly could be used for other purposes. *We* are not afraid of conversion, or of unemployment. If anything, we have a shortage of labor. Our villages haven't enough men."

"How," I said, "did Khrushchev come out on top? Why he, rather than Malenkov or Molotov?"

"There's no mystery about it," said Vasili Petrovich, "he had the personality, the originality, the drive, the sort of dynamic qualities the others lacked. Also, as First Secretary of the Party, he had more pull than the others. Further, he represented some new trend which corresponded to the mood in the country, and consequently, inside the Party. . . ."

"Why 'consequently?' "

"Because the Party keeps its finger on the people's pulse. And people here want peace—and an understanding with America."

"But it *was* touch-and-go for Khrushchev in 1957, wasn't it?"

"Well, yes," said Vasili Petrovich reluctantly. "The truth is, as you know, that the Twentieth Congress, which was very largely the work of Khrushchev, unleashed certain forces, both inside the country and, worse still, abroad, and in Poland and Hungary things got out of control. Khrushchev was blamed for it. But the general trend he represented was still the correct one, despite the Hungarian business. He personally regretted to have to get so tough with the Hungarians, but he had no choice after the defiant stand taken by that idiot Imre Nagy. . . . All the same, he was in favor of a certain liberalization, both inside the country and in our foreign relations. And, in spite of Hungary, his one *idée fixe* was coming to terms with America. Here he met with opposition from our 'pro-Chinese.' Molotov was against making any apologies to Tito and also (very wrongly) against the evacuation of Austria. And Khrushchev was, at the time, also criticized for his Virgin Lands scheme (which *seems* to have turned out all right), for his maize drive, for his emphasis on prosperity (after *he* had criticized Malenkov for the same reason!) and even for his familiar, garrulous, undignified ways! It wasn't always easy for him. He had to blow hot-and-cold. He couldn't allow our young people—*some* of our young people—to start spouting dangerous thoughts, to get starry-eyed about the 'freedom fighters' of Poland and Hungary, or out-Pasternak Pasternak."

"How serious then was the 'revolt of the young,' of which we used to hear so much in the West?"

"It didn't amount to nearly as much as you people in the West made out. No doubt, there was a bit of a ferment at both Moscow and Leningrad universities. There was something of a revolt against Stalinism and, in the arts, against Zhdanovism. Dudintsev caused quite a stir. Already before that Ehrenburg's *Thaw* had been snatched up in a few hours. There was a growing interest in all that was happening in the West. With the liquidation of the NKVD empire a spirit of freedom swept the country. *But* remember this: *all these young people, however delighted they seemed over the new liberalism that seemed to be sweeping Russia, very soon became aware of one very important fact: and that was that both the trouble in Poland and the revolt in Hungary were essentially* ANTI-RUSSIAN. *And that had a very sobering effect.* The Hungarians are rather alien to us; while the Poles—well, they are Poles, and we in Russia have always distrusted them. And all those jolly little jokes that they produced in vast quantities in Warsaw were *not* thought funny, because *all* these jokes were *anti-Russian* jokes."

"In short, these young people's nationalism proved stronger than their liberalism?"

"That's just about it. Our young people are tremendously nationalist. Or rather, the correct word is 'patriotic.' This does not mean that they objected to liberalism, far from it. And liberalism, or 'destalinization,' as you call it, is going on all the time—not at a mad tempo as it did in 1956, but it's going on all the same."

"At which point, would you say, did Khrushchev become immensely popular? Was it at the time of the Sputniks?"

"Yes, the Sputniks were the biggest single factor which made this country enormously self-confident; and Khrushchev became very popular as a result. I know, it wasn't all his doing. But he was lucky it happened that way. It gave him the supreme opportunity to pursue his peace-with-America policy. First Mikoyan went to America, and it was a relative success. Then Dulles died. And then Eisenhower invited Khrushchev to America. It was Khrushchev's crowning achievement. And today he's on top of the world. Very different from four years ago when he went to England, and the Queen and Prince Philip just deigned to invite him and Bulganin to a cup of tea. . . ."

"I remember," I said, "how even then the people around Bulganin and Khrushchev were saying: 'We don't give a damn about this trip to England, but it is a first step towards America; and that's the thing that matters.' But, tell me this: they seemed to get on remarkably well; why did Khrushchev get rid of Bulganin in this rather shabby way?"

"I don't know that there was anything sinister about it. Bulganin was getting pretty old and useless and, I have reason to believe, Bulganin was *not* as wholehearted about this flirtation with America as Khrushchev was. . . ."

"Tell me," I said. "What was the real effect in this country of the so-called secret report on Stalin?"

"I must say this. Officially, there was *no* secret report on Stalin. The majority of people still had it only at second- or third-hand. But those who had it at firsthand took it with very mixed feelings. Two generations had been brought up in the cult of Stalin. Lots of people had suffered under Stalin, but many more, who had been brought up under Stalin, had made their careers, or had gone into battle crying '*Za rodinu! za Stalina!*' Millions of people in their thirties and forties were deeply shocked."

"Were you?"

"To tell you the truth, a lot of the things Khrushchev said jarred on me. I know all about the camps; I know about the very shady side of the purge trials—and everybody in this country rather shuddered at the thought of Vyshinsky, no matter how brilliantly he debated with Acheson at the UN; there was really something snake-like in that old Menshevik; there were the Leningrad Affair and the Jewish Doctors, and all sorts of beastly things; and yet we had somehow lived together with Stalin through the days of defeat and the days of victory, and the greatness of the Soviet Union was somehow inseparable from the name of Stalin. When I was a student in the 1920s, we were sharply divided into what was called 'Stalinites' and 'Trotskyites.' From the start I had not the slightest doubt that Stalin was right and Trostky wrong. Stalin, if you like, appealed to our primitive nationalism, our primitive patriotism. We were going to make Russia, the Soviet Union, a great country and not put the cart before the horse, the way Trotsky did. We suffered hardships during the first

Five-Year-Plan, but it was all part of our life, part of our effort. Our young people don't realize how hard life was in the 1920s and 1930s. But we stuck it out. So when Khrushchev produced his 'report' many of us thought it—how shall I put it?—in poor taste. *Was* it necessary, many wondered, to make the break with Stalin such a sharp and brutal break? Was it necessary to tell lies about him—to say he was no good as a war leader when we all know that it was he who kept Russia together in the bad days of 1941 and 1942? That if the place hadn't been called *Stalingrad,* perhaps it would have been surrendered? No doubt he went paranoiac towards the end, suffered from senile persecution-mania; and yet. . . . Khrushchev did not make himself popular with the Stalin Report. And there was a feeling that he was gambling recklessly."

"Well, he got away with it. . . ."

"Yes, he got away with it, but not because of the Stalin Report. This very nearly cost him his job, his political future, perhaps his life. It was touch-and-go, as I said, in the summer of 1957. But his 'liberalism,' supported at that time notably by Zhukov and Mikoyan, saved him—for a time. And then came the Sputniks, and after that he sat pretty. . . ."

"You don't seem to be altogether sure that his 'pro-Western' policy is the correct one, do you?"

"Oh, I am quite sure he is right to be trying it out. The Americans have no choice. We are militarily stronger than they are at present. So they've got to grin and bear it when he says the world, and especially the underdeveloped countries, are more and more on our side, and that we'll be as rich as the Americans are in ten years from now, and that we'll win the peaceful competition and that the 'Socialist order' will, in the end, 'bury' the capitalist order. . . . But there are still an awful lot of Americans who hate our guts, and who are regretting the good old Cold War days, and who imagine that if they intensify the arms race, they can bust us economically. Or at least delay our economic victory. But if Hitler couldn't bust us, no American economic pressure will. . . ."

"You seem to have a very, very soft spot for old man Stalin," I remarked.

"That's not quite correct," said Vasili Petrovich. "But I

read a good number of Western books and periodicals, and, to tell you the truth, it jars on me when Stalin is represented as a kind of monster, as a personification of evil, somebody as bad as Hitler, or worse. Yes, he could be ruthless. But, to us Russians, Stalin was the man who, in the twenty-five years when he was supreme boss, turned our pretty miserable backward country into the second-greatest power in the world, thus paving the way for total Russian supremacy in the world. Lenin gave the new regime a start, but it was under Stalin that the real job was done. . . ."

"And the 'personality cult?' "

"Well, I'll grant you, it was overdone; but you were here during the war; and wasn't it understandable, in a way? At a certain stage of development the 'personality cult' has its points; I shouldn't perhaps say so, but in China there's a 'personality cult' of Mao Tse-Tung just now. Maybe it's necessary and normal at this stage of Chinese development that there should be such a cult. It's a sort of cement that keeps things together. . . . At our present phase of development it's no longer necessary. But I'll grant you, we are finding Mao's aloofness towards us a bit disconcerting at times, as well as the 'Chinese' tendencies Peking tries to implant in the Communist parties here and there. To the Chinese, Formosa is a symbol of their past enslavement—something enormous. To us, it's something fairly small on the international chessboard."

Chapter 11

STUDENT OF LITERATURE

ONE DAY KOLYA ANTONOV phoned me and said that Grisha Kononov, the student of literature I had met at the wedding, was coming to dinner on Sunday, and he would like to meet me again.

Except for Vanya, who had gone home for the week end, they were all there, and Anna Ivanovna was again fussing like mad in the kitchen.

Grisha, a dark-haired handsome boy of 24, was training to be a teacher of Russian literature, and was writing a thesis on the early poetry of Mayakovsky—the pre-revolutionary phase and the civil war phase.

Pointing at Kolya and Valya, he remarked: "Of course, these young people with a high technical training rather despise us these days. These technicians and engineers have an awfully high opinion of themselves; the way they talk, one would think each one of them had invented Sputnik!"

"Nonsense," Kolya laughed. "You literary people now talk of us the way, I suppose, poor peasants—*derevenskaya bednotà*—used to talk of the kulaks! Don't worry, there's room for everybody in our society, even for relatively useless people who study literature!"

"It must have been quite a landmark," I said, "when they erected a bronze statue to Mayakovsky a few years ago.

> Mne naplevat na bronzy mnogopudie
> Mne naplevat na mramornuyu sliz. . . .

'I spit on the tons of bronze, I spit on the marble slime'

104

—and now they've put up in the center of Moscow a great big hefty bronze statue of Mayakovsky, the very kind of thing he said he was going to spit on."

"It occurred to a lot of us," said Grisha, "when they put up the Mayakovsky statue. *Mne naplevat na bronzy mnogopudie.* But it just shows that Mayakovsky today has become a classic. We read Mayakovsky today just as we read Pushkin. But you haven't finished the quotation: 'Let Socialism, built in the midst of battles, be the common monument to us all'—

> Pust nashim obshchim pamiatnikom budet
> Postroyennyi v boyakh sotsialism . . . .

"Yes," said Grisha, "this *is* Socialism, and Mayakovsky got both kinds of monuments in the end—the one he wanted, and the one he despised. Perhaps he didn't really despise it; he was immensely vain and abitious, and it was at least partly out of pure frustrated ambition that he shot himself in 1930."

"Do you know," I said, "that I met Mayakovsky in Paris in 1929?"

"Good God!" said Grisha, "you *must* be old!"

And I had to tell him what little I remembered offhand about that brief encounter with Mayakovsky in Povolotzky's Russian bookshop in the rue Bonaparte.

"You actually *met* Mayakovsky!" Grisha said. He couldn't get over it. It was as if somebody had told me he had met Dostoevsky. "To us," he repeated, "Mayakovsky has become a classic. But what an epoch! What an exciting epoch! First, that 'futurist' period of Mayakovsky's before the Revolution—*Oblako v shtanakh* (*The Cloud with Trousers on*) and *Vladimir Mayakovsky* with their mad imagery —the cloud with a little wrinkle round its mouth—'like a woman who expected a baby, but God chucked a one-eyed little idiot at her. . . .' and then the ROSTA posters during the civil war, which Mayakovsky painted himself, and for which he wrote those pungent rhymes. Propaganda—but by a great poet!

"But when I say Mayakovsky is a classic, that's really only half the story. Everybody in Russia reads Mayakovsky, because he's pungent and entertaining and—tremendously topical. Yes—topical. His writings buzz with the revolt of Negroes and Chinese and other colored peoples. And when he writes:

> And if I were an elderly Negro
>   I would still, without boredom or laziness,
>   Learn Russian if only because
>   It's the tongue that was spoken by Lenin. . . .

Good God, that's just what *is* happening now, with African students rushing to Moscow, and Chinese students all over the place. And he was also full of 'Communist morality,' down on bureaucrats, down on hooligans, down on God and on bourgeois survivals of all kinds—house plants and lace napkins and drunkenness and promiscuity. And yet, he lived in the midst of the mad crazy '20s. Everything in Mayakovsky was exaggerated, everything in his poetry was hyperbole. Talk of the *kult lichnosti,* the 'personality cult'—didn't Mayakovsky start it with all he wrote about Lenin? Even though Lenin couldn't stand Mayakovsky's poems, Lenin to him was a kind of deity, a vast elemental force, wind and storm and thunder and lightning and, as we'd now say, a million atom bombs rolled into one, a superhuman force which was going to turn the whole world upside down. What an exciting time the '20s must have been!"

"You little idiot," said Anna Ivanovna, "*you* should have lived in the '20s. We think of the days of Lenin as the really hungry years, when the whole world was against us. There was complete *razrukha*—economic chaos—even here in Moscow. During the civil war we had to live on frozen potatoes and other filth: a little castor oil in which to fry whatever muck there was; and when there wasn't any castor oil, we'd use candle-grease. And you couldn't plant anything in the garden here, it all got stolen. . . ."

"But, Anna Ivanovna," Grisha exclaimed, "Mayakovsky *did* write about all that in *Horosho!*—about the famine in Moscow, with his presenting his girl with the fantastic present of half a log for the stove and of two carrots for the 'dinner!' He, as a privileged person, used to get occasionally a little piece of horse flesh! It's all there! All the same, wasn't the cultural life of Moscow terribly exciting then? Mayakovsky, Yessenin with a top hat and a monocle, crazy theatres

—Meyerhold—crazy paintings—Nathan Altman—crazy music—the young Shostakovich."

"It may have been all right for the intellectuals," said Anna Ivanovna, "they were getting rather special rations—bits of horse meat, as you say. But as a young girl, I had my first job then and it wasn't funny, I can tell you. I remember sending my mother to the *likbez*—the 'liquidation of illiteracy' school; but it wasn't much good; the old girl wasn't interested. Things got rather easier under the NEP, but it didn't do people like me, without money, much good. And then later, in the Sretenka, they opened a beastly thing called *Torgsin*—and there you could get liqueur chocolates and cream cakes if you paid in gold. People took along their wedding rings to buy a few cream cakes; it was a pretty disgusting business watching hungry kids looking into the *Torgsin* window. . . . If I were you, Grisha, I wouldn't get all worked up about the glorious '20s or the glorious early '30s. We had a terribly hard struggle for existence. Under Lenin, there was *nothing*. During the first years of Stalin, there wasn't much either. For five or six years before the war, things got much, much easier. And then came the war." And, turning to me, she said: "And you remember what that was like. It wasn't so bad for you, living at the Metropole, but you remember what a thin time Kolya and I had."

"Yes, I remember," I said.

"Well," said Anna Ivanovna, "it's not surprising we should be so happy now. When I look back on my 58 years, I reckon that during most of the time I didn't have enough to eat. It was *very* bad from say, 1916 to 1922; very middling from 1922 to 1934; then a few good years; then the war and its aftermath which were pretty bad, too. Now at last we are reaping the harvest. Now we are the greatest power in the world. But we had to struggle and work and suffer an awful lot, and every time things started looking up, we'd get a new war, or some such damned thing. Only this time they won't *dare!* Some idiots say: Let's have more shoes and cheaper shoes, and to hell with Sputniks. I say: No, let's have Sputniks. Sputniks and not shoes will frighten off the Americans. And we've got shoes, anyway!"

"There she goes again," Kolya laughed. "Mother likes to feel sorry for herself."

"I am not sorry for myself," said Anna Ivanovna, "but it needed a lot of patience and a lot of work to reach our present state of prosperity! And remember that your brother Misha was killed in 1941 by the damned Germans. Life is easy for *you* boys. . . ."

"Mother, you talk like the Komsomol decree of—let me see. . . ." He took down a big red tome from the shelf. "Here it is. February 27, 1957:

The whole world knows that Soviet youth is a good, hard-working youth. It deeply appreciates the care given it by the Soviet State and is conscious of its duties to its country. But the educational work conducted in Komsomol organizations must not overlook the fact that the present generation of the Komsomol has not gone through the hard school of revolutionary struggle or the same hardening process, and has known nothing of the hardships and privations that fell to the lot of our older generation—our fathers, mothers and elder brothers. It is therefore understandable why a part of our younger generation doesn't realize by how much sweat and blood the present living conditions have been conquered. They often take these conditions for granted, as something quite natural, without realizing the immense effort made by the Soviet people.

"There you are, Mother," Kolya smiled, "you talk just like a Komsomol decree. And it goes on:

Some young boys and girls betray parasitical tendencies, and while insisting on their rights, they tend to forget their duties to society, demand a lot from the State and give it very little in return. Occasionally insufficient demands are made on young people, and these are allowed to grow like hothouse plants, unadapted to any serious trials and ordeals; and when they come up against difficulties, they just collapse. There are also parents who spoil young people, and even say that this young generation might as well have a good time, since its fathers shed their blood so that their children should have a better life, and may these, therefore, not have to encounter any difficulties at all. This is a wrong approach, which renders a poor service both to the children and to society as a whole—that society which expects young people to overcome all difficulties in the hard battle towards our final aim, Communism."

"That's very true," said Anna Ivanovna. "Only I must say we've never had any parasites in our family—except, occasionally, *you,*" she said, pointing at Peter Ivanovich. "You were pretty impossible when you came back from the war. Just wanted to have a good time."

"That's ancient history," said Peter Ivanovich morosely. "But then lots of us, who'd been at the front, thought we could relax for a bit once the war was over. But old man Stalin wouldn't hear of it."

"And damn right, too," said Anna Ivanovna. She looked slightly annoyed, and I feared she might start on that postwar girl friend, but she refrained.

"Yes, I can see," said Grisha, "that the '20s were a difficult time; but, looking at it all from this distance, they must have been pretty exciting all the same. Mayakovsky really thought in terms of a Leninist world revolution; it didn't quite come off—blast that German working class, in whom Lenin seemed to have so great a faith. Always the Germans. . . . I suppose it's going to be a world revolution in the end; I mean, the world will gradually go Communist. Khrushchev scandalized the Americans no end by saying so. But it won't happen quite the way Lenin—and Mayakovsky—expected it. It's the Chinese who started this 'second wave,' and then it'll be the Africans and the other Asians, and the Latin Americans perhaps. And the advanced capitalist countries will be last on the menu. . . . The reformists of the privileged working classes of America, France, England seem to hate us even more than the capitalists do. All these Kautskys of today! . . ."

"What Russian literature," I asked Grisha, "are you going to teach?"

"Oh, the whole of the nineteenth and twentieth centuries. Right up to Mayakovsky, anyway. And, of course, a little bit about the eighteenth century and earlier periods. After all, Soviet literature is a continuation of Russian literature. Pushkin, Lermontov, Gogol, Turgeniev, Leskov, Tolstoy, Dostoevsky, Chekhov, Gorki—they're all terribly *close* to us. On the face of it, there's not much connection between our life and *Oniegin* or *War and Peace* or *The Three Sisters,* or less still, with Leskov's characters or Ivan or Mitya or Alyosha Karamazov. But we have pretty well abandoned the way of approaching all these writers from a kind of sociological angle—calling Pushkin an 'aristocratic' writer, or

Leskov a clerical-reactionary writer, or Dostoevsky a mystical-religious reactionary. Instead, we look upon them all as part of our *national heritage*. There are practically no taboos in pre-revolutionary literature any longer. Anyone can now buy the *whole* of Dostoevsky, including *The Idiot*, the *Karamazovs*, *The Possessed* and even his reactionary political writings. Dostoevsky is such a stupendous literary genius that *everything* he wrote is of interest. Bunin, Leonid Andreiev, though they were anti-Soviet, but are fine Russian writers, are now being sold all over the place. The symbolist and 'imaginist' poets, the 'Acmeists' and the rest of them—Gumilev, Viacheslav Ivanov, Innokenti Annensky, Feodor Sollogub—all those poets of the 1900s and 1910s, who were treated with such contempt and disdain in the past as so many 'decadents,' are being reprinted—also as part of our national heritage; some are being reprinted if only as historical curios. And you saw how *Literary Gazette* went into raptures the other day over a volume of collected poems by Anna Akhmatova. I am glad the old girl has lived to see it. A few years ago Zhdanov treated her as 'half-nun, half-harlot.' Now, there are a few 'reservations'—they talk about her 'complicated, tortuous road'; but, on balance, she is declared to be (as she should be) one of our major poets. . . . There is an enormous liberalization going on in our whole approach to the literature of the past. Also, Soviet writers who were taboo or under a cloud have been rehabilitated—Babel, for instance. His collected stories—and wonderfully good stories they are, too—came out recently with an enthusiastic introduction by Ehrenburg."

"Yes, I know," I said, "the poor devil was purged in 1938. I remember meeting Marshal Budienny at a reception soon after the war, and I said: 'In my early youth, I learned a lot about you from Babel's *Konarmia*. What happened to Babel?' And the Marshal muttered: 'Fifth Column,' and turned his back on me."

"Mistakes were made, some bad mistakes," said Anna Ivanovna. "Khrushchev says it won't happen again. But then, with Hitler preparing to attack us, I suppose we couldn't be too careful. . . ."

"And the Big Purges?"

"I'm not sure about that. Some dirty business. Of course.

All the same, could anybody really feel sorry for chaps like Kamenev and Zinoviev?"

"There are a few writers," said Grisha, "who still wait to be rehabilitated. Or rather, to be reprinted. There's a marvelous writer you may have heard of—Evgeni Zamiatin. Really in the great Leskov tradition. A bit ironical about the Soviet regime, I daresay. . . ."

"I knew Zamiatin very well in Paris; he arrived there in 1931; a few years later he was dead. It has since struck me that Orwell, in *1984*, borrowed an awful lot from Zamiatin's *We*. His wife was pining to get back to the Soviet Union; but he hesitated; tried to adapt himself to the West, went into films, it was no good. . . . He went abroad with a special permit from Stalin; so he could have gone back."

"Pity he didn't," said Grisha, "he might be with us yet. Or —he might have been purged like Babel. *We* was a pretty poisonous book. And a writer's life was risky in those days. . . . Curious how many suicides there were among writers: Mayakovsky, and Yessenin; and, latterly Fadeyev. I was upset about Fadeyev," said Grisha. "It was quite clear to all of us what had happened. He was a Stalinite, a 1000 per cent Stalinite; and he was not going to readapt himself. He had the honesty of his convictions. They were all Stalinites, but now Simonov and the rest of them keep beefing about the 'personality cult.' Fadeyev wouldn't do it. He was genuinely devoted to Stalin. It was mean to say in the official announcement of his death that he killed himself because he was an alcoholic. . . . In the case of Yessenin it was true; he was a hopeless drunk. He and Isadora Duncan—what a pair! Mayakovsky—well, that was a more complicated sort of suicide. Dirty intrigues by his fellow-writers, particularly by the RAPP group, with real rats like Averbach; no encouragement by the Party high-ups for his 1930 exhibition; perhaps a feeling that the 'exciting' period of the Revolution was over—though it was in 1930 that he wrote his most magnificent poems; also, awful sentimental complications. Something of a split personality perhaps; a love for the Revolution, and a bitter hatred of some of those who, like the RAPP rats. claimed to be better revolutionaries than he. Curious, all the same, he wasn't a Party member. . . . I also heard it said he had syphilis, but I don't believe a word of it. . . ."

"Who then are your favorite nineteenth-century writers?" I said.

"I don't know," said Grisha, "I love them all. Not much in common between us orderly Soviet citizens and Pushkin's Oniegin or Lermontov's Pechorin, or Chekhov's stories and plays—and yet we feel a kind of closeness to them all; every character in *The Three Sisters* and *The Cherry Orchard* we seem to know personally. Or rather, no; that's not quite true. *The Cherry Orchard* is a period piece; but *The Three Sisters* has a kind of permanent psychological value; in a different context, all these characters exist in Russia today. We have them all in the Soviet Union—whether Chebutykin, the old army doctor, with his futile but warm humanity and tenderness, or that prickly bitch, Natasha. Yes, *we* have our own bitchy Natashas all right! As well as Olga, Masha and Irina and Masha's nice, silly, self-satisfied husband. The nineteenth-century classics are, as somebody called them, our 'eternal companions.' There is more connection between our ordinary life and the classics than in any other country, don't you think so? Even after 42 years of the Soviet regime we are constantly reminded of *some* character in classical Russian literature. There was a time—not now—when people currently compared Khrushchev with a certain garrulous and extrovert character in *Dead Souls!*"

"Nozdrev?"

"Of course," Grisha laughed. "And Soviet literature is, after all, the heir of Russian nineteenth-century literature. Only there's this—and that's what's been bothering us quite a lot. Our writing tends to be uniform, partly perhaps because our writers keep on being told: 'Write like Tolstoy, like Turgeniev, like Chekhov.' And there's something wrong there. Mayakovsky, our greatest Soviet poet, and a real revolutionary poet, would have been absolutely hopeless if he had tried to write say, like Pushkin. Also, there's a certain contradiction in terms, as we all know (though we seldom say so) in the phrase 'Socialist realism.' It means realism which has got, in some measure, to be didactic. That, in itself, has a restraining, a distorting effect on *realism*; our writers can't write *quite* as freely about Soviet reality as Tolstoy, Turgeniev, Chekhov or Gorki wrote about Tsarist reality; and so our writers fall between two stools. But some of the younger ones are now trying to get out of the vicious circle.

In the 1920s writers were less conformist in their style, less given to copying the classical realists of the nineteenth century. They wrote more complicated, more dynamic prose; some wrote more like Leskov, others invented a style of their own. In poetry, Mayakovsky has *no* predecessors; in prose, a new style was used by the early Vsevolod Ivanov, by Babel, by the young Leonov. The 1920s, about which you were so rude, Anna Ivanovna, produced some really exciting literature, in the Leskov tradition, if you like, or in no tradition at all—like Mayakovsky, with his magnificent neologisms and verbal jugglery. Mayakovsky invented hundreds of new words; who ever invents a new word now?"

"Yes," I said, "Zamiatin was in the Leskov tradition. Young Leonov, as you said, also wrote a complicated kind of prose, brilliant stuff, Vsevolod Ivanov, too. Even Ehrenburg, with his *Julio Jurenito*. And, among the poets there were Khlebnikov and Pasternak. . . . Leonov and Ivanov now write much the way others do. And Pasternak is in the doghouse."

"He won't be there for long," said Grisha. "You'll see."

"Have you read *Zhivago*?"

"Not yet, but I've been promised a copy."

"What I find disconcerting," I said, "is that no funny books are produced in Russia any more. In the 1920s there was Zoshchenko; and there were Ilf and Petrov. But now?"

"Now—not much, if anything. Zoshchenko is old hat. Russian life *was* funny in the days of the NEP; and even funnier NEP books are the two Ilf and Petrov novels. But what is one to be funny about in Russia today? There are rogues and crooks in Russia today, but they haven't the monumental quality of Ilf and Petrov's Ostap Bender. They are worth a *feuilleton* in *Komsomolskaya Pravda:* that's about all. *Krokodil* keeps hammering at the same old themes—*stilyagi,* hooligans, red-tape, bureaucrats, inefficiency at this or that factory or *kolkhoz,* drunkenness, servility, toadying to the boss, hankering for 'Western culture,' and all that. But both the themes and the jokes are prefabricated, as it were. I very seldom get a real laugh out of *Krokodil.* The theatre is rather better in that respect. Korneichuk can still be funny. Though not wildly so. Obraztsov's puppet theatre is magnificent—but his most brilliant satire is directed at the USA and the West—Hollywood, Paris 'glamour,' and so on. But real big satire, the sort of thing Saltykov wrote in the nineteenth century—well, there's just not much scope for it in Soviet society—if you accept the system. And we *do* accept it."

"Would you like to hear a nice bit of satire, all the same," Kolya said. "Here's one of the best Arkadi Raikin records."

He turned on the rather fancy gramophone.

This was Arkadi Raikin, the highly entertaining head of the Leningrad Miniature Theatre:

"Will you come tomorrow," the chairman of the *datchas* trust said. I came on the following day. I waited an hour, and he did not see me.

"Don't come tomorrow. He's having a conference," said his secretary. "Come the day after tomorrow."

I came the day after tomorrow. I waited an hour. But he didn't see me. I went out of the office. And just at that moment a firebrigade rushed past. And I thought to myself: "How wonderful it would be if our government offices worked as promptly and punctually as our firebrigades. And what would happen if our firebrigades worked the way some of our government offices do?"

And then Raikin impersonated the chief of *such* a firebrigade.

(*To his secretary.*) Zinaida Petrovna, I told you not to put through any calls to me. I'm busy. What do you say? A fire? (*Silence.*) Oh. All right. (*Takes the other receiver.*) Yes . . . (*silence*). Yes . . . (*silence*). Yes . . . (*silence*). A fire . . . Yes, I was already informed. (*Silence*) . . . And what's on .fire? Enumerate. . . . A chacha. I see. What kind of chacha? Can't hear, speak more slowly. What? Oh, a *datcha*. (*Silence.*) I see. And what do you want *us* to do about it? What? Oh, put the fire out? (*Silence*). (*Slowly:*) Yes, I suppose . . . I suppose we *could* try. Anyway will you send an application and two photographs. . . . Whose photographs? But of the *datcha,* of course. What? Every second counts? Well, the house isn't on fire, is it? Oop, sorry. . . . I'm sending you the fire brigade at once. (*Takes other receiver.*) Chief accountant, please. (*Slowly:*) That you, Peter Ivanovich? There's a bit of trouble we've run into. What? A funny story? (*Keenly.*) Yes. . . . yes. . . . (*roars with laughter*). What's that? A fire starts at the *datcha*. Yes . . . yes . . . I can't hear. Say it again! Oooooh! The husband arrives. And the wife running around screaming: "What'll I do? What'll I do?" . . . Yes? . . . And the other one. . . . He what? Got into the closet and is whispering from there . . . what? What was that? "Carry out the furniture!" (*Coughs and chokes laughing.*) Oooooo-oh? Oooo-oh! (*Splutters.*) And then? . . . Ooooh! Oh, there's another story I know: also the husband arrives . . . and the wife . . . M-mmmm. (*Mumbles*) Oh, I've forgotten how it goes. But it was *frightfully* funny, too. I'll remember. I'll phone you up when I do. (*Silence.*) By the way, why did you phone me? Oh, *I* phoned you, did I? What on earth did I phone you about? Yes, yes, of course; there's a man who called up saying his *datcha*'s on fire. How do we stand for funds? (*Long silence*). Yes . . . Yes . . . Well yes, that'll be for the next quarter. (*Chokes laughing again.*) So he said "Carry out the furniture." (*Laughs.*) Well, good-bye, good-bye. Take care of yourself. What a story to think up! (*Chokes laughing.*) (*The other phone rings.*) (*Impatiently.*) Yes, yes, what *is* it? Who's speaking? Oh, it's *you!* (*Laughs uproariously.*) Still burning, eh! (*Silence.*) But no, no, no, don't misunderstand me. I am not laughing at your sorrow. Only I just heard such a frightfully funny story. All right, all right. What, you'll complain? But I am *sending* you the fire brigade. What? Too late? The *datcha*'s already burned down. I see. (*Bellows.*) Then why the *devil* do you have to disturb me? (*Slams down the receiver.*) One hasn't a moment's peace with these people. How can one get any work done at this rate?

The way Raikin impersonated the "bureaucrat" was really extremely funny. Everybody laughed.

"Good, very good," said Grisha. "But when you come to think of it, that's about as far as satire in Russia today will go. In our society there isn't room for very much more. It's the penalty one has to pay for a fairly uniform, fairly disciplined, society. The transition period—the 1920s—could throw up objects for satire like the magnificent Ostap Bender and his fellow-crooks. At a pinch, you could trace back his family tree to Gogol's Chichikov. Ostap Bender was, in his own way, defying the new society, he was a survivor of the capitalist system, its criminal fringe. Now the scope is much more limited, unless—one started making fun of the people right on top. But that wouldn't do.

"But, in the last few years, literature has, all the same, been getting out of its rut. Subjects are now being touched upon which were wholly taboo a few years ago. But these are serious subjects: our losses in the war, the NKVD, and so on. But new funny subjects—hardly. Pity, in a way, there's no scope for a Gogol, a Saltykov, even a Chekhov in his lighter vein. . . .

"The most we can afford in that line are a few little irreverent jokes, like the one about the porcupine. Do you know it?"

"No."

" 'What are the three occasions on which you like to sit on a porcupine?' And the answer is: 'If the porcupine has been shaved. Or if you can sit on it with somebody else's behind. Or if you do it by order of the Government and the Party.' "

"Also, one used to hear a lot of jokes about Khrushchev until a couple of years ago. But no longer."

"Tell us one."

"Oh, no!" said Grisha. "But I'll tell you one about Molotov at Ulan-Bator. Only it's not terribly funny. . . ."

He told it, and it wasn't very funny.

"Actually," Grisha said, "Molotov was the only one in the Anti-Party—i.e. anti-Khrushchev—group people felt sorry about. Pretty big figure in our history, after all. . . ."

"Well," said Kolya, "let's put on the other side of the Raikin record; here you get jokes just for the jokes' sake."

This was an amusing miscellany of songs and a variety of impersonations and funny stories. This one, for instance:

The Doctor: Well, well, what can I do for you? Take a seat. What are you complaining of?

The Patient: That thing again. What d'you call it? Yes, alcohol.

The Doctor: You drink a lot of vodka?

The Patient: Oh, not so very much. Two quarts a day.

The Doctor: And you've been drinking for a long time?

The Patient: Oh, not for very long. Just since childhood.

The Doctor: All right then, I shall give you treatment. But on *one* condition: a pint of vodka a day. No more.

The Patient: I see. A pint a day.

The Doctor: And you'll come back in three days.

(*Three days pass.*)

The patient comes in, bellowing an incoherent song.

The Doctor: But, my dear fellow, how did you managed to get so sozzled on a pint?

The Patient: So you think you're the *only* doctor I go to?

Another story. A public meeting:

The Speaker: Comrades, we must discuss today a problem of the greatest, of the utmost importance. As you know . . . (*Screams at a woman leaving the hall*): *Where* are you going? *Woman No.* 1: You know I've got a child at home.

The Speaker: Comrades, as I was saying, this is a problem . . . (*Again screams at a woman leaving the hall*): *Where* are you going? *Woman No.* 2: You know I have a child at home.

The Speaker: As I was saying, comrades, this problem . . . (*Screams at a third woman leaving the hall*): Where are *you* going; you haven't *got* any children! *Woman No.* 3 (*furiously*): If I have to spend all my time at public meetings, I shall never have any children *at all!!!*

Chapter 12

THE "TRANSITION TO COMMUNISM"

MOST SOVIET CITIZENS, both young and old, to whom I put the question: "When will the transition to Communism be completed, and what is it going to be like under Communism?" were either very vague about the whole thing, talked in terms of "wait-and-see," or made rough guesses about the process being completed in 20 or 30 or 50 years, adding, however, Khrushchev's remark that "no calendar date could be fixed."

A usual qualification was: "Much will depend on what happens in the outside world, and even on whether anything like a uniform rhythm in the progress towards Communism can be maintained in all the Socialist countries." The more erudite or pedantic tended to quote Lenin or—Khrushchev's speech at the Twenty-first Congress, or at some recent Plenum of the Central Committee. But none of this was particularly conclusive either.

Nevertheless, a good deal of theorizing has been done on the question; and one of the principal boasts of present-day Soviet theorists is that today they could see more clearly than the "Marxist classics" could the way in which the fundamental principle of Communism—"From each according to his ability, to each according to his needs"—would materialize in practice. *In short, under Khrushchev, and as a result of recent scientific developments, the future Communist society is treated by the Party theorists as a much more tangible reality than ever before.*

Thus, T. Stepanian wrote in *Communist* (No. 14, September 1959.) :

Many of the things which could not be scientifically foretold by the classics of Marxism-Leninism before the victory of the Socialist Revolution, or even during the building of Socialism, can be foretold today, in the present conditions of a direct transition from Socialism to Communism. . . . The danger of falling into Utopianism has been eliminated.

The main arguments, then, are these:

There are two phases of Communist development. The two phases have many features in common, but, in other respects, the second (higher) phase is different from the first phase.

Both phases are marked by "the social ownership of the means of production," by "the identical action of economic laws, aiming at the planned development of Socialist production, which, in turn, aims at the satisfaction of the ever-increasing needs of the masses;" and by "work according to everybody's capacity, such work being the citizen's first duty towards society." Both phases of Communism are also marked by the absolute unity of society, a unity achieved as a result of the liquidation of all social, class and national antagonisms. There must also be a systematic liquidation of "nonantagonistic contradictions." Throughout the process, there must be a constant heightening of ideological consciousness, of Communist morality and general culture.

But Communism grows out of Socialism; and Communism has certain features which don't exist under Socialism.

Economically, Communism is marked by an unprecedented and all-round development of the powers of production. This creates conditions for a change in the whole nature of labor, and in a general technical and cultural development of the masses. The two forms of Socialist property (state and cooperative) change to a single form of people's property; distribution according to labor is replaced by distribution according to needs, i.e. without money or trade. (Under complete Communism neither will be necessary.)

There will be a complete elimination of the essential differences between town and country, between physical and mental labor; the signs of any class divisions will disappear; workers, peasants and intellectuals will all have become workers of a classless society. All "survivals of capitalism" will have disappeared, such as religion and an idealistic outlook.

A large part of present-day humanity will probably skip
the classical capitalist phase of development—i.e. move (like
China and Mongolia or the Soviet East) from semi-feudal to
Socialist forms.

In the more highly developed capitalist countries (USA, Britain) capitalism itself lays the foundations for a Socialist system. The transition can be speeded up through the working
class taking power. But there can be no direct transition from
capitalism to Communism.[1] Socialism alone can gradually create
the material and psychological conditions for a transition to
Communism.

Khrushchev's 1955 "line" that each country could follow
its own Socialist road has now been fully abandoned—
"national-Communism" is now treated as a dangerous heresy.

The purpose of the revisionist doctrine of "national-Communism" was to prevent the Peoples' Democracies from building a
Communist society together with the Soviet Union. The successes achieved by the USSR, China and the other Socialist
countries struck a fatal blow at "national-Communism."

And then:

A decisive factor in the building of Communism is the constant creative activity of the masses, of all social organizations,
and of the Communist Party with its guiding and organizing role.
The development of democratic freedoms and particularly of
the freedom of the individual cannot be achieved without certain forms of organization; otherwise the result may be an-
archism; while organization without human freedom may lead to
bureaucratism. Under Communism there can be neither an-
archism nor bureaucratism.

But will the State wither away? Here everything depends on
the international situation: under Communism the State will
go on existing so long as there is any danger of an attack
from outside.

Moreover, the unification of nations, even after they have

---

[1] The veiled Russian criticism of the "peoples' communes"
in China is directed at the alleged "skipping" of the "Socialist
stage" in the transition from capitalism (or even feudalism) to
Communism.

achieved the Communist stage, will take several decades.

Also "complete Communism," which "will become a reality in the near future, does not mean something final or static; there will be further evolutions, and the Communism of the relatively near future will be different from the Communism of 100 or 200 years hence."

What then will be the "material and technical base" of Communism?

Already today we can see the outline in the development of Socialist production, especially in industry. Here we are witnessing a scientific and technical revolution—mechanization, automation, electronics, the new developments in the chemical industry, in the all-round electrification on the basis of both old and new sources of energy, including atomic and, before long, thermonuclear energy, in the ever-growing productivity of labor, the essential condition of Communist prosperity and abundance. . . . The new forms of energy will go on playing an ever-increasing role in developing the material and technical base of Communism. Machines will be produced on a gigantic scale so as to create the perfect conditions for the complex mechanization of labor and the automation of production.

According to Khrushchev, speaking at the June 1959 Plenum, the equipment under Communism would still have to be renewed, on the average, every five years. Khrushchev stressed in this connection the extreme importance of developing an immense network of research laboratories of various kinds; as a result of this development, the number of "scientific workers" would, proportionately to "manual" workers, increase enormously.

But technical equipment was not enough, in itself, to constitute the base of a Communist society; it was essential to produce a new type of worker "who would combine harmoniously highly-developed mental work with health-giving physical work."

Together with the creation of the material and technical base of Communism goes the gradual shortening of the working day and the increase of leisure time, as well as the radical reconstruction of all the phases of national education, and the strengthening of Communist education, all of which aims at training men and women of all-round development. . . . Naturally, Lenin's profound phrase that, under Communism, men should be able to "do everything" mustn't be taken literally. A superficial know-all attitude is not what's needed; but every man must be acquainted with the main principles of social production. In this way only can we eliminate the lifelong enslavement by one particular trade, and make it possible to change, if necessary, from one trade to another. This also would help to eliminate the borderline between mental and manual labor. . . .

When then will the "material and technical base of communism" be ready?

Here we are told that "its main elements should be completed within the next 15 years."

The further development of the material and technical base of Communism, the ever-growing use of atomic and thermonuclear energy, new economic and cultural achievements, the further growth in the prosperity of the masses, as well as the front rank that will be given to social means of satisfying needs will mean that, in the main, Communist society has been built.

The concept of personal property will undergo two essential changes with the coming of Communism:

The working masses will be getting more and more consumer goods: good and beautiful clothes, wireless sets, TV, etc.

Secondly, there will be a gradual withering-away of those elements of private property which are in contradiction with the growth of social property. In the more advanced *kolkhozes* we find, already today, that the peasants voluntarily give up their private plots and their private livestock. Similarly, there will be no need for a form of private property like private savings. But the liquidation of trade and money must not be carried out prematurely; they are an essential part of the Socialist phase of development. . . .

Under Communism, as Lenin said, labor would be voluntary and in the nature of a social service.

But in reality, "Communist labor, which will be done without norms, without regard to remuneration, will be possible only if the Socialist principle of material self-interest is consistently observed."

Here there seems to be a contradiction; but it's explained away as follows:

Communist labor presupposes not only a high degree of development of the social means of production, but also a Communist consciousness. . . . With labor becoming the primary vital urge, the transition will take place from distribution according to work to distribution according to needs—a principle which, to this day, bourgeois ideologists regard as Utopian. . . . But this, in reality, will be achieved along two lines—an ever-improving distribution from public funds and the growth of the private incomes of the workers. The social services will include the general development of communal feeding, a vast amount of new housing, kindergartens, crêches, schools, cultural and medical institutions, sports stadiums, etc. . . . Most of these elements already exist . . . and, already before the war, social services represented more than the workers' monetary incomes. At the end of the Seven-Year Plan incomes of workers and employees, as well as peasants, will have increased by 40 per cent, while the State's expenditure on social services will have gone up by 50 per cent. This process will gradually lead to a diminution and, ultimately, to a final elimination of inequality in the material condition of people. . . . Between 1959 and 1965 minimum incomes will increase far more than higher incomes. . . .

How will this look in practice?

In practice this means that, before long, the social forms of satisfying human needs will provide free food for all school-children, that all children will be able to go, free of charge, to boarding schools. Everybody will be able to acquire the necessary food, elegant and good clothes, in accordance with each individual's tastes and requirements. We must emphasize this elementary fact since bourgeois sociologists have been thinking up, since the Twenty-first Congress, new arguments against Communism. According to them, Communist abundance would smother the freedom of personality, since distribution would be done regardless of private tastes, but according to a standard pattern laid down by the State. . . .

Of course, all the details of this transition to Communism cannot be easily distinguished yet. Only practical experience will determine certain concrete ways of applying the main principle of Communism. As N. S. Khrushchev said:

"The completion of the building of Communism will take place once we have created complete abundance for satisfying the needs of all people, and once all people will have learned to work according to their capacities so as to multiply and accumulate social wealth."

In conclusion the *Communist* article returns to the question of the development of Communism in other countries:

> The general principles and rules of the building of Communism must be strictly observed everywhere; but this does not mean that there cannot be variations in the concrete forms and methods . . . arising from historical, national and other peculiarities of the country in question. Such variations will be inevitable so long as the complete victory of Communism throughout the world will not have been achieved.

Here, it seems, was an attempt to find a kind of middle way between the "uniform" progress of Communism in the different countries and the revisionist heresy of "national Communism" of which Titoism was, of course, the most extreme example.

It is, of course, extremely difficult to say what Soviet citizens generally think of all these arguments. But I attempted to discuss all this with both young people and with older people, with people who were Party members and others who were, more or less, "unpolitical."

The Party members argued that this was "the sort of general pattern we have in mind, though it's no use being too precise about the details." For one thing, the tempo of the "building of Communism" would be partly determined by outside factors. If there was a long period of international peace—which was one of Khrushchev's main aims—and if there was no need to concentrate unduly on armaments, the process would be a faster one than if war became probable once again.

Non-Party people, especially the older ones, were skeptical; they thought there was still an awfully long way to go towards the kind of relative egalitarianism which was being talked about in the theoretical journals; even assuming that each would get more or less the same housing conditions, the same kind of food, wouldn't there still be people who would have cars, while others wouldn't; and wouldn't there still be more deserving, and less deserving cases? And some people would be stupid by nature and others intelligent by nature, even if one assumed that both had the equal will to "work for the community."

And all this business about "communal feeding" and "boarding schools for all children" seemed in contradiction with the present tendency to cultivate the family, to give individual flats to every family—which meant getting away from the awful "communal flats" of the past.

The younger people took a different line.

Much of this, they said, had already been confirmed by practice. Science and technology would undoubtedly create unprecedented abundance in the Soviet Union within a matter of 15 or 20 years—if there was no war. Things that looked theoretical today might well become practical then. But the "egalitarianism" of all people, workers, peasants and intellectuals, they thought "a little remote." "No doubt," they would say, "there's a tremendous difference between the general cultural level in Russia before the Revolution and now; but there's even a wider gulf between a still pretty backward *kolkhoz* woman and a young scientist today."

Thus young Kolya said: "You can't get away from the fact that there is a technical and intellectual élite in this country today. And it'll take far more than 20 or 30 or 50 years to create any semblance of real equality. And even assuming there is going to be all this abundance in the Soviet Union, will there be anything like it in China or, say, Poland? And with all the revolutions that are likely to take place in the underdeveloped countries, won't we, apart from sending them scientists and engineers, also have to help them materially in a big way? And, to tell you the truth, we are not altogether sure about some of the other Socialist countries. In Poland, in particular, they seem to be terribly halfhearted about the building of Socialism. There's been no collectivization there; the Church is still powerful; a friend of mine who went to Poland recently said that the Poles hate the Russians, and keep looking towards the West. It'll take a good many years before the Poles 'accept' us. He said that every time, in Warsaw, he talked Russian, he got dirty looks. No doubt in the general evolution of the world towards Socialism and Communism, the Poles will have to conform in the end; but they are damned slow about it, it seems. In 15 or 20 years from now the Socialist camp will be producing far more than the capitalist camp; we'll have become a tremendous center of attraction to all the 'poorer' countries. But Khrushchev's idea of a smooth progress of Communism may not be so simple; the capitalist world is scared; and it'll do all it can to create difficulties for us. . . ."

Chapter 13

SOVIET MAN

THIS PROBLEM OF "gaining time" if Communism is to be built and if the Soviet Union is to develop according to plan (which, officially, mean the same thing) is the ever-recurring theme in all discussions, both private and official, on the future of Russia.

"The Soviet Union," writes L. F. Ilyichev, the present head of Agitprop, the Propaganda Department of the Central Committee, "must gain the maximum amount of time in its peaceful competition with the capitalist countries, and particularly with the USA. Somewhere around 1970, perhaps before, the USSR will take first place not only as regards the volume of production in absolute figures, but also in terms of *per capita* production." [1]

Apart from the "material and technical base of Communism," there must also be such a thing as "Soviet Man."

Does such a "Soviet Man" exist?

Ilyichev indignantly quotes certain bourgeois ideologists and propagandists who claim that Socialism "has not changed and cannot change human nature, since men will always be egoists and scroungers." He quotes, in particular, a West-German "expert" who "tries to prove that Soviet man does not substantially differ from bourgeois man, and that all attempts to "bolshevize the Soviet people" have proved a failure, and that a further intellectual growth of the Soviet people can only harm the Bolsheviks."

The truth is, with all due contempt for foreign commenta-

[1] *Communist,* No. 14, 1959, p. 47.

127

tors (Ilyichev argues) that, in the last 40 years, the Soviet people have not only changed the whole look of their country "but have changed themselves."

And Ilyichev, whom I knew in the past as one of the "hardest" of Stalinites (with a strong and undisguised dislike of the West), but who is now rightly regarded as one of Khrushchev's closest associates, proceeds to demonstrate this as follows, using, in the process, some of Stalin's phrases (such as "breaking the spine of the Fascist beast"):

Only men of great ideals and of a high spiritual uplift could have overcome the enormous difficulties and built Socialism in an atmosphere of capitalist encirclement. . . . Only such men could have broken the spine of the Fascist beast . . . or, abandoning the comfort of their homes, have gone out to the Virgin Lands or to the desert expanses of our Far North or Far East. . . . Of course, not all survivals of the past have disappeared yet; capitalism has left a legacy here, and one still finds traces, among Soviet people, of a private-ownership and individualist psychology.

Further, explanation and persuasion will continue to play an ever-growing part in our educational work, and coercion will hold a smaller and smaller place.

Stretching a point, Ilyichev goes so far as to say that "coercion never constituted the main method in conducting Soviet society"; but the time, he says, is not far off when it will be applied only to "specially vile anti-social and criminal elements."

But even now, with everything apparently moving in the right direction, there is still a danger that "for a long time yet, we shall have to resist the ideological offensive of imperialism, whose servants are doing all they can to revive the survivals of capitalism in the minds of Soviet people." *This ideological battle,* he argues, *will become all the more intense as the military and economic weapons of the capitalist world are proving more and more useless.* An interesting point which, broadly speaking, coincides with the views on the same subject of G. A. Zhukov, head of the Committee for Cultural Relations with Foreign Nations—with which I shall deal more fully later.

What then are the essentials of Communist education today? Ilyichev asks. The main thing is to "develop a Communist attitude to labor, to teach people to work like Communists." Not only must material goods but also "spiritual goods" be produced in ever-growing numbers, and of ever-growing quality—"remarkable scientific discoveries, good books, films, theater shows, ideologically and artistically valid works of music, painting, architecture, etc."

In time, the worker's role will more and more be reduced to working electronic machines and the instruments of automation. . . . And when all branches of production have been automated and man becomes the master of all machines, Soviet man will have ample time to develop his all-round culture. . . .

Or, as another Russian whom I met in Russia put it more graphically: "The finest democracy in human history, with the highest culture in the world, was the Athens of Pericles. Our future democracy will be the same—with just this difference: whereas Athens had slaves, we are going to have machines. The machines will be *our* slaves."

But this, in fact, is not quite Ilyichev's point of view. He believes in a sort of spiritual austerity, and is opposed to any sort of "Communist hedonism."

He even argues that the heroic spirit of the past is being neglected: "Not enough care is given to developing the Socialist patriotism and the national pride of Soviet people." The trouble is that—

Our young people can scarcely imagine what our country was like in the past, what gigantic strides it has made during the years of Socialism. The heroic deeds of their fathers in the Great Patriotic War are becoming to many of them a vague childhood memory. This cannot be allowed to happen. . . . Also, the deeds of our most valiant contemporaries must be given the greatest publicity. Soviet people are deeply grateful to N. S. Khrushchev for the wise and courageous manner in which he represented his Socialist country in the USA. Other great deeds by our contemporaries must be publicized; young people should have the opportunity of having regular talks with old Bolsheviks, with heroes of the Patriotic War, with heroes of industry.

That is to say, Soviet patriotism and national pride—which is not the same (Ilyichev stresses) as nationalist arrogance—must be developed by every means. Only in this way can capitalist propaganda and "the putrid ideas of cosmopolitanism" be properly fought. There must be no thoughtless imitation of the bourgeois way of life, bourgeois art, fashions, dances, etc.

And yet there are still many who tend that way, "just as there are still a good many profiteers, who try to grab from the State whatever they can; there are still plenty of red-tape bureaucrats, hooligans and drunks, thieves, slackers, and people guilty of bribery and toadying."

And Ilyichev argues in favour of reminding people more and more of the great heroes of the prewar and war years, and against an excessive emphasis in the press on "denunciatory" articles about all kinds of criminals, degenerates and moral monsters. Khrushchev was quite right, in short, to find the publication of a book like Dudintsev's *Not by Bread Alone* regrettable.

It is quite true, Ilyichev recalls, that the Twenty-first Congress had stressed the importance of "material self-interest" as a stimulus in production; but moral stimuli to work for the good of the country and society would, as the same Congress said, also play an ever-increasing role; the "combination of the material and moral stimuli" were the highroad along which Soviety society would move towards Communism, a society in which labor became man's most vital necessity.

Above all, Ilyichev argues, *it is important not to look upon Communism as a purely materialistic paradise*:

Those comrades are wrong who look upon Communism as being still a kind of distant abstraction. . . . But equally wrong are those who look upon it purely from a "consumer" or *obyvatel* [2] point of view. They even put across the idea that, under Communism, people are going to consume—and be idle the rest of the time. Some journalists, lecturers and propagandists are clearly guilty of taking the wrong line. The journal *Technology for the Young* went so far as to say that Communist development would be measured by the extent to which the belly is full. It literally wrote: "There can be real freedom only when man has to stop worrying about where his next meal will come from, and when he knows that his stomach will always be filled."

"Of course," says Ilyichev, "don't play down the prosperity

[2] *Obyvatel,* from the verb *byvat,* to exist, is somebody who merely exists, or vegetates.

that Communism will bring, but, at the same time, don't ever stop reminding people that under Communism everybody will have to work, and that work will be every's *prime necessity*."

Also, a Communist outlook, based on Marxism-Leninism, must continuously be cultivated; and Ilyichev sharply argues against the "technologists." And then comes this curious admission:

There are people in our country who already say that technical sciences matter enormously, but that social sciences don't—for there's nothing in them; nothing concrete, a lot of talk, discussion and blah.

For great though the scientific achievements of the Soviet Union are, they would have been impossible without the victory of Marxism-Leninism.

There can be no real Communist who confines himself to his narrow speciality, without trying to grasp Marxist-Leninist theory.

And here again we come up against this contradiction in Soviet thinking: the cult of the family, on the one hand, and the far better upbringing that children are likely to get in boarding schools.

Some parents are quite indifferent to their children's pastimes, friends, etc. . . . On the other hand, the boarding schools will go on playing an ever-increasing role in bringing up the young generation. No wonder they have been called the highroad to Communism. For here, in these schools, remarkable conditions have been created for forming a *new man*; here children are brought up in an atmosphere of labor, high culture and *in a spirit of genuine collectivism,* complete with a harmonious combination of spiritual and physical development.

The rest of Ilyichev's article covers the already familiar ground—the importance of using persuasion, rather than coercion; the importance of the educational role of the Komsomol, of the various factory, trade-union and house committees, and, if necessary, "Comrade Courts," all of which, in most cases, make it unnecessary to refer offenses to a regular law court.

In short the various "collectives" can be "ten times more effective" in making a young man mend his ways than the harsh hand of the law.

Very often an offender mends his ways much more rapidly and radically under the influence of the collective than as a result of a term of imprisonment. . . . The comradely care shown to such a person by his collective (factory, *kolkhoz,* etc.) not only protects him against the temptation to commit further offenses, but also tends to bring out in the man all that is good, healthy and honest in him.

Such "public opinion pressure" can do a great deal to put an end to bribery, corruption, hooliganism, drunkenness, "an uncomradely attitude to women," etc.

This Ilyichev pronouncement—which is by a man holding a key position in the whole educational and propaganda machinery of the "Khrushchev régime" (even though Ilyichev was—and still is—a type of the "harder" Stalin man) is of considerable interest. Only, to what extent, one may ask, is his picture of "Soviet man" theoretical rather than real? A vision of the future, rather than a living portrait? I think it has a little of both. Ilyichev's "Soviet man" seems a little unreal if only because what is "good" in him is "Soviet," and what is "bad" in him is "capitalist survival" or "un-Soviet."

And yet I am fully convinced that "Soviet man" exists, and has been evolving over the last three generations.

If certain fairly definite "ethical types" can, by a process of long conditioning, be produced in other countries—for instance, certain "typical" English or Scottish characters with their conventions and more or less well-respected codes of manners and morals—why not admit that, under a system of *infinitely more intensive conditioning* over a period of 40 years, a fairly definite ethical type can also be produced in Russia?

It is not as if this conditioning process was working on a perfect *tabula rasa*; below the surface of Soviet man, there remains much of the basis of the Russian national character; but the conditioning process has been applied, more or less successfully, to other nationalities, too; the greater the readiness to adopt Russian characteristics, the easier the adoption, too, of "Soviet" characteristics. This adaptation was quite simple in the case of the Ukrainians, who, with rare exceptions,[3] are less different from the Russians than are the Scots from the English, while the more "backward" Asian nationalities gradually took a pride in considering themselves Soviet, and also derived from the Soviet system very considerable material benefits. Material benefits are also underlying the gradual conversion to "Sovietism" of more obstreperous peoples like the Latvians and Estonians.

When I think of the countless Soviet citizens I met during and after the war, and now again in 1959–60, I feel that the image of "Soviet man" is becoming not less, but increasingly clear-cut. During the very bad days of 1941–42, the primary motive in resisting the Germans, as they did resist, in suffering greater hardships than any other people on earth, was in very many cases a kind of primeval Russian nationalism, combined with an acceptance of Stalin's leadership. The emphasis in the propaganda in both 1941 and 1942 was on "Russia." [4] After Stalingrad "Russian patriotism" was gradually transformed into "Soviet patriotism." In peace conditions, the emphasis has been more and more on "Soviet."

The main characteristics of "Soviet man," as we see him today—and you find these characteristics in all kinds of people: students, young technicians, army soldiers and officers, the average "intellectual," the factory executive, the higher-grade worker, the polished young Soviet diplomat—are, I should say, the following:

(1) an immense national pride, with a definite—even if only relatively-recently intensified—superiority complex derived from several things: the conviction that the Soviet people have made, and have proved themselves capable of making, a more sustained effort over a period of 40 years than anyone else, and of having made more sacrifices than anyone else in World War II; the realization that, despite the terrible human and material losses suffered in World War II, the country has recovered, in a fantastic degree, in the last 15 years.

(2) A tremendous optimism arising from the conviction

[3] To those who will tell me about a pro-Nazi "Ukrainian nationalism," I would point out that, in the Red Army during World War II, the record of the Ukrainians, in proportion to their numbers, was as good as that of the Russians.

[4] See the author's *The Year of Stalingrad* (London, 1946).

that the Soviet Union is *the* great rising power in the world, which is not only catching up, materially, with the richest capitalist countries (notably the USA), but is also the country to which ever-growing sections of humanity are looking for inspiration; which has the immense multitudes of China "on its side," while, in terms of influence, the capitalist world is shrinking. The various "liberation" movements in the world are all, though not always openly, sympathetic to the Soviet Union—whether Cuba, Iraq, Guinea or Algeria, not to mention bigger fry like India or Indonesia. So even if the Soviet Union is not actively "missionary," it is at least passively "missionary." This "missionary" spirit—implying great national unity—is often much stronger than the hankering for purely personal freedom.

(3) In more individual terms, the consciousness, among millions of young Russians, of being "in on a good thing"; the young Soviet citizen today only has to compare his material position, or his level of intellectual development, with that of his parents or grandparents to realize the difference— a difference far more striking than in most similar cases in Western Europe or America. Also, the Soviet Union is a country of immense opportunities for the young.

(4) The more or less general consciousness, due to a lengthy process of conditioning and education, that a new kind of society has been built up, in which certain rules of personal behavior and of an ethical code should be, more or less, strictly observed, complete with the "respect for the human person," based on the very important psychological factor of "comradeship." No doubt, there are different income groups in the Soviet Union and consequently also a certain amount of "toadying to the boss"—which is less of a "bourgeois survival" than a phenomenon inevitable at the present stage of development of Soviety society; nevertheless, there are fewer class distinctions and class snobberies than elsewhere. And while it would be idle to deny that these exist, the "aristocracies" in Russia are aristocracies of merit, rather than of income. It is true, of course, that, occassionally, this "merit" is not very genuine. All the same, the feeling of "comradeship," of "being in the same boat," of belonging to a "superior" system, more or less unites all Soviet citizens. And the "heroic" sides in the Russian character are very much alive: it is not surprising that the whole world was

impressed by the extraordinary endurance and lack of personal hysteria with which the four Soviet soldiers (one Russian, two Ukrainians, one Tartar) survived their 49-day drift across the Pacific, before they were picked up by the American aircraft carrier. Their exploit was comparable to some of the most extraordinary feats of down-to-the-last-bullet endurance performed by groups of encircled Russian soldiers during World War II.

Whether "Soviet man" sees very clearly, or not, how he is going to enter "full Communism," he is extremely conscious of working and living in a society which has proved itself to be in very good working order, and one from which he is deriving more or less substantial personal benefits in terms of material advantages, education, sickness and old-age security, etc. And, with all its faults, he approves of this system; he is determined not to allow it to be seriously disturbed, still less destroyed, by the outer world.

Russians, we are told, are "friendly" to foreigners. This is not quite true. There may not be any objectionable kind of xenophobia, but there is a mighty undercurrent of distrust (for excellent historical reasons: the Intervention, the delays in the Second Front, Hiroshima, American bases, etc.) towards the "West." On the other hand, to China and the "underdeveloped" countries the attitude is friendly even if, occasionally, somewhat patronizing.

It seems, therefore, that "Soviet patriotism" is a blend of (a) great-power Russian nationalism (which is shared by most Ukrainians and more and more members of the other Soviet nationalities); (b) the sense of constituting an immense physical and moral power in the world ("defense of the colonial underdog—and never mind about Hungary and Poland which, for a time, will still be rotten with Westernism"); (c) a sense of immense physical achievement, whether Stalingrad, Leningrad, the reconstruction of Russia since 1945, or Sputnik; (d) the consciousness of belonging to a society which, despite many ups and downs, mistakes and even tragedies, has proved its enormous vitality. And even if, in this society, "Soviet man" occasionally hankers for an American car, or gets drunk, or behaves in an "uncomradely way" (Russian version of "ungentlemanly!") to a girl or goes to church, or goes starry-eyed about *Doctor Zhivago,* these are only relatively minor deviations from the very broad and fairly straight road he sees ahead of him.

I have deliberately not mentioned the peasantry; this is still, in varying degrees, lagging behind the rest of Soviet humanity; in the industrial enterprises in Central Asia there is still something of an old-time industrial proletariat; also, until recently, there were some particularly wretched underdogs inside the Soviet system itself—particularly in the camps. But the tremendous machinery of the Soviet educational system is producing millions and millions of good specimens of "Soviet" citizens, each endowed with a certain sense of his own dignity and importance and with more or less good prospects ahead of him or her. The immense numbers of engineers, technicians and scientists turned out every year are a weapon of spreading Soviet influence throughout the world in its ever-growing "peaceful competition" with the West.

Whether the present "prosperity era" is going, in time, to "spoil" the type of Soviet man aimed at seems, despite protests to the effect that there is nothing to worry about, to disturb the Party hierarchy all the same. Hence Ilyichev's warning against neglecting the maintenance of the "heroic traditions," against the young "forgetting" about the industrial and military battle fought by their elders; hence also the Komsomol's warning against the toleration of "parasitical" tendencies amongst the young.[5]

The problem of "Soviet man" is not a simple one by any means; all the same, talk to any Soviet citizen of the categories enumerated above, and, in nine cases out of ten, you will find that he is there, as large as life. An attractive person? Matter of taste. Personally I like him, though, occasionally, he can be narrow-minded, pigheaded, and rather maddening.

[5] See page 108.

Chapter 14

A DIGRESSION ON LENIN: LEGEND
AND REALITY

ILYICHEV'S COMPLAINT THAT a certain proportion of young
people, particularly engineers, technicians and scientists, are
passionately interested in the accurate, precise and concrete
sciences, and tend to neglect the study of Marxism-Leninism,
raises quite a number of questions.

Every even slightly educated Soviet citizen is given, in the
course of his upbringing, a certain amount of Communist
theory; but, except for a minority, there does not seem to be
any passionate interest in the writings of Marx, Engels or
Lenin, and no serious attempt even to master the fundamentals of the doctrine. No doubt, this is done by prospective
Party members, but whether even these studies are more than
skin-deep is difficult to say.

A great deal is empirical in the present stage of Soviet
historical development; and the attempt to show that the
Khruschev policy marks a return from some sort of "Stalinist
deviation" to "pure Leninism" is plausible in only a very
limited sense. Conditions in the world have changed in so
many respects since Lenin that many references to Lenin
are inevitably arbitrary and artificial.

As for the hyperbolic cult of Lenin, as practised by public
speakers and the press, there seems a fairly obvious attempt
here to find a harmless sort of substitute for the much more
far-reaching "personality cult" of Stalin . . . or of Khrushchev.

I talked to many young Russians about Lenin; they assumed he was "an immense historical figure." But he was
remote to them. As for the advice proffered in the press "al-

ways to read Lenin," they thought that this was going a little far. There were Lenin books like *Imperialism, the Final Stage of Capitalism* which were still of great topical importance; but to read the whole of Lenin was unrewarding: what he had said of the revolt of China and of the colonial peoples was prophetic enough, but many major problems of today (or even of yesterday; such as the Fascist phenomenon) —above all, nuclear war—obviously weren't touched upon by Lenin at all. Also, his reliance on the revolutionary temper of the working class of Western Europe had badly misfired, at least up till now—despite some vital and pungent criticisms he had made of the West European reformists.

On nuclear war—or anything like it—no reference at all could be found in Lenin, apart from one lucky find: according to his wife, Krupskaya, Lenin had "foreseen the time when war would become so destructive that it would become altogether impossible," and that he had been "very excited at the idea." [1]

In one of the largest bookshops in Gorki Street there were always, I noticed, mobs of people in the literary section and even larger mobs in the science and technology sections, but very much fewer people—sometimes hardly anybody—in the political section, where Marxist-Leninist literature is chiefly sold. What they *did* buy there were, above all, topical books like *For Peace and Friendship,* describing Khrushchev's visit to the USA—of this 600,000 copies were sold in a few days!

Among many young people the view tended to prevail that Marx, Engels and Lenin could, up to a point, be taken as "read," and that if there was anything to learn from Lenin on any particular subject, somebody would be sure to make a speech, or write a *Pravda* article with an apt Lenin quotation, complete with the reference: *"Works, vol. 30, p. 467."* And many young people were a bit puzzled at the mental acrobatics with which so many articles on Lenin were being written, ostensibly with reference to the present world, but in which the 25 years of Stalinism were, somehow, skipped altogether. Although it was possible to find an occasional Stalin book in the big bookshops, the publication of his *Complete*

[1] *Pravda,* April 23rd, 1960.

Works (which had gone up to vol. 13, covering the year 1934) had been discontinued in 1953, and all these first 13 volumes were now hard to come by.

But Lenin was being boosted very deliberately—and chiefly along three lines: (1) he was the real founder of the Soviet State, an immense genius, a man with a "gigantic brain" (every "personality-cult" hyperbole was permissible in his case); (2) he was the "gigantic brain" who had foreseen how Socialism would conquer more and more parts of the world, and how capitalism—which had reached the decaying stage of imperialism—would lose more and more ground throughout the twentieth century, till it finally disappeared altogether; (3) finally, Lenin (and the constant implication was: "unlike Stalin") was profoundly humane, kind, considerate, a man with "an unforgettable infectious laugh" and with a "captivating smile."

And yet, what did this Lenin Cult add up to? In April 1960, almost entire issues of newspapers (*Pravda* and the rest of them) and of periodicals (*Communist, Novy Mir,* etc.) were devoted to celebrating the 90th anniversary of Lenin's birth.

On April 22, old man Otto Kuusinen made a long speech at a memorial meeting at Luzhniki, in which he showed how Russia today was following in the footsteps of Lenin. In 1920, in the midst of complete economic collapse, Lenin, he said, proclaimed with "the eagle eye of a genius" his doctrine of electrification as the true basis for the development of a Socialist economy in the Soviet Union. True, Lenin's extremely modest GOELRO plan was admittedly only a very small beginning; for by 1965 the Soviet Union would produce 70 times more than the 8.8 billion kwh Lenin had in mind—namely 620 billion kwh, while in 1980 it would be producing 2 trillion 300 billion kwh!

In the small beginnings of the new educational system of 1920, in the first kindergartens and crèches, Lenin also saw "the first young shoots of Communism." And after a reference to Lenin's prophecies about the revolt of the colored and colonial peoples, Kuusinen went on to say that Lenin had been "for co-existence"—since he had proclaimed: "The ending of wars, peace among the peoples, the stopping of all looting and robbery and violence—such is our ideal" (vol.

21, p. 264). If, in the West [Kuusinen did *not* mention China!] there were some who were trying to show that *Lenin believed in the inevitability of war,* they were, "with craven dishonesty, taking out of their context phrases written or uttered by Lenin at the height of the civil war and the imperialist intervention." On the contrary, said Kuusinen, "remember the instructions Lenin gave the Soviet delegation at the Genoa Conference in 1922." Also the convenient Krupskaya quote was brought in at this point.[2]

For all that, Kuusinen said that, in proclaiming at its Twentieth and Twenty-first Congresses the "absence of the fatal inevitability of war in our conditions, and the possibility of averting it," the Party had *"added a new word to Marxism."*

The great bulk of the Kuusinen memorial discourse on Lenin was little more than a survey of the internal and international situation in April 1960—with a flourish at the end to the effect that the Soviet Union—and indeed, the world—were continuing a process which had been begun under Lenin.

It was, with all due respect to Otto Kuusinen, a little like the famous Chekhov "lecture" *On the Dangers of Smoking* in which tobacco is mentioned in the first sentence and then in the last sentence, while the rest of the discourse is a digression on the henpecked old fellow's daily troubles with his wife and six daughters! All the same, the speech was, ideologically, important as an implied criticism of the Chinese "left-wing deviation" on the "inevitability of war."

In the special 160-page issue of *Communist* (April 1960), devoted to Lenin, everything too was, a little artificially, linked with Lenin: the articles were entitled: Leninism in Action; Towards the Victory of Communist Labor; Triumph of Lenin's Ideas on the Friendship of Nations; Lenin and the Achievement of the Ideals of Democracy; The Vitality of

---

[2] Significantly, too, at Bucharest, on June 22, 1960, Khrushchev (with an eye apparently on the Chinese and other *ultras*) explained why certain Lenin statements on "the inevitability of imperialist wars, so long as Socialism had not triumphed throughout the world" could not be taken literally:

"It is no use repeating, like children, what Lenin said in historical conditions which are entirely different from ours." See below, pp. 316–8.

Lenin's Principles in the Party Structures; Lenin on the Economic Competition of the Two Worlds; Lenin and Culture; etc., etc.

A certain artificiality of the whole thing was further strengthened by the *tour de force* of surveying the progress of the last 42 years, *without once mentioning the name of Stalin* throughout the 160 pages!

In *Literary Gazette, Komsomolskaya Pravda,* and many others the emphasis was more on the "humanity," the "kindness," the "human warmth," the "modesty" of Lenin.

Thus, in *Literary Gazette* (April 16, 1960) in an article called "Lenin's Smile," a Czech poet, Irzy Taufer, recalled that Lenin (unlike Stalin) was a modest man who did not meddle in things he knew little about:

A. V. Lunacharsky recalls that although Lenin was attracted by art, in which he saw a fruitful field for a Marxist theorist, he often complained that he "just hadn't time to study art problems," and "since he hated any kind of dilettantism, he preferred not to make any utterances on art." He refused to turn his personal likes and dislikes into leading ideas or guiding principles.

More characteristic still of the somewhat idyllic presentation of Lenin were the countless little "human-interest" stories about the man published in the Soviet press, particularly during April 1960. Thus, all kinds of elderly men or women who happened to have seen Lenin only casually at the Kremlin or, before that, at the Smolny in Petrograd—or who, at least, claimed to have talked to him—recalled various casual remarks made to them, all of them oozing human kindness and consideration. Or else, there was a long article by L. Slavin in *Literary Gazette* (April 23) telling how, during his convalescence at Gorki, near Moscow, Lenin took lessons from an old peasant woman, Maria Kirillovna Benderina (now a 76-year old *kolkhoz* woman) in—making wicker-baskets.

And here, after nearly 40 years, the old woman recorded word-for-word all that Lenin said to her during these lessons.

"And he was so considerate, so considerate; after each lesson there was a lot of litter round us. I would go down on my knees to pick it up. But no, no; he'd never let me do it, he'd always do it himself."

Or else, there were naïve little stories like this one (*Novy Mir,* April 1960) extracted from the archives of the writer Efim Zozulya:

THE MUSHROOMS

An old woman was wandering through a forest, with a basket of mushrooms, and she met Vladimir Ilyich [Lenin]. And Lenin said:

"What are the mushrooms like, grandmother?"

"Bad, my dear, very bad. Ever since the godless Bolsheviks have come here, no good mushrooms grow any more."

Suddenly a crowd of village kids came out of the neighboring birchwood, and they had whole baskets of lovely mushrooms; and Lenin pointed to them and said: "Well, grandmother, you spoke too soon; look what lovely mushrooms grow under the rule of the godless Bolsheviks."

Or else, a similar story about a village lad who refused to believe that the bald, elderly man wearing a simple shirt and trousers could be Lenin. "Oh hop it," said the lad; "you're not Lenin; Lenin wears golden robes."

This overhumanization and oversentimentalization of a very hardheaded man like Lenin struck me, even before this April 1960 orgy, as somewhat absurd and childish, and a bit reminiscent of the various Stalin-is-our-Sun-and-our-Moon-translated-from-the-Yakut sort of thing, of which there was so much in the late 1930s.[3]

I asked Vasili Petrovich what he thought of it.

"To tell you the truth, it doesn't make much sense, all this Lenin-told-to-the-children stuff. Insofar as it means anything, it's an attempt, through his person, to arouse a greater interest in his *ideas*; it may also mean that, since we are

---

[3] Another point always emphasized is the non-doctrinaire, non-scholasticist nature of Leninism: in Lenin's view, *concrete* conditions must always be taken into account; and in at least two articles in April 1960 there is a reference to Lenin's love for German poetry—for Heine and Goethe's *Faust,* with his significant affection for that perfect "empiricist" quote:

"Grau, theurer Freund, ist alle Theorie
Und grün des Lebens goldner Baum."

rather in the habit of going in for 'personality cults,' we might as well go in for this harmless one. But, on the whole, the thing strikes me as a bit artificial and unnecessary. I was a youngster when Lenin died; but I remember the years before that: years of civil war, and hunger; exciting but, for all that, hard, terrible years in the story of our country; years when Moscow was full of bandits and homeless, hungry and delinquent children, and when Dzerjinsky's Cheka was shooting people (rightly or wrongly) by the thousand, here and in Petrograd and all over the place. So all these little stories about Lenin and the Mushrooms and such-like pleasantries leave me completely cold. I doubt whether they impress anybody else either, except five-year-olds. Lenin was a tremendous figure—but he was no Father Christmas.

"Also, when he died in 1924, this country was still in one hell of a mess. The real test of our vitality in this world (and after all, let's face it, the Intervention of 1918–20 was a pretty halfhearted sort of thing, which could probably never really have won) came in 1941. It was during the 12 or 13 years before *that*, that the real foundations were laid for the immensely powerful country that we are now."

"Good for *papa* Stalin," I said.

"You're damn right," said Vasili Petrovich. "All the same," he added, "what Lenin said about colonialism is now coming true with a bang—with thousands of bangs! Stalin had neither the time nor the desire to worry about Africa. Anyway, Africa wasn't quite ripe yet in his day. Now it's ripening at a fantastic rate."

"But are Russians *really* interested in Africa?"

"Yes, we are—though how *actively* we're interested only time will show. Depends a little on how much Africa will be interested in *us*."

Chapter 15

SOVIET MAN: PRIVATE LIFE
AND SEX

IN RETURNING TO this question of "Soviet man," it is impossible to overlook the question of his private life and morals
—which, in fact, we are told, are *not* private, since nothing
is strictly private in a Socialist society.[1]

Most foreigners visiting Russia these days have a slightly
morbid, and usually wholly unsatisfied, curiosity about the
"love life" of Russians. Occasionally, they hear of glamorous
police spies who are planted on influential foreigners; but
few, if any, have ever seen them. Outwardly, Soviet life is
extremely decorous, almost "Victorian"; on two occasions, in
the Moscow subway, I was tapped on the shoulder by scan-
dalized-looking citizens because, sitting with my legs crossed,
I showed an inch or two of bare leg! You scarcely ever see
any necking or petting or even kissing in Moscow parks or in
the subway; and present-day Russian films and novels and
plays do not, as a rule, go very deeply into "that side of
things"—though there have, recently, as we shall see, been
some notable exceptions, such as Galina Nikolaeva's *Battle
on the Road.*

But is this anything specifically "Soviet?" Has not reticence
about sex been characteristic of the whole of classical Rus-

[1] This is, however, a point on which one should not be too
categorical. Recently, both *Literary Gazette* and *Komsomolskaya
Pravda* complained that there was sometimes a little *too much*
public discussion of some people's personal problems—problems
which were of no great importance to the community and which,
in fact, the people concerned could best sort out and settle between themselves.

sian literature, for instance? No doubt, there are traces of a
good deal of eighteenth-century French frivolity in great Russian writers like Pushkin and Lermontov; no doubt love—
though not specifically sex—holds a very important place in
the novels of Tolstoy, Turgeniev and Dostoevsky, but sex as
such is always treated delicately, by suggestion, as it were,
even by a volcanic, passion-ridden writer like Dostoevsky.
Not a single even remotely "erotic" piece of writing can be
found in either *Anna Karenina* or the *Brothers Karamazov,*
and not until he was a very old man did Tolstoy, in works
like *The Kreutzer Sonata* or *Resurrection* squarely face sex
(as distinct from love) as a major social and religious issue.
But again, little or no gloating, even though, as an old man—
notably in a famous conversation with a slightly scandalized
Chekhov—Tolstoy liked to recall that, in his youth, he was
"an insatiable f——er." Pushkin, too, had made a point of
drawing up a list of his 103 love affairs. No doubt, there
was, in Tsarist days, plenty of promiscuity, particularly in
the villages, while in the cities, large-scale prostitution was
a widespread phenomenon, complete with licensed brothels;
the fact remains, however, that Russians have always tended
to be reticent about sex, above all in their writings. It was
not till the final years of the Tsarist régime (and not without some indirect encouragement from Tolstoy's late writings) that some very bold and near-pornographic novels and
stories began to appear, some even dealing with "unheard-of"
things like homosexuality—though, in a hush-hush way, this,
too, had existed on a small scale, particularly in the theatrical
and musical world—Tchaikovsky being, of course, the most
famous case of all (a fact, by the way, never referred to in
any Soviet book on Tchaikovsky).

The Revolution, in the course of which much was made
of the "emancipation of women," produced a few years of
extremely lax morals. This "equality of women" was interpreted by the young generation as an encouragement to
"free love," and Madame Kollontai, who later became a
leading Soviet diplomat, even wrote novels in favor of this
"free love," as part of the revolutionary spirit. Lenin was,
however, wholly in disagreement with this, as we know,
especially from his (later published) conversations on the
subject with Clara Zetkin, the German Communist leader.
To Clara Zetkin he said that proletarian and Socialist morality

implied a strict social and personal discipline in these matters.

What is the position today, more than forty years after the Soviet Revolution of 1917? As already said, novels and films provide only few clues; in most of them, everything is highly respectable, and any breach of Communist morality is denounced, as a rule, as being "anti-social." No doubt, a good deal of "sinning" goes on in Russia, where as a result of the war, there are far more women (55 per cent) than men (45 per cent)—this resulting, especially in the villages, in some absurd situations in which love-starved middle-aged women are found "chasing" young boys of 14 or 15. Funny things also go on in the towns, especially among the *stilyagi* and "juvenile delinquents." Yet the fact remains that most Russians one meets are respectably married, with a cult of the family, and a real devotion to their children. Economic and social conditions have much to do with this: it is easier for a married couple to get a flat than for single persons or "free unions"; also, "social pressure" plays a considerable part in keeping people "respectable"; in the Party, in the Komosomol, promiscuous living is frowned upon, and may even lead to serious trouble if overdone. In the cities, too, lack of privacy is often an obstacle to "sinning."

But, as already said, Russians (though they don't mind, on occasion, telling some "dirty stories" are extremely reticent about sex; one might even say that there is a widespread conspiracy of silence on the whole issue; the Soviet press likes, of course, to talk about the depravity of Western bourgeois societies but, apart from an occasional denunciation in the press of some particularly black sheep, or an occasional general discussion on divorce or "illegitimate" children, very little is ever said about "these things." There is no such thing as a Soviet *Kinsey Report,* or anything even approaching it.

That is why a book published in Moscow in 1959 by a prominent medical man, Dr. T. S. Atarov, who has the official title of "Physician of Merit of the RSFSR," and has the high academic degree of "Candidate of Medical Sciences" must be looked upon as something of a major novelty. The book, called *Problems of Sexual Education,* is, as far as I know, the first book of its kind to deal with the problem in popular form. A hundred thousand copies of the book were printed in 1959, and these were sold out within a few days.

One of the most important points made by Dr. Atarov was that, in the Soviet Union, far too many parents and teachers treated sex as a taboo subject, surrounded by what he called a "conspiracy of silence," young people being, more often than not, left to find out the "facts of life" for themselves. More important, he argued that, owing to this "conspiracy of silence," no scientific study had ever yet been attempted on the sex life of the Soviet Union.

The book starts, of course, with a "Marxist" introduction on the subject, with long quotations from Marx and Engels, dealing chiefly with the "enslavement" of women, first in feudal, then in bourgeois, society.

It denounces the bourgeois convention of the "double standard"—men being allowed to do anything, and women not. Also, in bourgeois society, financial considerations had much to do with marriage and sex relations.

The Soviet Revolution swept away a lot of the old cob-webs, including prostitution "for which there is no longer any social basis." The institution of monogamy was, however, preserved, but was transformed from bourgeois monogamy to Socialist monogamy, not at all the same thing. The equality of women, the joint social sense of responsibility of husband and wife, plus mutual affection and respect made all the difference.

It would, however, be a mistake to imagine that the transition has been fully completed. . . . There are still, in our present society, plenty of old ideological survivals. Many of our men still think nothing of being unfaithful to their wives, and many boys (and even girls) take a light view of premarital relations. Worse still, among our young people, there are some who tend to reduce their relations with the opposite sex to a mere satis-faction of their physical urge without any spiritual or moral connection with the person concerned. . . .

Some of these moral lawbreakers have a peculiar "philosophy" of their own. They claim that the promiscuity they go in for is an inevitable substitute for the prostitution of the past. These "philosophers" also claim that society requires a certain freedom in matters of sex, since it is "biologically natural," whereas monogamy artificially restrains man's impulses.

This, Dr. Atarov said, was wholly contrary to Lenin's

views, who held that "free love" was no solution in a well-ordered Socialist society.

It was also quite untrue that sexual laxity was a good substitute for prostitution; in bourgeois countries there was plenty of social laxity, as well as prostitution; under Socialism, there was no need for either.

Then, in Chapter I, called "Sexual Education and the Schools," the author starts with some general considerations on finding a happy and harmonious solution, which would combine "freedom and discipline"—a solution equally important in sex as in many other matters.

Harmonious behavior is achieved when the interests of freedom and the personal desires of the person coincide with, or at least do not contradict, the interests of the people around him or her, as well as the interests of society as a whole.

Most young Soviet people, having completed their studies in a co-educational school, then are given a job, and "as far as their work is concerned, there are seldom any criticisms we can address to them."

Yet in their private lives, the shortcomings of our education can often be clearly observed. Things are done which are wholly contrary to Communist morality. . . . There are still people who think nothing of swearing eternal devotion to a young girl and of seducing and then abandoning her; or of getting married and, a year or two later, "getting tired" of their partner, and of abandoning him (or her), as well as the child or children; or, in the case of married people, of having casual affairs on the side. . . . Such immoral behavior is usually practiced by men, but it happens in the case of women, too. Needless to say, in saying all this, we are merely referring to a small minority in our country. . . .

And Dr. Atarov attributes many of these regrettable actions to a tendency, on the part of teachers, to ignore sex altogether in educating and bringing up children; it is not only a case of teaching young people "sex hygiene" in a narrow sense, but of also discussing with them the proper relations between men and women both in early and later life.

Of course, sex must not be treated as a distinct and separate subject in education; but, on the other hand, it is wrong to ignore it completely and absolutely. . . . It should be simply part of the *general* system of education, as part of the young person's formative process, as part of his or her social education. . . . For as long as possible, parents and teachers should try to divert the attention of children and adolescents from the "intimate" sides of life; yet sometimes there are awkward moments when children and adolescents put awkward questions to parents and teachers about the way children are born, etc. Most parents and teachers know how to deal with such questions by referring, for instance, to the lives of animals and plants. But some blunder terribly. Thus, some tell children that "it's a shame" to ask such questions; or they look awkward and embarrassed, and this only whets the children's curiosity. . . . Of course, there can be no fixed rules about dealing with "sudden" questions children may ask. But parents and teachers should refrain from telling them a lot of nonsense about "storks" and about "finding children under the cabbages." Such questions should be answered in more general terms, but *without going into details*.

Dr. Atarov deplores a certain "neutrality" displayed in these matters by both teachers and whole organizations concerned with the education of the young, and their tendency to "leave things to chance."

Also, it is wrong when teachers are mysterious about sex, as if it were a subject on which it was awkward to say anything; on the other hand, it is wrong when any manifestations of the sexual urge in children and adolescents are automatically treated as a sign of depravity or immorality. . . . It is essential to put an end to both "neutrality" in these matters, and to the prevalent "conspiracy of silence."

There follows some advice to parents: they mustn't spoil children, and satisfy all their whims, however unreasonable; for this gives children the idea that "everything is permissible." Spoiled children later tend to lead a disorderly sex life.

There then follows, without its being specifically mentioned, a reference to the housing shortage in Russia, under which whole families live in the same room:

One cannot emphasize too strongly how important it is that the intimate love-life of grown-ups should be concealed from children. Unfortunately, many adults forget about this. Sometimes, they are too affectionate to each other in the presence of children. Sometimes, in the same or in the next room, they go in for sexual intercourse, believing that the children are sound asleep. They overlook the fact that adolescents often pretend to be asleep. In many children sensuality is prematurely aroused as a result of such careless behavior by their parents. . . . In the presence of their children, parents should also behave with mutual respect, and things like suspicion, jealousy or irritation should not be displayed in front of the children. . . .

Further, bad language should be avoided:

Cultured speech is an important part of sexual education. Unfortunately, bad language is still common, and some, especially young people, use a dirty word in almost every sentence. Such dirty words are often learned from adults. These are the kind of words which distort the understanding of the proper relations between men and women. Hence an immoral attitude to things, and immoral actions. Children who go in for foul language tend in later life to behave immorally.

The campaign for clean speech is an important element in sex education; and public opinion and the various collectives should be persuaded to give this matter all the attention it deserves.

Next, care must be taken not to allow children to read the wrong books, see the wrong plays or films, or take part in the wrong games, all of which might tend to arouse their sensuality.

Further, alcohol. Heavy drinking in the presence of children often leads to disgusting scenes, including fights. Such scenes can only have a disastrous effect on the formative process of a child.

Persons of either sex lose control over their sexual instincts under the influence of alcohol. Under the influence of drink, marital infidelity is most frequently committed. Similarly, under the influence of drink, young boys and girls often start an unnecessarily early love-life. Alcohol, taken in excess, leads to premature old age and impotence. . . . Parents should be strongly condemned for allowing children and adolescents to take part in binges. . . .

In all these matters the law is not of decisive importance. More important in creating a worthy Socialist everyday life is the pressure of public opinion.

Dr. Atarov then deals with what he calls "hypocrisy" in sex matters.

Some teachers resort to ostrich tactics when questions of sex are raised by any pupil. Others go to the other extreme, and adopt an attitude of extreme intolerance to any manifestation of the sex instinct in young people. Sexual relations between very young people, though inadvisable, do not always have to be treated as something fundamentally wicked; such relations often end in marriage. Indeed, when such things do happen among young people who have not reached full maturity, teachers should not be self-righteous about them, but should simply try to see to it that such sex relations do not lead to dissoluteness; they should, in fact, try to persuade those concerned to marry as soon as they have reached the age of marriage.

In short, what's wanted in such cases is the proverbial happy ending.

Dr. Atarov then says that, in the case of young people of 18 or more, they should be given special talks by the teacher or doctor, each sex being lectured to separately. Similarly, there should be short talks between father and son, mother and daughter. But, as things are at present, everything "tends to be left to chance," and "questions of sexual morality receive practically no attention in our schools on the part of either teachers or doctors."

In short, there is a "conspiracy of silence" about the whole thing; nobody has approached the question of sex in the Soviet Union scientifically, or "subjected the sex life of our population to any kind of rational scientific analysis."

The author then argues that it is high time sex education in schools be given some systematic attention; and suggests the setting up of joint committees comprising members of scientific organizations, and of the ministries of health, culture and education.

The next chapter, dealing with "Sexual Maturity," stresses the difference between puberty and sexual maturity, which are not the same thing, and deals with the "difficult years" between the two. After a lengthy description of the reproductive process among higher animals, and of the male and female sexual organs, Dr. Atarov then discusses the more important first manifestations of puberty, and here we come acrosss some curiously "Victorian" passages in the midst of much plain common-sense:

A sign of puberty in young males is "pollution"—which occurs spontaneously, usually at night and during sleep. This spontaneous emission of semen is usually accompanied by dreams and an orgasm (a voluptuous feeling). Usually pollutions begin at the age of 15 or 16 and occur, according to the individual, at intervals ranging from 10 to 60 days. Pollutions, usually followed by awakening, do not cause any objective or subjective disturbance. But a first pollution may arouse in a boy alarm, astonishment and even fear. Parents should remember this, and if pollutions become frequent, measures should be taken to reduce any outside influence tending to increase sensuality. Some boys have few or no pollutions, but this is nothing to cause alarm. But when pollutions take place during the day, they point to a departure from normal conditions and a doctor should be consulted.

As regards girls—

Menstruation starts between the ages of 13 and 15, though the age may vary according to climate, geographical latitude or personal peculiarities. The beginning of menstruation is an important moment in the life of every girl, and is often accompanied by a complex psychological crisis. That is why the girl's mother (or an adult female friend) should explain the process to her and give her the right hygienic advice; it is unnecessary, however, for them to dwell on details or on the importance of menstruation in later life.

There then follows practical advice on how to deal with menstruation ("on no account should cotton wool or gauze be inserted into the vagina, as many women wrongly do. . . . The external organs should be washed twice a day with boiled warm water . . . heavy physical work, mental overexertion, sports—especially riding and cycling—should be avoided during menstruation"), etc.

After a scientific discussion on internal secretion glands, the author then deals with other symptoms of puberty—pubic hair, breasts, growth of beard, etc.

Parents and others should not draw attention to these perfectly normal developments, still less make them the objects of parental joy or, worse still, frivolous jokes. For this intensifies young people's interest in sex, and tends to increase their sensuality. . . .

In young males and females, the sexual feeling often awakes very early—any time between the ages of 5 and 14, though, in most cases, after 14. . . . Only in a small minority of cases is this feeling spontaneously awakened; usually this awakening is due to outside causes—the influence of schoolmates, grown-ups, games, books, films, etc.

Dr. Atarov reiterates that puberty and sexual maturity are not the same thing. Such maturity is usually reached, in the case of boys, between 18 and 21; in the case of girls, between 16 and 19. There may, however, be variations in either direction.

Another tricky problem, usually arising during the "difficult" years, is onanism, or masturbation; boys go in for it more frequently than girls.

"Under Soviet conditions," Dr. Atarov says, "masturbation is no longer the mass phenomenon it used to be in the past" —i.e. under Tsarism; all the same, it still exists.

Various factors, some psychological, others mechanical, he says, encourage masturbation.

Thus, tight clothing in the lower regions may arouse sensuality through constant friction of the genitals . . . other causes of masturbation are certain bad habits in boys, such as keeping their hands in their trouser pockets, or under the blanket, the frequent lying on their stomachs, mutual tickling under the armpits or in the chest area, etc. . . . constipation and a full bladder also tend to encourage masturbation.

Conducive to masturbation are also the reading of exciting books, cynical conversations and the contemplation of the sex life of animals.

Other bad influences are: an unduly sedentary life, isolation from the collective and personal solitude; and, needless to say, alcohol.

Early masturbation may also be brought on by purely physical malformations: an unduly tight foreskin, etc.—in which case medical advice should be sought.

These and other reasons may cause masturbation long before sexual maturity is reached. Environment almost entirely determines the frequency of masturbation or the duration of this practice: the fewer the factors arousing sensuality, and the better the physical, mental and labor training of children, the less are they likely to resort to masturbation. Regular meals, exercise, walks, sports, physical culture all detract the child's attention from sex. . . . In this matter, sleeping habits are very important; a hard bed is essential; it is also important that a child or adolescent should not look at the sex life of animals or fowls. Any tendency, on his part, to use bad language should be nipped in the bud. . . .

After enumerating other factors which tend to encourage masturbation, and saying again that "the experience of doctors shows that, under Soviet conditions, masturbation is no longer the mass phenomenon it used to be in the past, though it is not to be entirely excluded even in our conditions." Dr. Aratov emits the somewhat "Victorian" view that it is a very bad and harmful practice:

There is not the slightest doubt that masturbation has a bad effect on the nervous system and the adolescent's general condition; he becomes irritable, apathetic, easily tired, and indifferent to both physical and mental labor. If the problem is correctly approached, and the adolescent or youth is properly watched, he usually gets rid of this bad habit, and his health is fully restored.

Having said that, Dr. Atarov, however, admits that Russian scientists are not entirely agreed about the phenomenon. Thus the great I. I. Mechnikov attributed masturbation "to a certain disharmony in human nature, and to a premature development of the sexual instinct. He thought sexual attraction often existed in children even before puberty and the capacity for reproduction."

All the more reason (Dr. Atarov argued) why parents should see to it that their children avoid the bad influence of schoolmates, or exciting games, books and films; also they themselves should avoid making the wrong gestures which would stimulate the children's genitals; small children should not be carried in such a way that their genitals are constantly rubbed; nor, in bathing a child, should a mother rub these parts too hard.

Worse still, there are "loving parents" who, in going into raptures over the beauty and innocence of a child, caress it unnecessarily and smother it with kisses. It is particularly harmful when such kissing concentrates on the chest, stomach, etc.

Such caresses inevitably arouse premature sensuality and such doting parents do great harm to the child. Such doting also points to a very low cultural level in the parents.

This is followed by a lot of advice on hygiene.

The correct organization of daily life is very important, as well as the interest in sports and physical culture. From early childhood children should acquire the habit of washing frequently in cold or cool water. They should keep their bodies clean, take baths regularly, wash their hands after games and work, after going to the lavatory, and before meals. . . . Boys should wash their private parts regularly with soap and water every day, and girls should wash their outer organs with boiled water.[2] But in washing these parts, an excessive amount of rubbing should be avoided.

Also, says Atarov, there are certain trades from which, for sexual and moral reasons, very young people should be debarred:

Thus, they should not be given jobs as waiters and waitresses in restaurants, cafés or beer-houses. The atmosphere in these places, with their constant coming and going of all kinds of people, has a bad effect on young people working there, and tends to encourage them to embark on premarital relations: young unmarried people should not be given jobs in such places.

In Chapter III, called "The Moral Education of the Young," Dr. Atarov again stresses the difference between puberty and sexual maturity.

The two are not the same; though some young people wholly misunderstand this: just because there is sexual desire, and puberty means that the sexual act and reproduction are possible, they come to the erroneous conclusion that this desire must be satisfied, and that chastity is bad for you, and contrary to the laws of biology. This erroneous view justifies in their eyes the beginning of a premature sex life. Medical science completely rejects this "theory." No diseases have ever been caused by

[2] "Boiled water" suggests that in some parts of the Soviet Union tap water is still considered unsafe; before the Revolution and for some years after, tap water was undrinkable even in a city like Leningrad, where it was associated with cholera epidemics, etc.

chastity. Chastity is completely harmless, not only for young people, but also for adults who, for one reason or another, have temporarily interrupted their sex life; people practicing chastity practically never complain of any ailment arising from it: such is the experience of medical science. On the contrary, such people are full of energy and creative power. On the other hand sexual promiscuity often leads to premature old age and impotence.

But it is not only, Dr. Atarov argues, the alleged dangers of chastity which make people lead a disorderly sex life. They behave in this undesirable way in virtue of certain ideological survivals.

Some people imagine that in having an "affair" with somebody they scarcely even know, they do nothing wrong—provided there are no serious consequences, and everything remains hush-hush. Some such people refuse to realize that, for the sake of getting a momentary physical pleasure, they may have seriously upset the inner world of another human being. Girls are usually the victims of this kind of primitive approach to sex. Thirdly, there are some who think nothing of having a little "fun" on the side, even though they are married.

And then:

Such people have no moral sense. To treat sex life as a simple physiological function is contrary to all the moral standards of a Socialist society. Under Socialist morality, there cannot be any sex life based entirely on the physiological urge, and without any spiritual intimacy between the two partners.
. . . And yet, there are Soviet citizens who imagine that all this talk about "past survivals" is a lot of nonsense: "Why," they say, "talk to me about bourgeois survivals when I was born long after the Revolution and have never been in a bourgeois country? The laws of nature *must* be right."
Those who talk like that show that they have been badly brought up.

He then gives three typical examples of the wrong kind of upbringing:

(1) *The Seducer:* Boris was a turner, 20 years old. He did not complete his secondary education and his parents did not protest when, at the age of 15, he took a factory job. As a worker,

Boris did very well, and was well looked upon by his chiefs and comrades. But his private life was dissolute and disorderly. . . . One night, in a dance hall, he met a girl. They soon became friends, and two or three days later, under the influence of drink, intimacy took place. Boris had not even bothered to find out what her surname was, or where she worked or studied. But he was eloquent enough to persuade her to surrender to him. The friendship did not last long; in less than a month, Boris started avoiding her, and then vanished from her sight altogether.

What surprises one in this sad story (Dr. Atarov commented) is not only the behavior of Boris, but also the boundless confidence of the girl who could not resist the insolent advances of her casual acquaintance. Both the girl's parents and the school where she was taught are responsible for what happened.

As for Boris, his attitude, Atarov said, would not bring him much joy in the long run: "by such behavior he will condemn himself to loneliness; he is not likely to know the joys of family life and the chances are that, in the end, he will contract VD."

This equally "Victorian" threat of VD as the wages of sin, as the ultimate Nemesis, is a little comic, since, later in the book, the Doctor emphatically declares all forms of VD today to be completely and easily curable.

(2) *The Promiscuous Rat:* Peter, a 26-year-old student, was living maritally with a girl. One day, while on holiday in a rest-home, he met another girl; they became intimate, even though they did not know each other's surnames. When, some time later, he returned home, he promptly infected his "permanent" girl with VD contracted from his casual holiday acquaintance. This "Don Juan" attitude is quite disgusting. Peter looked upon sex like an animal. For all that, he is an excellent student, and his fellow-students think very highly of him.

(3) *The Vamp:* Vera, a municipal official, had, at 20, a well-paid job. Her father had died young, and she had been brought up by her mother, a woman of small culture. She had started her sex life at 19 after a dance, where she had got drunk. She thought it quite "normal" for a girl of 19 to behave like that. But a few months later, she lost interest in her boy friend; they had no common interests and no mutual legal obligations.

By this time, she had met another young man. Changing lovers all the time, she finally contracted VD. Vera had clearly been given the wrong upbringing; her mother was a stupid woman; nor had the office in which Vera worked done anything to influence her frivolous and unworthy behavior.

In Dr. Atarov's view, "such people constitute only a small minority in our Soviet society; and most Soviet people, above all the young, do not share the views of the three sorry heroes we have just described.

"The real basis of all comradeship, friendship and love among Soviet people is the feeling of mutual *respect*. . . . It is only when *respect* for fellow-humans is absent that disgusting stories like the above become possible. . . . Such love and friendship should not be allowed, in the name of 'natural' behavior, to be marked by vulgarity and excessive familiarity—least of all in the relations between boys and girls. And promiscuity was rightly branded by the Soviet poet Schipachev, who wrote:

One day you kiss the one, next day you kiss the other
In clouds of blue cigarette smoke.
Maybe it is useless for the poet to reproach you.
But it is frightening to grow old,
Knowing that you have scattered your love like small change
Among people you don't even know."

In Chapter IV, the author deals with a variety of other sex problems, which I shall summarize only briefly:

The minimum age of marriage has been fixed by Soviet law at 18, which is the age at which the body matures, especially in women; maturity in young men is reached a little later. But the purpose of the law is to prevent unduly early marriages, for these are harmful to both partners, as well as to any offspring. Marriages in the Soviet Union generally take place at the age of 20 to 22 (girls) and 22 to 24 (young men); these are also the ages at which the young people have taken up their position in society. The time lag between puberty and marriage is thus much shorter than in bourgeois societies. Thanks to this, Soviet society is not marred by such bourgeois phenomena as late marriages, bacherlorhood, spinsterdom, horrible immorality and professional prostitution on a vast scale.

In short, 20 to 24 is the perfect marriage age, when young people, as a rule, have completed their education, got a job,

and are in the best possible condition for sexual intercourse, pregnancy and childbirth.

True, says Dr. Atarov, touching this time on a very tricky
Soviet problem, as a result of the two world wars,

there are far more females than males in our country; and this
disproportion has led to some disturbances in questions like marriage, the family and sexual relations. But, thanks to the peace
policy of the Soviet government, this anomaly will gradually
disappear.

Happy marriage: there can, says Dr. Atarov, be no successful and happy marriage unless the feelings of devotion,
attachment, attraction and love between the two are mutual;
incompatibility may also arise from a very different unbring-
ing, very different levels of culture, premarital relations, etc.
Some marriages also break down because they have been
entered into, by one side or both, for some sordid material
reasons:

When a young person thinks of getting married, parents should
not remain completely neutral. In the USSR marriage is not
merely a personal matter; it is connected with the interests of
society and the State. Parents should, therefore, take a discreet
but genuine interest in the prospective marriage of their children, so as to prevent bad marriages, as far as possible.

People who look upon marriage as a temporary amusement,
who lightly break up a home, and abandon husband or wife
(and a child) are committing a crime against Socialist morality.

There then follows a section on sex hygiene: more about
menstruation and pregnancy: "sexual relations must be
completely stopped during the two months preceding, and the
two months following child-birth."

Unfortunately, as we know from doctors, men often completely ignore these pregnancy rules; while others, finding it difficult to restrain themselves, think it "natural" in the circumstances, to look for satisfaction outside the home. Need we say
how utterly immoral such an attitude is!

The section on *Birth Control* starts with a description of a
common practice, the *coitus interruptus;* but this may lead to
nervous upsets among both men and women; and it is better

to resort to contraceptives, of which the condom is the best; there are also other devices used by women.

Abortion. "Today in our country [as distinct from a long period which began in 1936] women are able to decide themselves about effecting an abortion. Every provision has been made for performing these by qualified medical personnel.

At the same time, both the State and public opinion condemn a frivolous attitude to abortion—i.e. those carried out without some very good reason of a personal or social nature. Some women resort to abortion for purely selfish motives. Even more serious is when husbands urge their wives, for purely selfish motives, to have an abortion performed; such an attitude should be sharply condemned.

A clear distinction appears to be made here between married women and unmarried prospective mothers.

Women should also remember that abortions are not completely harmless, especially when frequently practiced. They may lead to sterility and premature old age, as well as to various nervous and gynecological complications.

Sterility: In cases when medical science is unable to remedy this and, provided husband and wife, anxious to have a child, get on well together, the best solution for them is to adopt a child from an institution.

After a section on VD—"against which gigantic progress has been made in our country," but which still, unfortunately, exists, despite such measures as compulsory treatment and compulsory examination—the author then deals with "sexual morality."

What, in the author's view, are breaches of sexual morality in a Socialist society?

(1) Premarital relations; these, however, are not necessarily wicked, especially if they end in marriage.

(2) Marital infidelity—very bad.

(3) Getting married for mercenary reasons, without any mutual affection and love uniting the two partners.

(4) Seeking a divorce without some very strong reason, and, of course, abandoning a family without divorce.

On divorce Dr. Atarov says:

Divorce is allowed in the USSR, but it is a right which should not be abused. Often frivolous reasons are given for a divorce petition, such as "incompatibility of character," cooling-off of love, sexual frustration, etc. In reality, these are sometimes mere excuses in an attempt to contract a more advantageous marriage. Under our laws, the main condition in granting a divorce is that the children's interests be respected.

Actually, the divorce procedure in Russia today is extremely unwieldy; there has been much controversy in the press in favor of easing-up divorce; the present difficulties in obtaining a divorce no doubt largely account for what the author indignantly describes as "de facto divorces," when husband (or sometimes wife) sets up a home "on the side." "Usually such 'divorces' are due to dissolute sexual behavior, drunkenness or, in a few cases, unwarranted jealousy."

From such situations, children suffer, of course, most of all.

The book ends with a rather lofty discussion on two "painful situations"—first, when a married person falls genuinely in love with a third party; in this case, he demonstrates that it is best if "duty is made to triumph over passion"; and secondly, what happens in cases of unrequited love?

Unrequited love sometimes causes deep emotional and mental disturbances, especially in the case of very young people. Sometimes only a great effort of willpower and time can cure the sufferer. But such unrequited love should not be looked upon as a final failure and as a great life's tragedy. Under Socialist society, in which public service is the main thing, and provided the sufferer has enough inner discipline, he should get over his troubles. Work and the moral support of his comrades should be of the greatest help.

And to conclude:

In our country, public opinion severely condemns divorce when there are no strong reasons for it. Similarly, it condemns weakness and defeatism arising from failure in love. The law cannot deal with all cases of immoral behavior, but the pressure of public opinion should continue to play an ever-growing part in fighting all forms of immoral behavior.

There can be no doubt that this kind of "puritanical" approach to sex is very much part of Soviet upbringing; that, for a large number of reasons—such as the advantages of an "orderly" existence, and also because of the housing problem —a very considerable proportion of the young generation, especially in the cities, adhere to these rules. This seems particularly true of the young technical élite, who are interested, above all, in their work and in "getting on," and who are aware of the fact that "scandalous" behavior can be damaging to their careers. I mentioned before Kolya and his various friends, who, broadly speaking, do follow the "Atarov code."

No doubt, Dr. Atarov overstates many of his points; love and marriage are, to him, so much a matter of "social significance" that one would think people made love, not for pleasure, but merely as a social duty. The sexual act is also reduced by Dr. Atarov to its simplest and most primitive form, without any "refinements" of any kind, whereas "dreadful" things like homosexuality [3] are not mentioned at all, as if they just did not exist. Similarly, there is no mention of complex psychological problems, partly on the ground that Freud has always been treated in the Soviet Union as some-

---

[3] In the standard textbook on Psychiatry (*Uchebnik Psychiatriyi* by O. V. Kerbikov and others, Moscow 1958, p. 313) we find the following on this point:

Why are sexual perversions so unusual in our country? Because phenomena like homosexuality (which are acquired and not innate) have nothing in our environment to encourage them. . . . In the capitalist world, with its sadistic films and books, there is a good deal of sadism. In prewar Berlin there were three papers for homosexuals, and 120 widely advertised clubs, beside numerous cafés where people sharing this tendency met. The healthy atmosphere in which Soviet youth is brought up provides no conditions which would encourage the development of such perversions; and these are very unusual in our country. Under our law (Art. 154-a of the Criminal Code of the RSFSR) homosexual practices between males are punishable, and although homosexuality is a morbid phenomenon, persons guilty of such practices are considered responsible for their actions, and cannot plead irresponsibility.

thing of a charlatan,[4] as he is, indeed, according to the Russians, by serious scientists in the West as well.

As Dr. Atarov says, however, no proper statistical or scientific study of sexual behavior has ever been attempted in the Soviet Union, partly because of the "conspiracy of silence" surrounding the whole problem.

Actually, the silence has not been all that complete; and there has lately been a great deal of controversy in the press, particularly on two problems—divorce and "illegitimate" children.

Opinion seems to be strongly divided on whether divorce —which was absurdly simple in the early years of the Revolution, but was made extremely difficult in the 1940s—should not be made a good deal easier again; there are those who think that "unhappiness" and "incompatibility of character" should be sufficient ground for divorce, if both parties are agreed, and if the children's interests are safeguarded; others hold that only adultery (if no reconciliation has been achieved), impotence, insanity and a long prison sentence should be valid grounds for divorce.

As regards illegitimacy, an interesting discussion was opened on April 2, 1960, in *Literary Gazette,* by an article by a well-known writer, V. Kaverin, who told the rather banal story of an 18-year-old girl, Larissa, who, after a very brief acquaintance, allowed herself to be seduced by, and set up house with, a young engineer called Yuli Solyakov. They lived with her parents in Leningrad; but Yuli seemed in no hurry to register the marriage; when, finally, a child was born, it turned out that the man was already married, and had a wife and child at Ferghana. When the poor girl

---

[4] "From the very start at the beginning of this century, leading psychiatrists refused to treat psychoanalysis as anything other than a sectarian current. Freudism is of no scientific value. Its popularity must be sought in its ideological significance: it is highly profitable to the ruling classes since, instead of dwelling on the hardships brought to the masses by the capitalist system, it dwells on the alleged psychological chasms of human nature, on its unconscious urges and instincts. People with only a superficial understanding of clinical psychiatry are taken in by it. As W. Mayer-Gross, E. Slater and M. Roth say in their study, *Clinical Psychiatry* (London, 1954) it is 'popular only amongst half-baked amateur psychologists, journalists, writers and critics, and is much disliked by neurologists and psychiatrists with long clinical experience.'" (*Uchebnik Psychiatriyi*, p. 20.)

applied to Court for alimony, she was turned down. Kaverin argued that there was something seriously wrong with the law, if fellows like Solykov could get away with it.

Another writer, V. Beliayev, argued, as against this, that Larissa deserved no pity; no self-respecting Soviet girl would have behaved in such a way; instead of putting her suitor through the ZAGS (registry office) test, she was carried away by the same kind of irresponsible pleasure-seeking instincts as he. No doubt, it was hard on the child, but then its mother should have thought of *that*.

The most interesting contribution to this correspondence came from a Leningrad woman-teacher who said that, in her ten years' experience, she found that 20 per cent of her pupils were fatherless; in their birth certificates, opposite the father's name, there was a blank. This caused terrible complications amongst the children themselves; it was common for "legitimate" children of 12 or 13 to taunt the "illegitimate" children by calling them "Father-Blank."

Like Kavarin, she was all in favor of revising the wartime law of 1944 under which the State took on the financial burden of all "illegitimate" children, and not only prohibited any action for affiliation but also prevented fathers from recognizing their children voluntarily, if they were not married to the mothers.

Interesting were also the Readers' Letters, which took very different attitudes to the sad case of Larissa:

A Moscow reader said it was quite right that enamored couples should go to the registry office *first*; in this way alone could an end be put to promiscuity. Girls should be taught the "facts of life" accordingly.

A Leningrad reader asked whether Shakespeare's Juliet should, like poor Larissa, also be treated as a "fallen woman." "On the contrary, Larissa deserves a helping hand."

A lawyer, on the other hand, wrote: "In Socialist society marriage is not a purely private matter. The State cannot be expected to protect *any* unions, but only those properly registered. We lawyers know how difficult it used to be to embark on any action for affiliation, if the defendant was unwilling. Therefore, the 1944 law is right, and should not be changed."

A judge from Tarnopol (not an *old* Soviet territory) argued that the law *should* be changed. Too many dissolute men were taking advantage of it; as a result, the number of "single mothers" was as great as it used to be, even 15 years since the end of the war, and despite the fact that abortions were now allowed. The present law of 1944, which was issued in war conditions, was valuable in the peculiar conditions created by the war and the occupation; but it "is now a distinct obstacle in the way of developing a high standard of sexual morality amongst the young, and in the upbringing of children."

What is one to conclude from all this? Briefly, that there is a distinct code of morals designed for "Soviet men"; that, for a large number of reasons, it is widely observed; but that "unregistered" marriages, more even perhaps than promiscuity, are still very common, and that only a change in the 1944 law can seriously improve the situation, notably by legitimizing at least a very high proportion of children born from "unregistered" marriages.

But the very fact that a sort of stigma is attached to "Father-Blank" points to a curiously "puritanical" attitude; as the above-mentioned Leningrad teacher remarked: "Aren't we reaching a stage when we shall start referring to our fatherless children by the revolting Western name of 'bastard?' "

In short—back to alimony and affiliation, whenever possible!

But what inevitably will complicate matters for a long time yet is, of course, the wide discrepancy between the male and female population.

Chapter 16

SOVIET MAN: THAT DAMNED
HOUSING PROBLEM

ALL OVER THE SOVIET UNION there are billboards with bright
colored posters, with charts and diagrams showing the increase in production in the various branches of industry,
agriculture and transport between 1959 and the completion
of the seven-year plan in 1965. Even every matchbox sold in
Russia tells a story: a large 1959 sugar-loaf marked 6.6 million tons, and a very much bigger 1965 sugar-loaf marked 10
million tons; or a little 1959 oil derrick of 113 million tons
and a sort of 1965 Eiffel Tower of 240 million tons. Or even
the comparative amount of hoisery—400-something million
articles in 1959 and 700-something million articles in 1965.
All this is very important and satisfactory, and there is every
chance that most of the seven-year plan will be fulfilled before
1965. With the immense army of skilled workers, technicians
and engineers, nobody doubts that all these targets will be
achieved. Russia is extremely conscious of being a going
concern, of being more and more a "have" and not a "have-
not" country. There may still be some inefficiency here and
ther, plans may go wrong and norms may be faked; agriculture in this or that part of the Soviet Union may be hit by
drought—many think the Virgin Lands rather precarious in
that respect—or by inefficiency, but this *should* be remedied
within a reasonable time.

Housing, on the other hand, continues to be a major worry
to a considerable part of the urban population. Will things
go quite as quickly and smoothly as Khrushchev seemed
to think? This was what he said at the Twenty-first Congress:

166

Housing is one of the most acute problems of the human race. According to the *Book of Facts* issued by the Democratic Party of the USA 15 million people still live in slums. . . . The housing shortage and high rents representing 25 to 30 per cent of a family budget constantly pursue the toilers in the capitalist world. In the Soviet Union, on the other hand, an ever-growing concern is shown for improving the living and housing conditions of the workers. Rent, including communal services, amounts to only 4 to 5 per cent of the family budget. In the villages, houses are built with the help of the *kolkhozes* and the State. There are no such possibilities for the workers in any capitalist country.

The target set in 1957 by the Party and the Government to settle the housing problem in the next 10 or 12 years is being successfuly carried out. In the last two years some 120 million square meters of housing [i.e. about 3 million dwellings] have been completed. During the next seven years we intend to build 650 to 660 million square meters of housing, i.e. about 15 million flats. This is more than the whole urban housing fund built since the Revolution. One of our aims is to distribute this new housing space on the principle of "one family, one flat."

The very fact that this "principle" should be put forward as almost a major innovation is significant in itself. It might be argued that Russia has suffered from a housing-shortage for the last two centuries. In Tsarist Russia the contrast was appalling between the luxury in which the rich, and the squalor in which the poor lived. Between the Revolution and 1941 the new housing had no connection whatsoever with the vast increase in the urban and industrial population. The rather sumptuous seven-room flat where I spent my childhood in Tsarist St. Petersburg, I found occupied by five families just after World War II—and Leningrad was then still one of the *least* overcrowded cities. They were all sharing the kitchen, bathroom, etc. In Moscow the overcrowding was much worse. During the war thousands of villages and hundreds of towns were completely or partially destroyed; the villages were built up quickly, if not well; the rebuilding of wholly-destroyed cities like Stalingrad, Rostov, Sebastopol, Voronezh and dozens more, and of half- or more-than-half-destroyed cities like Kharkov, Odessa and Kiev—to mention only the largest—was an immense job which was, in the main, completed around 1952–53. Very striking is the fact that in all these cities the population is larger today than it was before the war; and this can only mean—another housing shortage.

Even in Moscow, in 1959, despite a very spectacular effort that was being made in the housing line, there was still plenty of grumbling; the more "irresponsible" citizens were arguing along the lines that, instead of sending rockets around the moon, *they* had better hurry up with the housing program—"the kind of deplorable attitude we've always had among some citizens—the kind of people who in the past used to say: 'Why not more sugar, rather than the Dnieper Dam?' "

One day, talking to a taxi-driver, in Moscow, I heard this story:

"I have two rooms, in which I live with my mother and sister. Now I want to get married. But there isn't a chance in hell of my getting a flat in less than two or three years. And neither I nor my future wife wants to live together with my mother and sister—carry on, as it were, under their very noses. So I've been thinking of taking a single room in a flat belonging to somebody else; but they want 400 rubles a month for such a room; and that's a pretty big hole in my budget—even though my wife and I are going to earn about 2,000 rubles between us. But then thousands of people are in the same position; you've only got to look at the small ads in *Vechorka*.[1] No doubt people get handsome grants and credits for building their own houses in the country and also in new towns like Igarka, in the depths of the Siberian North. But lots of people soon get bored living in Igarka—or even in small provincial centers like Orel, though housing conditions there are obviously far better than in Moscow; but then, damn it, housing isn't everything."

Housing isn't everything, no doubt; and there are plenty of people in the big cities ready to rough it, rather than live comfortably in a provincial backwater or—at Igarka. Officially,

---

[1] Short for *Vechernia Moskva,* the Moscow evening paper. Where, I wondered, were these "rooms to let?" I found that most of these were in *new* houses; thus, if a fairly large family had a three-room flat, and had only a small income, they were content to cram into two rooms, and let the third one for good money. A lifetime spent in "communal-flat" conditions had largely conditioned them to sharing a flat with a stranger.

there are about 5½ million people living in Moscow; but, unofficially, probably at least a million more.

I saw all kinds of houses in Moscow, ranging from the Antonovs' extremely primitive but relatively spacious izba and some badly overcrowded and shabby "communal flats," where several families still shared the kitchen, to the rather monotonous two-or-three-room standard flats (rented usually, but not yet always, on the one-family-one-flat principle) in the southwest area of Moscow, and to the rather snappy-looking new blocks in the Kutuzov Prospect, with a rather more "Western" appearance than the others. But whether in the southwest, or elsewhere, all people living in their *own* new flats seemed extremely pleased—even though they did occasionally have some complaints to make about the paint and plaster peeling off even in some almost brand-new buildings, and also the elevator being frequently out-of-order.

And there are hard-luck cases—plenty of them still. I visited one day a man I had got to know just after the war. He was still suffering from the effects of shell shock; drank heavily, and wasn't quite sane, from what his wretched wife told me. And there they were, the two of them, and three children, living in two small rooms of a damp basement, dark and pretty horrible. He was getting a pension of 600 rubles; and she had a minor job of sorts, but they were miserable, unhealthy, and waiting desperately for a flat, but fearing they'd have to wait at least another year. And the wife's bitter last remark, as I left, was: "Shedding your blood for the country is all very well—but look at us now. . . ." However, she was hoping to get the two older children into a boarding school.

To get an all-round view of what was really going on in Moscow in the building line, I asked for an interview with Yuri Mikhailovich Rodin, a very impressive senior official —Head of the Technical Department—of Glavmosstroi (the "Chief Moscow Building Organization"), who received me, together with an American colleague—who knew no Russian, much to Comrade Rodin's annoyance; for he had no interpreter, and also muttered something about "correspondents coming to the Soviet Union, as though it were Afghanistan." Also, the American colleague at one point asked me to translate his question why practically nothing had been built in Moscow during several years after the war; at this

Comrade Rodin exploded, and grabbed a book, from which he read out the number of cities destroyed during the war in Western Russia, the Ukraine, etc. *"There!"* he spluttered, "does *that* answer your damned-fool question?"

The gist of what he said was this (I shall omit some technical details); his story reflected, in a curious way, something of the whole history of Moscow—and even of Russia:

The "housing fund" of Moscow in 1912 was 11.8 million square meters for a population of nearly 2 million people, i.e. a little over 5 square meters on the average, but very unevenly distributed. No building was done during World War I.

In a small way building was resumed in 1923, and rather more substantially in 1928; in 1920, with famine conditions prevailing in Moscow, the population was very small; but in 1928 it was 3 million, whereas the amount of actual housing (apart from government offices) built between 1923 and 1928 was still very insignificant, especially when one considered that during the famine years some 2,000 houses had been pulled down for fuel. Between 1928 and the beginning of World War II only some 5½ million square meters had been built—or the equivalent of about 120,000 flats.

Up till 1954 a large number of government offices were built; and it was, in fact, not till that year that the Central Committee and the Government decided to reorganize the whole housing program for Moscow; it was then that the Glavmosstroi was set up, and it now dealt with two-thirds of all the building in Moscow; before that the work had been shared by some sixty(!) ministries.

Allowing for the fact that much of the new building during the years between 1945 and 1953 was that of offices, very little actual housing was built during those years. The figures for the total building were as follows:

	1000 *sq. meters*			1000 *sq. meters*
1946	. . .	90	1953 . . .	812
1947	. . .	130	1954 . . .	910
1948	. . .	270	1955 . . .	1065
1949	. . .	406	1956 . . .	1360
1950	. . .	585	1957 . . .	1810
1951	. . .	735	1958 . . .	2330
1952	. . .	782	1959 . . .	2700

If very little was built in Moscow, by way of housing, before 1954, it was, of course, because the destroyed cities of the West and South had inevitably to be given priority.

Already in 1958 two and one-half times more housing space was built than in 1954—and that, thanks to increased mechanization, without a large increase in the actual number of workers employed.

Under the seven-year plan (1959–65) 20,500,000 square meters of housing space would be built—the equivalent of over half-a-million flats; this was more than had been built in Moscow during the whole of the first 42 years of the Soviet régime (1917–59); it was the equivalent of twice the whole of 1913 Moscow.

In 1959, 70,000 flats would be completed in Moscow, i.e. 14 flats per 1,000 inhabitants.

By the end of the seven-year plan, the rate of building would go up to 20 flats per 1,000 inhabitants.

The "useful" floor-space of the flats was calculated on the basis of 9 square meters per person; the one-room flats would be up to 20 square meters; the two-room flats, 25 to 33 square meters; the three-room flats, 42 to 45 square meters (only the "useful" living space was counted; in addition there were corridors, etc.).

The one-room flats would account for 10 per cent of the total.

The two-room flats for 60 to 70 per cent.

The three-room flats for 25 per cent.

In all new houses there would be central heating, hot water, baths, toilets; in many also rubbish-chutes, etc. The central heating would often cover as many as a hundred flats.

In the last four years alone close on 250,000 new flats had been completed in Moscow, which meant that *about one million people had been resettled.*

Comrade Rodin went into a variety of other questions; such as the building materials used; the enormous progress in mechanization; the techniques employed in the assembly of the various kinds of prefabricated panels and other parts, etc. The discarding of ordinary bricklaying, he said, represented an enormous saving. He described the various building-material "trusts" employed by Glavmosstroi—those producing the sanitary, plumbing, electrical and other equipment, those dealing with interior decoration, etc.

Surprisingly, he declared himself "wholly dissatisfied" with the present rate at which houses were being built in Moscow; there was a lack of co-ordination between the actual building and the plumbing, electric-wiring and other "subterranean" operations; the actual building, he said, was simple—"one quarter of the job"—large blocks of flats could be assembled in two months; but, owing to the imperfect co-ordination with the plumbing, electrical and other operations, it now took from nine months to a year to finish a job which it should be possible to complete in four or five months.

Another surprising point he made was that the principle of one-family-one-flat had not begun to be applied until 1958; even so, not all flats built in 1958 were one-family flats. However, now this principle was being strictly observed.

The standard type of block was now the five-story block of flats; occasionally blocks went up to seven or eight stories, but this was unusual. The "skyscrapers" had been completely abandoned; they were absurdly expensive, and Khrushchev had rightly observed that people mostly liked to live on the ground floor, while hardly anybody wanted to live on the 26th floor, least of all with children or old people.

Now there were no more than 50 standard types of houses; he (Rodin) had recently visited Finland, and found that every architect had fancy ideas of his own; all this was "chaotic" and "a waste of money." The 50 types of houses to choose from were adequate from any point of view.

There were, of course, he said, long waiting lists for flats; and it was the Housing Department of the Gorispolkom (City Executive Committee) which examined the urgencies and priorities; priority was, for instance, given to the inhabitants of primitive wooden barracks condemned to demolition.

All this immense amount of new housing also required many other new buildings; during the next seven years, 260 new schools would be built (one per 800 pupils), including 56 boarding schools.

There would also be built new cinemas with 42,000 seats ("twice as much as we have built in the last 25 years,"), including supercinemas with 6,000 to 8,000 seats; further, there would be new hospitals with 19,000 beds; and new kindergartens and crêches for 100,000 children.[2] Moreover, during the next seven years, three new theaters would be built, a Pioneers' Palace in the Southwest, a new Congress Building in the Kremlin, besides a multitude of swimming pools, public baths, laundries, etc. Twelve hundred acres of trees would be planted; there would be an increased water and natural-gas supply, this gas being brought from Stavropol in the Northern Caucasus.

Also, the Palace of Soviets, which had been abandoned at the beginning of the war, would be started, but in the new southwest part of Moscow, and not on its present site, and in a style different from the originally-planned "wedding-cake" with the Lenin statue on top.

Comrade Rodin, while sounding reasonably starry-eyed about the gigantic tasks with which the Glavmosstroi ("biggest building company in the world," he said) had been entrusted, still thought the building techniques and tempos were "slightly behind" the best American building concerns. He grumbled about the various "trusts" with which the Glavmosstroi had to deal, and said they'd have to pull their socks up. But with growing automation, the building-material industries would certainly make rapid progress in the next few years. The actual building process did not allow much room for automation; true, experiments had been made with teleguided cranes; but it had not, so far, gone beyond that.

In answer to a question Rodin said that the eight-hour working day would be reduced, in 1960, to a seven-hour day, without any diminution in wages. The present builder's wage was, on the average, about 1,200 rubles a month.

He also said the population problem in Moscow was still a difficult one; the city was so overcrowded that it was almost impossible to pull down any more or less habitable houses, no matter how old and unlovely they were; that was one reason why a large proportion of the new building was going on on the outskirts of Moscow. "All the old rubbish inside Moscow will have to remain standing for a while yet. If a lot of central Moscow goes on looking a mess, it can't be helped."

[2] It is not true, as is widely believed abroad, that there is enough room in these for *all* children.

"But after all," I said, pointing out of the window, "nearly the whole of Tverskaya was pulled down, and Gorki Street built in its place."

"Well," said Rodin, "that was done in Stalin's days. He liked to do things in a rather spectacular, and not very economical way, and it was necessary, I suppose, to have at least one grand spectacular new street in the center of Moscow. I don't think we would have built Gorki Street quite the same way now—far too many frills, and spirals, and turrets, and statues and little balconies, and floral designs and things. At least," he laughed, "we knocked down that ballerina dancing on top of the corner building at Pushkin Square. She looked so damned silly."

"The seven-year plan won't really 'settle' the housing problem in Moscow, will it?"

"Not entirely," said Rodin; "Khrushchev said our housing problem would take 10 to 12 years to settle; and I rather think that Moscow, at any rate, will be overcrowded, *whatever* we do! Everybody seems to want to come to Moscow, Indians, Chinese, Americans and a good proportion of the 200 millions of our far-flung country. I sometimes wonder," he grinned, "what they think is so wonderful about this place! Is it the GUM department store, or is it because Moscow is like 'a banner of flame' as Mayakovsky said? 'Banner of flame,'" Rodin repeated; "that's one side of it, and the other side is how to get the plumbing fixed without undue delays in all the thousands of blocks that are going up. That's 'revolutionary romanticism' of another kind. . . . More difficult, in a way, than thinking up fine phrases."

Chapter 17

SOVIET MAN: "BOARDING SCHOOLS,
THE HIGH ROAD TO COMMUNISM,"
AND ALL THAT

AT A RECEPTION in New York on September 17, 1959, Khrushchev said:

Our higher educational establishments turned out last year
nearly three times more engineers than yours did: we turned
out 94,000, and you, 35,000.

And at the Twenty-first Congress in January 1959, he
said:

During the 1959–65 period our higher educational establishments will turn out 2.3 million specialists, as against 1.7 millions during the previous seven years. The total number of specialists with higher education will be 4.5 million persons in 1965.

This spectacular increase in the technical élite of the Soviet Union—which is important in terms of industrial development and "peaceful competition" with the West in the underdeveloped countries and elsewhere, as well as in terms of the Soviet Union's "taking first place in all-over, as well as *per capita* production by about 1970" [1]—is merely one

[1] "Allowing for the fact that the Soviet population will then be larger than that of the USA by about 15 to 20 per cent, we shall require another five years after the completion of the seven-year plan in order to catch up with, and exceed, the USA in terms of industrial production. By then, or maybe even before, the Soviet Union will take first place both in terms of the absolute volume of production and in terms of *per capita*

aspect of the vast and complex Soviet educational program.

The program was, clearly, not going without some hitches. But this was not surprising. "The reorganization of secondary and higher education (in accordance with the Central Committee's "Theses" on "Strengthening the Bonds between School and Life and the Further Development of Education," approved by the Presidium of the Supreme Soviet on December 24, 1958)," Khrushchev said, "will require a certain amount of time and a great deal of work." In 1959–60, therefore, these changes were still far from having been completed.

In the same speech Khrushchev also laid stress on that peculiar innovation, the "boarding schools" which, by 1965, would have "no fewer than 2.5 million pupils" (out of a total of some 30 million children of secondary-school age).

In future, we propose to make it possible for all children to be educated in boarding schools, as this will help to settle successfully the problem of the Communist education of the new generation, and to include many more millions of women into the active building of Communist society.

One day I had a long talk with A. M. Skrobov at the Ministry of Education of the RSFSR. Skrobov, a very impressive-looking official, was Deputy Chief of the General Administration of Schools in the RSFSR (i.e. Russia proper).

I shall summarize only briefly what he said about the present system of "bringing life and school closer together," with its emphasis on all pupils spending part of their training "on production."

The general scheme, which will not be fully completed until 1963, would, Skrobov said, be like this:

All secondary education would be transformed by 1963. And all schools would be "eight-plus-three" schools; but

production. This will be an historical victory, on the world scale, of Socialism in its peaceful competition with capitalism in the international field." (*Khrushchev at Twenty-first Congress of the CPSU*: January 27, 1959).

On other occasions he said that this also applied to the *per capita* production of food though on this point there continue to be some serious doubts, as was, indeed, made very apparent by some of Khrushchev's own highly critical speeches on "agricultural mismanagement," early in 1961.

pupils would not be required to spend the "extra three" years at the school; if anything, they would be discouraged from doing so.

The "mass-school"—i.e. *the first eight years*—*would be compulsory for all* (as against the present seven- or 10-year school, the latter of which was not compulsory).

After completing the eight-year school, some pupils would do their remaining three years at the same school, this three-year additional training being called "secondary polytechnic school, with productive training"; others would, as will later be explained, follow a different course.

The purpose of the eight-year "mass school," Skorobov said, was to give children not only a good general education, but also prepare them physically and psychologically for work; it would give them "the habit of practical work," as well as the "right psychological preparation for going into production" once the eight years were up.

During the last three years actually spent at the 11-year school, two-thirds of the time would be devoted to general education, and one-third to acquiring a trade or profession. Thus, one year in three would, in practice, be devoted to the latter task.

But this was not the only way of spending the last "three years."

How then, would the scheme work in practice?

At seven, children would go to school; then, on completing their eight years, they would follow one of three courses:

(1) Stay on at the school, on the above basis, for three more years.

(2) Transfer to technical trade school for highly skilled workers—these schools having, according to the trade, a curriculum of two or three years. After that, they could go "into production" but, at the same time, follow evening classes or take correspondence courses.

(3) The third possibility would be for an adolescent, having completed his eight-year school, to enter "a secondary special technical college," which could, however, be not only strictly technical, but also a teaching or medical college, with a three or four years' course; thus, a *feldsher*—a hospital assistant—would rank, after such special training,

as a specialist "of medium qualifications" who had completed his "full secondary education."

Having completed in these various ways the "secondary 11-year school" (by staying on at the school itself for the three "additional" years, by taking correspondence or evening courses while "on production," or by having done their three- or four-year "technicum") pupils would then have the opportunity of entering a VUZ (i.e. a "higher educational establishment," such as a university), according to their speciality, and upon passing an entrance examination.

There would, of course, be far more candidates than vacancies; but, with equal marks, preference would be given to candidates who had been "on production" for two years. (In other words, those who had stayed on at the school for the "extra" three years would be somewhat handicapped for having reduced their "production" work to a minimum.)

Those who had not been admitted to a VUZ could still take up their studies on an evening-class or correspondence course basis, with every prospect of getting the same diploma and rights as a "regular" student. There would be evening classes in medicine, though not correspondence courses; and provision would be made for allowing workers several weeks off to go to summer schools.

The last three years of the 11-year schools would be "attached" to some industrial enterprise (if the school was in an urban area); pupils would spend two days in the week working in this factory; during the first one or one-and-a-half years they would acquire a speciality (turner, metal worker, etc.), then pass an examination before the Factory Commission, and get a third or fourth degree (eight being the top rank) in technical proficiency; those willing to stay on in the said factory would usually do so, unless they preferred to try for a VUZ. Factories, as a rule, would like to keep on such young specialists. Once settled in the factory, such workers could still go on with evening classes.

While still at school, pupils "on production" would be paid piece rates.

In rural areas, pupils of the "last three years," would work in village schools, at tractor repair stations, etc.; there would continue to be much coming and going between town and country; not only were young pupils from the country drifting into the towns, but many from the towns were now going into the country—notably to the Virgin Lands. The Komsomol and the Party had strongly appealed to the young people's patriotic sense in urging them to go to the Virgin Lands, etc. "In the countryside tractor drivers, truck drivers, and many other young people with technical qualifications are quite fit to work in both town and country."

Such is the brief summary of Comrade Skrobov's long dissertation on the "new school." What he kept reiterating was that, with automation, electronics, etc., the difference between manual and non-manual labor was rapidly disappearing, as was also the borderline between urban and rural work. At the end of 1959 the system was in a state of transition; and he sometimes used the future, and sometimes the present tense. It was not entirely clear whether the transition to this "organic bond between schooling and production" was working quite smoothly yet; young people interested in industrial processes should, apparently, have no difficulty in adapting themselves to the new system; but what, for instance, were future language or literature teachers, or musicians or painters to do? On what kind of "production" would they be employed during their last three years at school? Must they do "manual" labor in a factory—or could they spend part of their last three years working in some capacity in a specialized school or institute? The impression I got was that there were still a few loose ends dangling about, and that nothing quite final had been settled in their case, or also in the case of some *outstandingly* good pupils. Was it absolutely essential for an outstandingly good budding mathematician, for instance, to go literally "into production?"

Insofar as the purpose of the new school plan was to reduce the difference between manual and non-manual labor, and to eliminate any kind of "intellectual class-snobbery," to what extent would the "production" duties be enforced?

It was significant, of course, that, in allowing access to a university, priority should be given *not* to those who had stayed on at the 11-year school (and had thus done only relatively little "production" work), but, on the contrary, to those who had worked "on production" (and had, at the same time, done evening classes or correspondence

courses), or else had substituted their "three years" at school
by three years of "technicum-cum-production."

In top academic circles, I gathered, there was a good
deal of disagreement about the effectiveness of the new
system; some were all in favor of it; they thought it made
for excellent *human* training, if nothing else. Others felt
that it might tend to *lower the standard of science,* by
"wasting" some of a gifted young man's or young woman's
best years with little advantage, and a third serious objection
came from factory executives who feared that the "invasion"
of their factory by unskilled students would merely interfere with the fulfillment of the factory's plan.

The young people themselves, I found, were rather divided on the question, too; young technicians were mostly
all in favor of it; students of literature, for instance, were
often opposed to it—if it meant "working in a factory"; but
would it? This question had, obviously, not been clearly
settled. The transition period, starting with 1959–60, was to
cover a period of four years.

In talking to other Soviet educationists both then and
much later, I got the impression that the whole system had,
from the very outset, been given considerable flexibility—
almost to the point of looking vague and imprecise—so that
it could be more easily adjusted to local conditions or individual cases. Thus, there was, by 1960, a tendency to allow
exceptionally promising pupils in mathematics, physics and
other fundamental sciences to stay on at the school during
the last "three years." It is true that the admission to universities and other VUZ's was, broadly, based on the following
principle: there was a sort of *numerus clausus* for those
who had not been (or scarcely been) "on production," with
the result that only those with *the very highest marks* were
admitted, whereas those with a fairly long production *stage*
were admitted even with substantially lower marks. Thus
only really *exceptionally* brilliant young people could afford to dispense (though not without some risk) with the
"production *stage*" entirely, apart from the "practical" work
done during the last three years at school.

Apart from the "moral" and "social" purpose of the reform, its principal practical aim was, obviously, to train a
very large number of so-called *medium cadres*, though without further educational outlets being closed to them. By

1961 it became apparent that a high proportion of those who had "entered production" for their last three "school" years were, in fact, already *in jobs* and did not necessarily strive to enter a university or other VUZ. Others again contented themselves with evening classes or correspondence courses for "raising their qualifications."

If this school reform had a strong ideological basis, there was an even stronger one underlying the Boarding Schools Plan.

When we speak of "boarding schools," we tend to think in terms of Eton and Harrow in England, or Exeter and Andover in America, and similar schools for turning out the upper-class élite. To what extent do the Soviet Boarding Schools pursue a similar object? Clearly, that is not their aim, though certain "boarding schools" which have existed in Russia up till now, notably the Suvorov Schools set up during World War II—which have been described by foreign critics as "nurseries for an army officer caste"—have tended to produce a rather distinct type of Soviet citizen.

The new boarding schools—which ultimately aim at educating the *whole* of the young Soviet generation and at thus taking over the *whole* of secondary education—are described as an essential machine for turning out the best possible *Communists* during the present "transition from Socialism to Communism."

Skrobov described the system to me as follows:

"The Boarding Schools (*shkoly internaty*) are a new type of school which have existed for only three years. The whole idea has caught on, and is very popular.

"The purpose of the boarding schools is to organize education *on a higher level* than that in the mass schools, and to turn out *highly-educated and politically-literate people*. For doing so, they are provided with all the necessary conditions. Under this system, children remain for a very long time under the supervision of their teachers. Spending their time constantly in the collective is very good for the children, and produces better results than the day schools of our mass education."

"Do you mean," I said, "that it is better for children to live separately from their parents; this, surely, doesn't quite fit in with the Soviet 'cult of the family.' "

"I'll come to that in a moment," said Skrobov. "But I can

tell you right now that, although there can be no question of 'separating' children from their families, we think that, by being in a boarding school, they, nevertheless, get away from a good many undesirable influences that still exist in our country. But don't mistake me: we are not forcing anybody to enter a boarding school; children are admitted only at the parents' request.

"They start at the age of seven, and there is no entrance exam. The curriculum is the same as in the day schools; in their fifth form pupils begin to learn a foreign language— English, French, or German; but in some schools they can also learn Chinese, Hindi or Urdu.

"These boarding schools will be either eight-year or 11-year schools, on the same principle as the mass schools. The schools are coeducational. The children spend the whole year at school, except for vacations, holidays and Sundays; these periods are spent with the parents; and the parents may, of course, visit them at school. As a rule, children go to a boarding school in the same town where the parents live; but when these live far away (this frequently happens in rural areas), then they join their parents only during long vacations.

"Only 20 to 22 per cent of the present boarding schools are in the rural areas, but this percentage is going to increase. By the end of the seven-year plan, as you know, there will be 2.5 million children in boarding schools, out of a total secondary school population of 30 millions.

"In the boarding schools, as I already said, young people are going to get more serious training than in day schools; also, they will develop more rapidly than others a strong collectivist mentality. We have called the boarding schools the high road to Communism and that is why we hope that, ultimately, *all* children will be brought up in boarding schools, though by the end of the present seven-year plan less than 10 per cent will yet be there."

"Do parents have to pay anything? And how are children selected for boarding schools?—for there must be a lot of people who'd like to send their children there," I said.

"There *are* lots of people; and this is a bit of a problem still. For the present we tend to give preference to children living in unsatisfactory family conditions (overcrowded homes, unmarried mothers, etc.). As for payment, parents pay, on the average, only one-tenth of the cost of keeping a child in a boarding school; this cost amounts to between 9,000 and 10,000 rubles a year and the parents generally pay about 1,000 rubles—something a little less, sometimes a little more, according to their income, or the number of children they have. In the boarding schools there are not only teachers, but educators as well; the great advantage of boarding schools is that they don't let children waste their time stupidly; outside teaching hours, they go in for sports, amateur theatricals, music; they have their various 'science circles,' labs., etc. In our experience also things like foreign languages are more quickly learned in the boarding schools than in the day schools; also boarding schools provide better opportunities for physical culture, for the development of musical and artistic talents, and so on. You see," said Skrobov, "the way we look at it is this: the future citizen of a Communist society must be a man or woman of very high ideals, of good health and physique; with a finely-developed artistic sense, intensely patriotic and internationally peace-minded. The knowledge of foreign languages is very essential; it makes for a better international outlook. We have every hope that most pupils who have been brought up in a boarding school will, by the time they are 16, speak fluently at least one foreign language; with the Soviet Union being what it is, our contacts with the outside world—both East and West —will become more and more frequent.

"As I said before, there are educators at the schools, as well as teachers, besides specialists in music, sports and so on. There is also a doctor at every boarding school. The educator is specially versed in child psychology, and can cope with any problems that arise during childhood and adolescence. The fact that the boarding schools are co-educational is very important; young boys learn from the start to treat young girls as equals—to treat them with that human respect which is part of a proper Communist attitude."

"Don't they feel homesick, and want to get back to their parents?"

"They may be homesick for the first few days; after that, more often than not, they feel 'school-sick' when they're at home. What we have arranged about the parents is this: at first, parents can come to see them any time; later they can come three or four times a month; there are also Parents'

Meetings and Parents' Committees which work together with the school."

"You say that, at present, there are more applications for admission to boarding schools than you can cope with; so, in all cases, the parents want the children to be admitted. But will the parents have any choice when *all* children are going to be brought up in boarding schools?"

"You are looking even further ahead than we are," Skrobov said with a slightly ironical twinkle. "So far, as I already said, we are planning for no more than 2.5 million children in boarding schools by 1965. Whether during the 20 or 30 years after that we will be able to build enough boarding schools to house 35, or 40 or 45 million children is still a bit early to say. But in a Communist society we reckon that *all* children should go to boarding schools; it won't be a case of 'busting up' the family; I should think the voluntary principle as regards parents will still hold—though it's asking rather a lot to tell you exactly how things are going to work 30 or 40 years hence! For the present we have, after all, only 326 boarding schools in the RSFSR, 47 of them in Moscow; the number of children in these vary, at present, from 250 to 600.

"The new boarding schools are now being built according to a special pattern—with the school itself in one building, the dormitories in another, complete with dining-rooms and sitting-rooms, recreation halls, etc. Then there are annexes like bathhouses, laundries, and so on. The boarding schools are very largely run on the self-service principle; the children must make their own beds, keep the place clean, and so on. Apart from that, there is, of course, a domestic staff, particularly in the kitchen, where the greatest care is taken of the right and sufficient diet.

"The children are not overworked; in the junior classes they have only four lessons a day of 45 minutes each, in the older classes five lessons. And then, of course, at 16, they choose one of the three courses I outlined to you before; it works the same as in the day schools. But although our experience of boarding schools is still only a short one—three years—we find that the general educational, cultural and what I might call 'civic' standard is higher in the boarding schools than in the day schools. A better collectivist mentality, a better Communist mentality, in short."

One could not but feel that here was, potentially, the most powerful weapon for creating a human society which would be very different even from present-day Soviet society—which has still so much variety and light-and-shade.

Only, how will it really work in practice?

Chapter 18

SOVIET MAN: NATIONALITIES—
THERE ARE *TWO* "JEWISH
PROBLEMS" IN THE SOVIET UNION

THERE ARE, of course, "nationalities problems" in the Soviet Union. Some were fairly acute until a few years ago. There were the "disloyal" nationalities during the war who sympathized or collaborated with the German invaders—the Crimean Tartars, the Kalmuks, some small Moslem nationalities in the Northern Caucasus like the Chechens and the Ingushi, and, of course, the Volga Germans. They were deported indiscriminately, *en masse*, "to the East" during the war, men, women, children and all. The North-Caucasian Nationalities and the Kalmuks—or those among them who survived—are "back home"; the Crimean Tartars and the Volga Germans have, apparently, remained out East.

Then there are the Balts: the Estonians, Latvians (Letts) and Lithuanians. A high proportion of their upper government cadres and of their bourgeoisie were anti-Soviet, and many were deported in 1940–41; in 1945 many more who had actively cooperated with the Nazis (and the Gestapo men of Latvian and Lithuanian nationality were numerous) either fled to the West or were sent East. After 1953 a high proportion of these deported Balts were allowed to return home. During recent years the Estonians, Latvians and even the predominantly Catholic Lithuanians have been no trouble. Propaganda has constantly (and fairly successfully) reminded them that they had "always" been "part of Russia" and that even if they didn't like it, there was nothing they could do about it, and had better adapt themselves as best they could; they have also been buttered up economically, more perhaps than any other part of the Soviet Union; they have been

186

flattered with Stalin Prizes; and, with an influx of a considerable number of Russians, especially into Estonia and Latvia, and the intensive industrialization in these two countries, there has been a good deal of intermarriage, particularly in Latvia, where the working class of Riga had always been largely pro-Soviet, anyway.

There are also other "minor" nationalities problems—a certain mutual dislike, for instance, between the Georgians and the Armenians. I remember in Tbilisi in 1946 talking to a Georgian girl who was going to get married, but who then broke off the engagement because her parents violently objected to her marrying—an Armenian!

But when, in the West, one talks about the "nationalities" problem in the Soviet Union, the question that is almost invariably raised is—the "Jewish problem" and "anti-semitism in Russia."

In reality there is not one Jewish problem in the Soviet Union; there are two; and in most cases those who talk about "anti-semitism in Russia" get hold of the wrong end of the stick.

There is, on the one hand, the problems of Jewish, specifically Yiddish culture, which was more or less forcibly stamped out in 1948–1949. In a recent issue of the French Catholic magazine *Esprit* there is the review of a book by Leon Leneman, called *The Tragedy of the Jews in the USSR*. According to this writer, there were, broadly speaking, five periods in the history of the Jews in the Soviet Union:

(1) The "good days"—from 1917 to 1930, when Jews were very active in the Party and held numerous high and responsible positions; the Yiddish press, publishing houses, theaters, etc., were flourishing as never before; but by the end of this period a large number of "old Bolsheviks" (many of them Jews) were liquidated; men like Trotsky, Kamenev and Zinoviev already made Jews suspect in Stalin's eyes.

(2) The 1930–41 period, marked by the unsuccessful Birobidjan (Jewish "national home" in the Far East) experiment; today there are only 35,000 Jews living there, "in the midst of an indifferent population."

(3) 1941 to 1948 is again a "good period." Jews played a distinguished part in the Army; American goodwill was being cultivated, and the newly-formed Jewish Anti-Fascist Committee was very active in its propaganda; the great actor Michoels

and the well-known writer Feffer were sent in 1943 to the USA to do propaganda for the Russian war effort.

(4) The worst period was from 1948 to 1953. In January that year Michoels was mysteriously murdered during a visit to Minsk, together with Golubov, a ballet critic, who had also been active on the Jewish Anti-Fascist Committee. Michoels was the real chief of Yiddish culture in the Soviet Union. It was said at the time that the NKVD had been ordered to "liquidate" him. It became even worse after the Soviet recognition of the new State of Israel and the rousing reception given to the first Israel Ambassador, Mrs. Golda Meier, by a few thousand Jews on her arrival in Moscow. This strongly confirmed Stalin in his view that "the Jews" were a foreign body in Soviet society, or, at best, people with divided loyalties. The Jewish Anti-Fascist Committee was dissolved, and the Yiddish press stopped, as well as the Yiddish theatre and publishing houses. In 1948–49 mass deportations of Jews started; 1952 was marked by the trial of 24 Jewish writers including Markisch, Bergelson and Feffer; they were all shot.

Then there was the Jewish Doctors' Plot, and, before his death, Stalin was said to be thinking of deporting the entire Jewish population.

(5) The post-Stalin period was more "liberal"; many of those killed, including the great writer, Isaac Babel, were rehabilitated; and the exiled Jews were, like others, allowed to return. But prejudice and discrimination continued and culturally, the Jews were never allowed to regain their autonomy.

Now, according to *Esprit* (and Leneman) there are "two scandals": "Communism denies the existence of a Jewish nationality in the USSR, though passports put opposite 'nationality'—'Jewish.' The constant policy of the régime . . . has been russification, integration, assimilation. . . . Birobidjan, with no historical tradition, could, obviously, not succeed."

The "second scandal" is this:

Russian Jewry does not want to break its bonds with the Jews of other countries, whatever the ideological differences. The point is that Soviet Jews speak Yiddish, and do not wish to abandon this language which is, to them, a source of irrepressible emotion and inspiration. So the Soviet authorities have done their utmost to crush the language and its culture, by suppressing Yiddish schools, theatres, books, newspapers, etc. In spite of all this, Russian Jewry is today more determinedly Jewish than ever.

Such is the "Yiddish" version of "Soviet anti-semitism"; but it seems to be a one-sided and rather lopsided story.

First of all, it is *not* true that all, or even most, Jews in Russia cling either to the Yiddish language or to Yiddish culture.

There is unquestionably a strong Soviet prejudice against Yiddish, which is associated not so much with a "nationality" as with a completely dead and "medieval" phase of the Jews' historical development—the Ghetto phase. Yiddish writers like Sholom Asch and Sholom Aleichem have lately been published in Russian in large printings—but as historic curios. The "ghetto tradition," which both Lenin and Stalin attacked in their polemics with the leaders of the Jewish Bund (it was "unproletarian" to observe the Sabbath, eat *kosher* meat, etc.) is something for which there is no room in Soviet society.

Secondly, the Soviet authorities are strongly anti-Zionist, and object to any Soviet citizen hankering for his "real country"; thus, both the "nostalgia for the ghetto" and the "nostalgia for Israel" are un-Soviet, if not actively anti-Soviet. The Jews' demonstration in honor of the first Israel Ambassador in 1948 added an anti-Zionist campaign in Russia to the already fairly active anti-Yiddish campaign, the grimmest manifestation of which was the savage murder of Michoels. Thus, in 1948, the anti-Yiddish and the anti-Zionist campaigns were merged into one. (A little paradoxical, since in Israel, too, Yiddish is frowned upon.)

Not only were the writers mentioned above "liquidated," but even an old Bolshevik like Solomon Lozovsky, who looked like an old Paris *boulevardier*, and was, as one of the Vice-Commissars for Foreign Affairs, the official spokesman of the Soviet Foreign Ministry for the foreign press during the first two years of the war. Lozovsky later became a member of the Jewish Anti-Fascist Committee, and as such, was ruthlessly bumped off in 1949. Anything more wicked and absurd than killing this harmless old man is difficult to imagine.

In 1959 the publication of books in Yiddish was resumed for the first time since 1948; the first of these were reprints of old writers like Sholom Aleichem, Peretz and Sforim; in 1960 some more recent books were published: by David Bergelson, who was shot in 1952, along with several other writers; by Asher Schwartzmann, as well as by three living Yiddish-writing authors, Vergelis, Dobin, and Samuel Halkin, who had survived the purges. According to Israel sources, these books are, however, chiefly meant for export and propaganda abroad, since most copies of these books have been exported to Poland, the USA and other countries with large Yiddish-speaking communities.

As against this assertion, there were the three very warm and laudatory obituary articles in *Literary Gazette* (September 24, 1960) after the death of Samuel Halkin, one of them signed by the Writers' Union of the USSR. He was treated as a "great Soviet writer," whose main works had all been translated into Russian, and whose plans, including his tragedy, *The Revolt of the Ghetto,* had been frequently performed. He was also highly praised for his translation into Yiddish of Shakespeare, Pushkin, Blok, Mayakovsky, etc. Later, after Stalin's death, he was "rehabilitated."

It was also in 1948–49 that a rather virulent kind of anti-semitism began in Russia. Russian writers of Jewish origin and "nationality" began to be referred to as "rootless cosmopolitans"; and it was all very well for Ehrenburg to laugh this off, when abroad, with remarks to the effect that "there are lots of idiots in Russia, too, and it only shows we've got a free press." A number of outstanding writers of Jewish descent like Vasili Grossman were ill-treated and victimized at the Writers' Union. (It is only fair to say that Ehrenburg strongly protested against all this.) The Slansky Trial in Prague had serious repercussions on the position of the Jews in Russia; in the midst of the "vigilance campaigns" and the widespread spy-mania the Jews began to be looked upon by some as something of a potential Fifth Column. (One should also add to this a certain irritation against "the Jews" during the years of hardship just after the war, when they were supposed to be more successful at wirepulling—getting flats, etc. —than others.)

Although Kaganovich was still one of Stalin's right-hand men, several members of the Politbureau—Shcherbakov (who died in 1945), Zhdanov (who died in 1948), and even

Khrushchev, as well as some others—were said to be more or less openly anti-semitic.

Recently an Israel-inspired publication (*L'Observateur du Moyen-Orient*) came out with a special issue devoted to "Khrushchev's anti-semitism," which he was supposed to have displayed both in the Ukraine during the years following the war, when he was, among other things, careful not to specify that most of the people murdered by the Nazis in the Ukraine were Jews (for "didn't the Ukrainians, on the whole, approve of these massacres?") and later, in Poland, when he was supposed to have told the Polish Government in 1956: "There are too many Abramoviches amongst you; and even an Abramovich who adopts a name ending in -*ski*, still remains an Abramovich." And then, towards the very end of the Stalin régime, came the Jewish Doctors' Plot (incidentally, a number of the "plotters" were pure Russians).

The stories about Khrushchev's anti-semitism sound, to say the least, rather apocryphal.

It seems to me that all those speaking of "the tragedy of the Jews in Russia" are arguing beside the point. They are speaking in terms of a relatively small and in any case, rapidly dwindling minority—of Jews who are either religious, or attached to their Yiddish tradition, or both, or who have strong Zionist and pro-Israel leanings.

The truth is that the great majority of Russian Jews do *not* speak Yiddish, are not greatly interested in Israel (if at all) and are, very largely, integrated in the Soviet community. As already said, the 1959 census showed that only 20.8 per cent of Soviet Jews considered Yiddish as their language, i.e. about 500,000 people.

The trouble of most Soviet Jews, not to say their tragedy, is not that they are *too* integrated and *too* assimilated, but that they are not sufficiently so. Trotsky, for example, who was often bothered by his own Jewishness, considered that the best thing for the Jews to do was gradually to "disappear," that is, to be wholly assimilated through intermarriage, through changing their names (as he did), and in other ways. This was perhaps putting it too strongly; and yet there is little doubt that *that*, broadly, is a solution which, openly or secretly, is favored by a very large number of Soviet Jews, who still feel that they are not "entirely accepted" as "complete" Soviet citizens.

There is both discrimination and non-discrimination; Soviet society resembles some Western societies in this respect. In the top echelons of the Party, the number of Jews are few—only one or two members of the Central Committee are Jews. Although, in the early days of the Revolution, there were many Jews in the diplomatic service, there are practically none now. The number of Jewish generals is insignificant. On the other hand, in science, in industry, in medicine, in literature and the arts Jews are very prominent. As Khrushchev remarked during his American tour, Jews played an important part in the development of Sputniks and rockets; in 1960, out of the Lenin Prizes for technology and science, about 10 per cent were awarded to Jewish scientists. One only has to look at the Academy of Sciences, or at scientific journals, to see that Jews hold a very prominent place there. They are as wholly integrated in Soviet society as can be. Jews also play an important role in the film industry; two of the most famous writers of children's books are Jewish—Lev Kassil and Samuel Marshak; so are many famous Soviet musicians—David Oistrakh, Emil Gillels, Leonid Kogan, old man Goldenweiser, and dozens of others. A very high proportion of composers of light music (including popular and patriotic songs) are (or were) Jews: Pokras, Dunaevsky, Blanter, Sigismund Katz, Boguslavsky, to mention only the best-known; the leaders of light entertainment (Zfasman, the jazz band leader, Raikin of the Leningrad Miniature Theater, etc.) are Jews. Some of the most famous war novels are also the work of Jews—Grossman, Kazakevich, etc.; in the official press Jews are much less prominent than they used to be in the days of Radek (apart from a few old men like Ilya Ehrenburg and David Zaslavsky), but they are prominent in "lighter" journalism, including *Krokodil,* and at least one leading political cartoonist (Boris Efimov) is Jewish.

So it is certainly excessive to speak of any systematic anti-semitism in Russia, least of all in relation to Jews who are "integrated" Soviet citizens, without any hankering for either Yiddish culture or Israel. Why, indeed, should a top-ranking Soviet scientist or industrial executive—or a man like Oistrakh—be interested in either?

In spite of it all, even some of the most wholly "integrated" Jews are in a slightly false position. Why are they described as "nationality: Jewish" in their passports? Can they get the "Jewish" changed to "Russian" or "Ukrainian" if they so wish? Can they, if they wish, change their names—i.e. not merely adopt pseudonyms, but change their names *legally,* and call themselves "Ivanov" and not just "Rabinovich, known as Ivanov?" These are moot points; and the Soviet authorities appear on the whole unhelpful in allowing Jews to become wholly assimilated and integrated.

In Moscow I talked to X, a rather eminent Jewish scientist, about this.

"On the whole," he said, "it doesn't bother me being described as 'Jewish' in my passport, or of having a name like mine. But there are lots of Jews, especially of the younger generation, who don't like it. Their parents are completely russified, don't know a word of Yiddish; neither do they; they, as good Soviet citizens, as real 'Soviet men,' are distrustful of Israel, and have certainly no sympathy for it, or interest in it. The whole thing is anachronistic: it's no use saying they are being 'disloyal to their own race'; *they don't feel they belong to any particular 'race'; they are good Soviet citizens of Russian culture and upbringing, and that's all.* To make them belong to some virtually non-existent 'national' minority is like asking an American to feel some loyalty for King George III. Well, yes—it's as simple as that! But just because we still have *some* orthodox Jews, and Yiddish-speaking Jews, and some who *are* squinting towards Israel, the Jews who are 100 per cent Soviet citizens are treated, not as suspects but—how shall I put it?—as 'potential suspects.' I suppose," he added, "that the Jews have a kind of skeptical and sophisticated streak which doesn't *quite* fit in with the Russian approach; they are—even the young ones—too sophisticated to be taken in by a lot of the official blah. But then, are the Russians always taken in by it? Frankly, no; but they disguise their skepticism better than the Jews do. In 'naughty' political jokes you nearly always find the Jew acting the Soviet Good Soldier Schweik, as it were. You know the one about Khrushchev making a speech: 'Next year, comrades, we shall go to the moon, and, before long, we shall travel to Mars and Venus.' Whereupon Rabinovich gets up and says: 'I want to ask a question. When will we be able to go to Paris?' The next day Khrushchev makes another speech: 'Comrades, next year we shall travel to the moon and then——' Somebody stands up. So Khrushchev says: 'I know, I know; you also are going to ask "What about going to Paris?" ' 'No, no, I only want to ask: What's happened to Rabinovich?' Well," said X, "that's just an example. It's in the hoary old tradition of 'Jewish anecdotes'—the Jew is always a little bit of a rebel. But it's all a bit unfair; my own view is that the law should be changed; that Jews who *feel* Russian and want to be considered as such, should be allowed to become legally Russian—name, nationality and all; even if it doesn't quite work in their case, it'll work all right in their children's case."

So there are, in fact, two Jewish problems in Russia: that of the minority of "old-time" Jews who are not allowed to be *as particularist* as they would like to be; and that of the majority of "modern" Jews who are not, as a rule, allowed to be *as fully assimilated* as they would like to be, and who combine complete Soviet loyalty with the lurking suspicion that even if they aren't discriminated against today, they *may* be discriminated against tomorrow, and that, in any case, their sons stand a much poorer chance than a "real" Russian of getting say, into the diplomatic service.

Chapter 19

SOVIET MAN: IS THERE AN
ANTI-GERMAN COMPLEX?

NO ONE WHO, like myself, has spent the whole period of the war in Russia can have any doubt about "Germany" and "the Germans" presenting a very complex psychological, and not merely political, problem to every Russian. It is something that Dr. Adenauer may pretend not to understand, though, being an intelligent man, he should understand it fairly easily.

There is scarcely a Russian alive whose life has not, in some way, been affected by the Germans—i.e. by World War II. Owing to the war, there are millions of widows and single women in Russia, millions of fatherless children, millions who have lost one or all their children in the war, millions who have been physically or mentally crippled.

At the meeting of the Supreme Soviet on October 31, 1959, Professor A. N. Bakulev, President of the Academy of Medical Sciences of the USSR, said, in the course of a speech in favor of joint medical research with Western scientists, that the last war was the most murderous of all, and that the Soviet Union had lost no fewer than *20 million people*. This figure, incidentally, was omitted from the press reports of the Supreme Soviet meeting on the following day; not that anybody could have doubted its accuracy. It meant that, in addition to the seven million soldiers who had lost their lives, either in battle or in German captivity, *13 million* civilians had, in one way or another, died as a direct result of the war—in deportation, in bombings, in massacres, or in famines like that of Leningrad, where, it now appeared, nine 'hundred thousand people had died of hunger. There had, in Russia, been not one but hundreds of Oradours and Lidices, while hundreds of thousands of war prisoners, taken by the Germans during the first two years of the war, were allowed to die of starvation. Very little was said about this in Russia while the war was in progress, but when the surviving prisoners began to return, Russians became aware of the full horror of what had happened to so many of their sons.

Also in liberated cities, one after another, mass graves were discovered by the advancing troops with hundreds and sometimes thousands of war prisoners and civilians massacred by the Germans.

In Western Russia the retreating Germans destroyed, when they had time to do so, every town and village; the destructions were almost as systematic in the Ukraine, particularly in industrial areas like the Donbas and Krivoi Rog; Byelorussia, too, was a waste land by the time the Germans had pulled out.

Everybody in Russia, except the very young, remembered the war; there was scarcely a person I talked to who hadn't some lurid memories of the war, or of the German occupation. Liza, one of the maids at the hotel, was telling me about the occupation in the Smolensk province. She was a woman of 35 or 36; dark, with a beautiful Madonna-like face; most striking were the two rows of perfect white teeth; like many Russians, she had that characteristic faint earthy smell of black bread. She spoke with the vaguely Byelorussian accent, typical of the Smolensk people.

"I am a simple *kolkhoz* girl," she said one day. "Near our village, not far from Smolensk, Gipsies used to camp in the wood; the women had rows and rows of beads round their necks, and they always wanted to tell you your fortune; and, at night, the Gipsy boys and girls would dance like mad round the bonfire; during the day, they'd come and beg in the villages. But when the war came, we hadn't anything to give them; and they had no cattle of their own; and then the Germans, thinking they were nomads or partisans, rounded them all up, and killed them all—women, children, everybody. And we, in the village, were made to dig the graves and dump their bodies. Even small children. I was only 17 then.

"We hadn't time to be evacuated; very soon after the war

had started, the German tanks arrived; and the soldiers broke into all the houses and farms; and they took everything they could lay their hands on—cows, chickens, pigs—and the cows and pigs were taken away in big trucks; and the soldiers took away all the butter and eggs; we were glad to get away with our lives. The Germans are, of course, hard workers; but they also made us work—and how! We had to dig trenches, and clear away the snow at the height of winter—22 degrees below it used to be sometimes. And I caught such a terrible chill one day that something went wrong inside me; and although I've been married for six years, I can't have any children. The Finns who later came were even worse than the Germans; they'd attack small girls of 13 or 14. In our village, fortunately, there was the German divisional headquarters, so the soldiers didn't run quite as wild as they did in other places; but they kept asking me if I was a Communist or a komsomol. I was a simple *kolkhoz* girl, and though I was 17, I was kind of under-developed; so they didn't take much notice of me, and I tried to look as dirty and as unattractive as possible. And then, one day, at the height of winter, we were marched off to Orel; and there we were again made to dig trenches and mend roads. But then, in the summer of 1943, they wanted to deport everybody to Germany, so I hid for several days in the fields inside a haystack till the Red Army came.

"I stayed on at Orel with my mother and aunt; my father was mobilized in 1941, and has never been heard of since; must have died a horrible death in a German death camp for Russian prisoners. My mother is very religious, but my aunt is not; and they often have rows; or rather, my aunt pulls my mother's leg about God.

"I don't believe in God either; I saw so much wickedness during the war, that it's hard to believe there can be a God who would allow all this to happen; why should they have killed all those Gipsies? . . .

"And then, in 1944, I came to Moscow, and got a job at the Rotfront candy and biscuit factory; but I didn't like it; too many sweets make you sick; also we were made to take two showers every day, and with my lungs in a bad state as a result of all the work I had to do for the Germans at the height of winter, I always got colds and flu. So, soon after the war was over, I took this dull and badly-paid job; but then, as I told you, I got married; and my husband works in a factory; but we have only one small room, and we are not very happy, because I can't have any children. . . ."

This seemed a routine kind of Russian story: there are others which are much worse.

And everything is done not to let the young generation forget about the war and the German invasion. TV frequently shows war films in which the Germans figure as so many fiends, even though, occasionally, there is among them a "good German." Regular films are also often concerned with the German invasion—among them are famous films like *A Man's Fate*, made after the Sholokhov story. "Anti-German" novels are written by the dozen; and the publishing house attached to the Ministry of Defense makes a point of bringing out millions of copies of old and recent war novels, such as Grossman's *In a Right Cause*. Similarly, recent best-sellers included Kochetov's *The Yershov Brothers*, in which part of the action revolves round a man whom the Germans had forced into the Vlassov Army, and round a woman, a pathetic creature, a broken reed, whom the Germans had sterilized, or *Deep in the Rear* by Boris Polevoi, also full of German atrocities, such as the bombing of a Volga steamer full of refugee women and children. In Polevoi's novel there is also a "good German"—whose father was a Communist in one of Hitler's camps, and who himself came over to the Russians. Not that he is entirely convincing; but this book, as a whole, is a sort of epic of ordinary Russian working people in a half-destroyed textile mill, where they keep on working, despite constant hardships, privations and a ceaseless flow of notices about sons and husbands killed at the front.

The memories of the war are vivid, and the resentment against "the Germans" continues to be deep. Yet, where present-day Germany is concerned, this resentment is, perhaps a little artificially, canalized against "Bonn," Adenauer and "the Nazi clique" surrounding him.

But although there is something slightly artificial in the build-up of Adenauer as Number One bogeyman and the tendency to divide Germany into an "absolutely bad" Western and an "absolutely good" Eastern Germany, there is a very genuine fear that, in years to come, the *revanchards* of Western Germany are more likely to run wild than anybody else, and to confront America and the West generally with the *fait accompli* of a Third World War. The frequent warnings given to Western Germany by Khrushchev and others that, should she try on any nonsense, she will be "the first to be wiped out" are not considered a sufficient guarantee that "the lunatics" will necessarily, and in all circumstances, stop to think.

As for the "good" Eastern Germany, there are, needless to say, some mental reservations about her in Russia, too. No doubt, the official line is that Eastern Germany is a very "good" country.

The tenth anniversary of the foundation of the German Democratic Republic was celebrated in East Berlin with great solemnity. In the absence of Khrushchev, the Soviet Government and the CPSU were represented by Frol Kozlov, who paid the warmest tributes to "that great son of the German People," Wilhelm Pieck, as well as to Ulbricht, Grotewohl, and the rest.

The line Grotewohl took at that famous meeting of October 6th 1959, was, briefly summarized, this:

At the end of the war, Germany's most essential task was to put an end to German militarism. The revolutionary-democratic reforms of Eastern Germany meant a defeat for the warmongers. The democratic land reform, the punishment of war criminals, the liquidation of the *Konzerne,* the democratic school reform were so many defeats for the imperialist-militarist powers.

The unification of the Communists and Social-Democrats into a single party in 1946 meant the end for all time of all conflicts inside the working class.

The Soviet Union had greatly helped the workers of the GDR, whose people "were full of sympathy for the Soviet Union."

After paying a warm tribute to Khrushchev's Disarmament Plan submitted shortly before to UN, Grotewohl went on:

The great tragedy of the German people was that only one part of Germany had learned a vital lesson from World War II. The other part was returning to a sinister, reactionary past.

The industrial production of East Germany had trebled since 1949, and she now held fifth place in Europe. Numerous new giant enterprises had been created in the country in the last ten years. The real "economic miracle" was to be found not in Western, but in Eastern Germany.

In agriculture already nearly 50 per cent of the "useful" land was in the "Socialist sector." The standard of living was rapidly going up, and the GDR had now commercial relations with about 100 countries. Its foreign trade was six times larger than in 1949 and would be nine times larger by 1965.

The GDR was the most advanced Western outpost of the Socialist countries, united by the Warsaw Pact, and more than half the world population was on friendly terms with the GDR.

He then proposed (a) the stopping of all nuclear tests; (b) rejection of all atomic armaments and the inclusion of both parts of Germany in an atom-free zone; (c) limitation of armaments and no conscription; (d) withdrawal of all foreign troops and liquidation of all military bases; (e) non-agression pact between the NATO and Warsaw Powers; (f) no more war and *revanche* propaganda; (g) the formation of an All-German Committee for preparing German unification and the peace treaty.

The only possible slogan for a United Germany (he said), was "Down with Militarism." Germany must become a country of peace and democracy. The unification could only be the final outcome of a gradual *rapprochement* between the two German states; in Western Germany meantime the militarists and *revanchards* must be put out of action. But, instead of considering such a *rapprochement,* Adenauer was still talking in terms of "liberating" the East, i.e. the unconditional inclusion of the GDR in the GFR. By 1965, Grotewohl concluded, the Socialist countries of the world would be producing more than the rest of the world; this would show that Socialism was superior to the capitalist system.

Frol Kozlov started by paying the GDR a number of compliments:

The GDR was the stronghold, on German soil, of the lofty ideas of Socialism for which the greatest leaders of the German and international working-class movement had fought in the past—Wilhelm Liebknecht, August Bebel, Rosa Luxemburg, Karl Liebknecht and Ernst Thaelmann. Thousands of the best sons of the German people had died in Nazi prisons for these ideals. They had not died in vain. . . . The GDR had a proud record behind it; its industrial production was nearly three times that of 1936; nearly 90 per cent of industry had been socialized. *The GDR's avowed aim, which was to raise the standard of living above that of Western Germany, was sure to result in Eastern Germany becoming an ever-growing center of attraction to the whole of Germany.*

After a further tribute to "your great fellow-countryman, Karl Marx," Kozlov devoted the rest of his speech to the "immense historical importance" of N. S. Khrushchev's visit to the United States, and to the warm welcome he had received from the American people. The Khrushchev-Eisenhower meeting was of the "greatest and most far-reaching importance."

And so on. It was obvious at that time that Khrushchev was hoping a great deal from the Summit, including a compromise on West Berlin, though, at the same time, it was clear that he was not going to press the matter too hard if it threatened to bring about a setback in Soviet-American relations. Nevertheless, on Western Germany the Russians continued to feel very strongly; they would not, however, force the Berlin issue if they could obtain some assurances about Western Germany not being rearmed to a "dangerous" extent. The two themes of peaceful coexistence and the ultimate victory of the Socialist system ran side-by-side even in a purely German context: far-fetched though it looked, the aim, within a foreseeable future, was to raise the standard of living in Eastern Germany above that of Western Germany. Were not the first signs of a "coming victory of the East" to be seen in the trickle of unemployed and discontented Germans moving from West to East?—even though the migration the *other* way was still *very* much greater.

On whether the East Germans could be looked upon as real friends of the Soviet Union, there was, of course, a good deal of skepticism in Moscow. To hold "free elections" in Eastern Germany would be asking for trouble. The Germans had voted *en masse* for Hitler not so very long ago; they were politically too irresponsible, one Russian told me, to be entrusted with universal suffrage; it was a "penalty they would have to pay for their past aberrations." However, they were *learning*; the young generation of East Germans was being more and more converted every year to the Socialist way of thinking, and once the living standard in Eastern Germany had exceeded that of Western Germany, there would be no great difficulties any more. Also, more and more and more people were having a vested interest in the GDR continuing. In fact, many Russians thought that the East Germans were, in many ways, "more malleable" than, for instance, the Poles. Also, they respected force; they liked to be on the wining side; and they were being gradually persuaded that the East, and not the West, was the "winning side."

Russian technicians and others who went to Eastern Germany had a good deal of respect for German efficiency, and if anything, personal relations were better with Germans than they were with Poles.

All the same, the Russian attitude to East Germans was rather reserved. At the Hotel Berlin (named in their honor) where I stayed in Moscow, there was a constant succession of East German delegations. There was a lurking suspicion that there might be quite a few secret Nazis amongst them. However, as the young waiter (the one who was taking evening classes to become, at the end of five years, a "restaurant director," and was studying, for the purpose, microbiochemistry and all sorts of elaborate sciences) told me: "I've seen a lot of these Germans, mostly young people, during the last couple of years I've worked here. They aren't a bad bunch, really. It's amazing how many of them speak good Russian. They are very polite to us Russians, and they like making nasty remarks about Adenauer; they think, I suppose, it makes a good impression here. Also, they all religiously line up, first thing, outside the Lenin-Stalin Mausoleum. Funny bunch. . . ."

However, after Russians have had a few drinks, the old anti-German feeling is apt to come up to the surface. One night in the "Berlin" restaurant, about a dozen young Germans—drinking East German beer, a great attraction in this place—sang in chorus a German folk-song; no sooner had they finished than a rather drunken party of Russians, including two officers, burst into song. What they sang was a wartime song—the *Song of the Bearded Partisan*—

But when we've driven out the Fritzes
We'll have time to shave again. . . .

The Germans listened sheepishly, pretending not to understand, and when the song was over, they clapped politely.

Chapter 20

MOSCOW CONVERSATION PIECES ON AMERICA, CHINA AND MUCH ELSE

DURING THE MONTHS that followed Mr. Khrushchev's return from his "historical and epoch-making visit to the United States" (for that is how it was usually described) the Russians I knew (some were old, other new acquaintances) were more candid and outspoken than they had been for a long time. The "international thaw" seemed to be in full swing, and conversations were informal and uninhibited—not, of course, with big official personages, who continued to be rather cagey and reserved, but with what I would describe as the near-top and medium layers of Moscow journalism. All these friends I met had more or less specialized in international affairs; several of them had been abroad, either as resident correspondents, or as reporters who had accompanied Khrushchev on his various journeys. All of them were highly-educated Soviet citizens, nearly all of them Party members, but open-minded for all that, with an often refreshing tongue-in-cheek attitude both to the outside world and to certain official lines taken by the Party and the government.

These conversations took place in the course of half-a-dozen lunches, dinners and other meetings; but I shall, as far as possible, divide them by subjects. I shall call these Soviet friends simply A, B, C, D, etc.

(a) AMERICA

First, about America. A and C had accompanied Khrushchev on his American tour.

I: Well, what was it *really* like?

A (*with a grin*)*:* You only have to read the Soviet papers: It was *exactly* as we described it there. Of course, we built up, as far as possible, the really nice sides, and played down a bit the nasty sides. We didn't deny that there *were* nasty moments. At one point, as you know, Khrushchev got so fed up that he told Gromyko to inform Washington that if all this rudeness continued, he'd cut his visit short; there was, of course, plenty of rudeness—a lot of it before that incident, and some (though much less) after it. The mayor of Los Angeles was vile, and so were the labor union leaders whom Khrushchev met at San Francisco. Really dishonest to a degree! The police could be pretty trying, too, not allowing Khrushchev to see Disneyland and other things. And then, some of those people at Hollywood were either unbelievably stupid, or else they deliberately tried to insult Khrushchev by putting on that lousy cancan show of theirs. He took it very badly. Oh, not that Nikita is easily shocked (he likes to make some off-color jokes himself occasionally) but it gave him a chance of showing his displeasure, as much as to say: "Well, if that is what you call American Culture, you can keep the damned thing." Even after it was over, he went on muttering: *"Vot uzh dermo!"* ("What real sh—t!") And yet, *on the whole*, there is something very nice about Americans, and, my God, it's an impressive country; and it's no use denying that Nikita was really impressed by their standard of living. Of course, he wasn't taken to the Deep South, or to the more sordid Negro and other slum areas of the USA; and he was terribly tactful not to say anything about the Negro problem—though I can tell you: he *did* mention it privately many a time.

I: Did he come away completely convinced that the United States had been won over to "peaceful coexistence and peaceful competition?"

A: Completely convinced—isn't that asking rather a lot? No; but it was a beginning, a tremendously promising beginning, as he saw it. For years it had been his ambition to go to the USA; the fact that he was invited there by Eisenhower convinced him that, thanks to our rockets and Sputniks and things, the Soviet Union was at last being accepted as an equal—in some respects a superior, and that the Americans were sufficiently scared of us (well yes, it *is* largely that) to want to work out with us some kind of *modus vivendi.*

And, rightly or wrongly, he put his money, as it were, on Eisenhower. He got on—or seemed to get on—remarkably well with Eisenhower. There was a certain sportsmanship about Ike which Nikita liked. When, on the first day, Nikita presented him with a model of the Soviet crest the original of which was now on top of some volcano on the moon, Ike took it like a man, and gave a gentle, if slightly melancholy smile; another President might have thrown it in his face. So when Eisenhower and he agreed at Camp David about peaceful competition and peaceful coexistence, and about discussing everything in a reasonable and even friendly way (Berlin and everything else) Khrushchev felt extremely pleased. Also, he found him personally simple, friendly—a good guy, in short.

I: But Ike isn't everything. There was Nixon whom, I gather, Khrushchev did not like. And Dillon, and some others, too.

A: I don't know about Dillon; but he certainly didn't like Nixon. If he'd seen Truman or Acheson, no doubt he wouldn't have liked them either. But there were others he did like—quite definitely: Adlai Stevenson, for instance. But Eisenhower was the man who mattered to him; he was, as it were, his own opposite number. He was *the* President of the United States; he, Nikita, the simple miner's son, was rather flattered talking to him as an equal; but it wasn't only that. Nikita didn't think for a moment that everything had been settled; but he felt it was a real beginning; if we—the Soviet Union—could get along reasonably well with the United States, if Nikita Khrushchev and Dwight Eisenhower could see eye-to-eye on coexistence, and agree to discuss disarmament and *even* Berlin in a reasonable, businesslike way (and Ike's implied future concessions in Berlin scared the pants off Adenauer), then there was no serious danger of war any longer. And that matters to Nikita more than anything else. I daresay he boasted—perhaps a little too much—about Communism defeating capitalism in the end; but then, after all, what other line could he take? To play down his Communism would have been wrong; people would merely have called him a liar or a hypocrite; the beauty of it was that he—the top Communist—*was* being fêted by the biggest capitalist country in the world.

I: Isn't "fêted" putting it rather strongly?

A: No; there were unpleasant moments, but, by and large, people were prepared to take Khrushchev for what he was: the "enemy" who had come to talk peace and friendship and who, within certain limits, meant it. Oh, Khrushchev knows perfectly well what he's up against—arms monopolies, the Pentagon, and the CIA; but the impression he got—perhaps he was being slightly overoptimistic—was that at least a part of Big Business wasn't entirely in favor of keeping up the Cold War, and that the American people generally were glad (even with some mental reservations) to come to terms with the Soviet Union. Mental reservations—well, of course, there are mental reservations there, just as there are a good many here. *We* remember the days of Truman and Acheson, the threats to blow up Moscow with atom bombs, and all that, and to "liberate" our European allies, and all the Containment and Roll-Back stuff. But the fact remains that today the head of the Soviet Government is received with great honors in Washington, and that in New York and other cities, American corporation bosses like to welcome Khrushchev as their guest.

I: But aren't you slightly overrating the importance of people like Cyrus Eaton?

A: No. We know perfectly well that Cyrus Eaton, though a man of some weight in—is it Ohio?—is not typical of the Big Business class generally—though we met hundreds of others who, without loving us, *were* willing (and anxious) to *talk.* But we like to think that Eaton is a forerunner of *other* businessmen who will believe in disarmament and conversion, and in developing the Russian and Chinese markets. As Khrushchev sees it, even if such people are not taken very seriously yet, the time will come—it may be in five years or 10 years—when they will *have* to be taken seriously.

I: Does Khrushchev really believe his Complete Disarmament Plan, which he put before UN, is going to be taken seriously?

A: His maximum plan—no; but his minimum plan, why not?

I: I doubt whether even the "minimum plan" will produce any early results.

A: Maybe you're right. Probably you are. But with a thing like disarmament one just *has* to go on trying.

I: While in America, Khrushchev did refer a few times to American bases around the Soviet Union; but what puzzled me was that he should not have made more fuss about them than he did. Didn't that strike you as odd?

C: That, naturally, is a problem about which we have always felt very strongly, though rather less strongly than we did before we had all these new ICBMs. But bases are, nevertheless, a very vital and acute question. Only, *what Khrushchev wants to do first is to get the machinery of negotiations going.* The elimination of the American bases is one of his main objectives; but it was no use, at this stage, getting all hot and bothered about them. In fact, I put this question to one of the people closest to Khrushchev: his line was that bases were going to form part of any serious Soviet-American discussions that would arise from the Camp David meeting; that we would certainly raise the question in a big way at the Summit Conference. As long as relations between America and the Soviet Union go on improving, bases will not, in the present circumstances, and considering what we've got by way of missiles, constitute an immediate threat to peace (at least we hope not—unless somebody goes completely crazy). But if there were suddenly to be a serious deterioration in American-Soviet relations, then the bases would get top priority treatment from us. Meantime we are trying to get everything settled *po-khoroshemu,* in a friendly spirit, and the scrapping of bases is part of both the disarmament plan and of the general "reduction of international tension," to use the usual phrase. I know the Americans are clinging like mad to their bases, but *if* we make any progress in our present policy, if there develops a real spirit of confidence and cooperation, the bases will surely become an anachronism.

I: Do you really and quite seriously believe in such great *confidence* ever developing between the capitalist world and the socialist world?

C: You are talking a bit like some of our Chinese friends. No, Khrushchev is not a hundred per cent certain that such confidence (which is putting it rather strongly) will develop; but he thinks that he *must* give this policy a chance. If it fails, it'll just be too bad.

I: Are you not kidding yourselves a bit about the Americans wanting to be such friends with the Soviet Union? The Khrushchev journey to America is being treated here as a world-shaking event; and it is *not* being treated as such in America.

C: Isn't it? It got a pretty tremendous press and radio and TV coverage, all the same. Plenty of malicious stuff in the press—but still, on balance, it was pretty good.

I: The coverage was bound to be good; it was first-class copy. But that's another matter. Now, I don't want to sound catty; but aren't you tending a bit, in the Soviet press, to build the whole thing up as an immense *personal* triumph for Khrushchev's own, very personal policy?

A: You're talking nonsense. Khrushchev's policy is *the* policy of the Soviet Government and of the Party. Only I tell you, it isn't a set and final policy. If the Americans don't play ball, Khrushchev will, with the Party's approval, produce an alternative policy; but we are convinced that *this* policy is the right one, and the most popular one with the Soviet people. And it *has* made Khrushchev popular. *We* don't want a return to the Cold War policy and, until further notice, we are satisfied that the Americans don't want it either.

I: How did you like the American newspapermen?

A: Some brilliant people among them—Lippmann, Reston, for instance—but, on the whole, a pretty rotten, disagreeable lot. They have, of course, been fed for years on the Cold War, and seeing "Mr. K" amongst them made a lot of them suffer almost physically. And they have a sort of impertinent, backslapping way which we don't like; familiarity is all very well, but they tend to treat somebody who is, after all, the head of the Soviet Government as though he were any Tom, Dick and Harry. Nikita, I must say, took it fairly well, but he sometimes had a bit of a job controlling his temper. When Eisenhower comes to Moscow, he'll be treated by our people with far greater regard and respect.

I: Khrushchev certainly got pretty mad when Bill Lawrence asked that question about the "secret report" on Stalin.

A: Bill Lawrence; well, he was in Russia during the war. He's just pathological about Russia. He hated our guts even at the time of Stalingrad.

I: Never mind about Bill Lawrence; I remember him during the war here in Moscow; I don't think he is the monster you make him out to be; he's just a rather common American type; there must be millions like him.

C: Well, no; there *are* still Americans like Bill Lawrence —and we met quite a few; but they're becoming anachronistic. Or am I wrong?

I: I am not so sure. There's an awfully strong anti-Soviet phobia in America still; I was there at the time of the Sputniks; they respect Russia much more than they did; they even have a sneaking admiration for Soviet achievements; but the distrust, the resentment, the fear are all there. . . . But let's talk about more pleasant things. You said Khrushchev was impressed by the American standard of living.

A: Yes—he was, and he wasn't. He liked the consumer goods; he liked the supermarkets and all that; but he thought the economy was run on absurd lines, all the same, with its incredible waste. And one thing he said he was not going to copy from America was its automobile industry; it struck him as economic nonsense.

I: How did the American Exhibition at Sokolniki go off here? Weren't people impressed?

D: I had to report on it. People were impressed, and yet not as much as one might have expected. A few, of course, were quite starry-eyed. But most of them thought it was too much like a department store, a sort of super-GUM, with a lot of very nice goods, rather better than ours; but, so what? We'd catch up with them in a few years where *that* sort of thing was concerned. *They* hadn't had a war the way we had; so what the hell? All the same, our young people went pretty crazy about their cars. You heard the funny story they told about it? A young man got so rapturous about a Cadillac that he asked an American guide how he could possibly get such a car. "You've got to show that you Russians are really tougher than we Americans." "What do I have to do?" "First you've got to drink a whole bottle of scotch in one draught; then you enter a lioness's cage, and shake her by the paw; then you've got to have sexual intercourse with an old Eskimo woman." So he drinks off the bottle of whisky without turning a hair; he gets into the lioness's cage; after forty minutes he comes out, looking badly bruised, scratched and tattered, and says: "Now, where's that Eskimo woman whose paw I've got to shake?" (*Laughter.*)

It's a very famous Moscow story.

I: The joke of it is that it isn't a Moscow story; it's a hoary old Texan story I heard in the States. It was about a Texan who challenged an Alaskan—or it may have been the other way round, I forget. And it wasn't a lioness, but a she-bear. But the Texan (or Alaskan) made the same mistake.

A (*laughs*): Anyway, it shows that American-Soviet cultural exchanges are in full swing. . . .

D: Where the American Exhibition went wrong was this: Our people are very industry-minded, and they expected to see real wonders of engineering, and something suggesting that America was really a tremendous industrial country; well, the Exhibition didn't dwell nearly enough on that side of things, and stressed far too much the consumer goods side, the "good living" side; people were *not* convinced that everybody in America was living quite as well as this Exhibition made out. The Poles recently had a much smaller exhibition in Moscow, but, in a way, it made a better (if not bigger) impression; the shipbuilding section—there was nothing like it at the American show—was really impressive; also the consumer goods were attractive, and the modern art (though our more orthodox critics fumed about it) interested people a lot. In the same way, people were impressed by the Czechoslovak glassware exhibition; impressed —yes, but again not overwhelmed; you don't overwhelm anybody in Russia with consumer goods, no matter how nice they are. Our people have a pretty good sense of proportion, you know. . . .

(b) CHINA

I: Is it true that when Khrushchev was in Peking after his American trip, he was given a fairly cool reception, and that, in the great Peking parade celebrating the tenth anniversary of the Chinese Peoples' Republic there were pictures of Mao Tse-Tung, Lenin, even a few of Stalin, but none of Khrushchev?

D: That's a story they had in the capitalist press. I don't think it's true.

I: Is it true, or isn't it?

D: I really don't know; but we probably would have heard about it if it were true. Khrushchev seems to have got on extremely well in Peking; and you also saw, no doubt, the big speech Suslov made at Peking before Khrushchev arrived. He dwelt, you'll remember, on the tremendous impact the immense resources and prestige of the Socialist camp were making on a very large number of countries in Asia and Africa; he also dwelt on the rapid decay of colonialism; also, he was fairly reserved in what he said about the Khrushchev-Eisenhower meeting, and Khrushchev's visit to America generally. He said it would, he *hoped*, help to prevent war, which was far too destructive in present conditions, but added that the end of the Cold War had not yet been achieved, and that in countries of "monopolist capitalism," especially the USA and Western Germany, there were still plenty of warmongers, and that *the world situation continued to be dangerous*. When Khrushchev arrived in Peking, he said, broadly, the same thing, with perhaps a little more emphasis on the value of his talks with Eisenhower.

I: Are you then suggesting that Khrushchev and Suslov have different views on China and the world situation?

D: That's an over simple "Western" interpretation; Suslov was speaking chiefly as a theorist of Marxism-Leninism, Khrushchev as a politician who was right in the thick of international negotiations. I know the Western argument about Suslov being a "Stalinite." In fact, there was nothing in what Suslov said to which Khrushchev wouldn't have subscribed.

I: All right, let's then agree that there was just a slight difference in emphasis.

D: You must, of course, realize (and I don't deny it) that it obviously annoys the Chinese, with 650 million people, to be kept out in the cold; they recognize the leadership of the Soviet Union; but, all the same, they feel all the time that the "Big Four" add up to 470 million people while they *alone* represent 650 million; so when they hear us glibly talking about the Summit of the Big Four, they don't feel too happy about it. To China, America is *the* enemy, who grabbed Formosa, intervened in Korea, split Korea and Vietnam in two, is keeping Japan in a state of subservience, has set up the essentially aggressive and anti-Chinese

SEATO alliance They feel the American "Pacific Front" much more strongly than we do. The Chinese do tend, of course, to interpret Lenin a little too literally—especially what he said about the inevitable aggressivity of capitalist imperialism. Some of their papers, recalling the Yalu and the threat to drop A-bombs on Manchuria, openly say that America will never cease to be aggressive as long as the imperialists are in command, and that it is just as well for the Socialist camp to prepare for a "just war" to smash the "unjust war" the Americans are preparing. There were certain things Khrushchev said at the Twenty-first Congress which the Chinese didn't like—for instance, that "a world war could be excluded from the life of human societies even while capitalism continued to dominate part of the world." Their answer to this was that "the Leninist theses on the warlike nature of imperialism were *not* out of date."

I: Somebody told me the other day that Sundström, the Finnish Ambassador in Moscow, had a talk with Chou En-Lai in Peking recently, and that Chou said to him: "I know you people in the West are scared stiff of a world war, and think it'll mean the end of the human race; we in China are so numerous that we think there'll be quite enough of us to survive and so witness the complete triumph of Socialism in the world."

D: Probably another Western fabrication, although he may, of course, have said something to *suggest* this pretty absurd idea. What the Chinese do say, though, is that the imperialist-capitalist system will not collapse of its own accord, and that it will be overthrown by proletarian and nationalist revolutions in the countries still under its tutelage. Of course, you will find some Chinese "theorists" saying that we Russians are becoming bourgeois, lacking in dynamic vigor, and sitting on our fat asses, waiting for even greater prosperity to come to us. One Chinese diplomat bitterly remarked at the time of Khrushchev's visit to the USA: *"The rich getting together."* The Chinese also say we are not sufficiently interested in the process of decolonization going on in the world.

I: It is rather striking, I must say, the extreme reticence with which the Soviet Union has been handling a case like Algeria, and the great sympathy—and more than sympathy —shown in Peking for the FLN.

D: That's rather a special case; here we are simply anxious not to discourage de Gaulle against assuming a more independent attitude towards NATO and America. But the Chinese do feel that the colonial and other underdeveloped countries are their natural allies, and that two-thirds of humanity is therefore on their side. Maybe they're overoptimistic in their estimate. We also think they are our allies, but we are not so blatant about it. We believe in coexistence with the capitalist world and in competition with it in the "underdeveloped countries." The Chinese tend to take a slightly different view: they know perfectly well that what help we give to Nasser, and Kassem of Iraq, or Nehru is given on a basis very different from that on which "underdeveloped countries" receive help from the West; but they still think that our trying to be rich uncles, too, to these countries (though perhaps more benevolent and more disinterested uncles than the capitalists) is playing a mug's game.

I: What do you mean by "disinterested?" There's no charity in international affairs, as you know.

D: I mean *financially* disinterested. Our loans and gifts to these countries bring practically no financial returns, but they *do* bring certain political returns. Our help encourages these countries to be more or less "positively neutral." It's something if we help them to resist being bullied into SEATO or CENTO. In short, we are content to encourage "neutralist" and "uncommitted" countries in the world. There are lots of things about these countries we don't like: why, for instance, should Nasser, who is supposed to be a friend of ours, persecute and murder the Communists in Egypt? But it's important for us that Egypt should not be "bought up" by the West, and never mind about her Communists. The Chinese don't agree with this. India is another case. We want India to be neutral. We have no grandiose illusions about the steel plants and other things we set up in India making an enormous difference to the mass of Indians, who continue to be exploited by their capitalists and the British investors in Tea and what-have-you. And the Indian masses are starving in the midst of their capitalists and their sacred cows. We think that, by peaceful competition, we shall gradually win over India; it'll gradually go Socialist; but it's no use forcing the pace, if we want to avoid a major showdown with the West. The Chinese take, of course, a different line: in 1949 they started from scratch; 10 years later, 500 million Chinese peasants were integrated in the rural communes; now there are also the "urban communes;" gigantic areas—about 20 million hectares—were irrigated; 600,000 engineers and technicians are trained every year now in China as against the 40,000 Chinese students whom *we* trained over the last few years; 100 million children go to school; hell—it's the most gigantic going concern in the world. Somebody calculated that, in these last 10 years, mostly by pick-and-shovel methods, the Chinese dug the equivalent of 500 Panama Canals! And, of course, every Chinese compares *this* with India, which is still not very different from what it was under the British Raj. So the Chinese think that giving a little technical aid to India, which we are doing, is not good enough; we ought to encourage the revolutionary forces in India. *We* think this is all pretty mad. We are not so sure that there *are* any serious revolutionary forces in India; and even if there were, would we want them to overthrow Nehru—who suits us perfectly well?

I: And after Nehru?

D: Well, we'll think of that when the time comes.

I: You think, all the same, the Chinese were right about Tibet?

D: That—yes. But when they start nibbling at Indian territory, then, as Khrushchev said the other day, "it's *dosadno* —regrettable, deplorable. . . ."

I: What you say suggests some rather fundamental differences between Russia and China.

D: No, the differences are tactical, rather than strategic, and ideological, rather than political. We think that their (hitherto mainly theoretical) tactics—I'm not counting the bombing of Quemoy, which *we* made them stop—are wrong, and, above all, dangerous. The Chinese are full of youthful revolutionary enthusiasm—and small wonder, considering what they've achieved in the last 10 years. But we believe Asia, Africa, even Latin America are moving in the right direction, but that it would be wrong to intervene too actively and possibly bring on a Third World War.

I: You say China is still dependent on you economically.

But will she still be dependent on you in 10 years from now, at the rate she's developing?

D: We don't mind how soon China becomes completely independent economically; the sooner the better. We've our ever-expanding home market, and there'll be plenty of other markets for us; meantime, China can afford to thumb her nose at Japan by closing the Chinese market to the Japs; let them stew in their own juice under American domination! As Suslov said in Peking, China is no longer flooded with goods marked "Made in the USA" and "Made in Japan." The Japanese are feeling the pinch. . . .

I: Aren't you worried about becoming a back-number in Asia and other underdeveloped countries if the Chinese start flooding these countries with their own technicians and engineers?

D: Hell, the underdeveloped countries are such a vast problem that there'll be plenty of room for everybody. . . .

I: But Chinese demographic pressure. . . .

D: There you go again! I know, the American correspondents here are looking all the time for "signs of tension" between Russia and China; one of your colleagues the other day hooted with joy when he saw an article somewhere in the Soviet press about Tuva and the fact that Tuva had—God knows when—been "under the heel of Mongol conquerors." "Ha, ha," he said, "the Ruskies are afraid the Chinese will grab Tuva again." No; we are not worrying about Chinese "demographic pressure." With their present rate of agricultural development and industrialization, there'll be plenty of room in China for 1,000 million people.

I: But when there are 1,500 million?

D: By that time new ways of producing food will have been discovered. I know you want to ask me whether the Chinese won't overflow into Siberia and Kazakhstan—the favorite hobbyhorse of all Western commentators. We don't have to worry about that—unless we start thinking in terms of science fiction. In that case, there may be nothing but Chinese in Australia and America. . . .

I: It seems a long way from China to Africa, or from China to Latin America; and yet the Chinese seem terribly interested in both these parts of the world.

D: Decolonization is in full swing everywhere, and it's going *crescendo.* We are really living in an amazing world, when you come to think of it. In Moscow, the other day, we had a state visit from Sekou Touré, the President of Guinea. Fifteen years ago, to you people in the West, a man like Sekou Touré was little more than an ape.

I: It's not quite true. Sekou Touré received a French education.

D: Well, perhaps not Sekou Touré personally, but most of his countrymen. Or else take the Latin-American students who threw stones at Nixon, Vice-President of the United States. Or Fidel Castro—what a fellow! And whom do the Americans back, I ask you—Batista, Syngman Rhee, Chiang Kai Shek, General Franco, that fellow in South-Vietnam— Diem, or whatever he's called.

I: But what are you going to do when the various pots start boiling over in Africa, Asia, Latin America?

D: We don't have to do anything; they'll just boil over— without any "hand of Moscow" taking part in it. We are not encouraging anti-Western revolts. That's part of the un-written bargain with the West. But they'll happen all the same. . . . And if the West starts crushing such national-liberation movements, then—*if it's not too dangerous*—we'll back such movements.

I: But to get back to China. Some time ago, a Chinese leader—Chen Yi, I believe—said that China wasn't afraid of war; the surviving 300 million Chinese could dominate the world.

D (laughing): Well, China is a big country, and some Chinese like to talk big. These things needn't be taken literally. But the Chinese have, of course, been treated like lepers by America over the last 10 years, and they are feeling as sore as hell. They'd like to kick back, not only verbally but say, by liberating Formosa. We are trying to restrain them. We are convinced that the time will come—and per-haps it won't take very long—when America will *have* to recognize China—and clear out of Formosa—to China, a "ninteenth century" humiliation.

I: And out of Japan?

D: Yes, out of Japan, too; the Japs themselves will take care of that. It's inevitable. The Japs are in a growing eco-nomic mess. And the Japs—and the whole of Asia—remember Hiroshima. *We* never dropped atom bombs on "Asiatics," and we don't strike those insufferable American and British airs of racial superiority when *we* go to Asia. We *are* partly an Asian Power ourselves.

I: You saw, all the same, what de Gaulle said the other day about the Russians having to gang up with the rest of the "white race" against the "yellow multitudes of China."

D: De Gaulle is ridiculous. The way he talks one would think that France was still the *pup zemli*—the Navel of the Earth. At the same time, we have a soft spot for France, and even for de Gaulle—so much so that, in reporting his speeches and press conferences, we leave out his more inept utterances (like the one about China) which would just make people here laugh.

I: And what do you make of England?

D: The English are very good at looking after their own interests. They managed never to get themselves into the jams the French got themselves into—in Indo-China, in Algeria. They have the cleverest of all the capitalists; these have even won over the British working class. And Macmillan is quite somebody! He also knew how much it mattered to his own career to come to terms with us—and look at the election results!

I: You certainly seem to prefer the Tories to Labor, don't you?

D: Yes, we prefer the honest Conservative whores to the ugly old Labor spinsters with their insufferable humbug. We had both Gaitskell and Bevan here recently: didn't like either of them. Gaitskell was patronizing, if you please, and Bevan silly and facetious. Thought himself *awfully* witty.

I: In fact, you think that the capitalist world has still a good deal of life in it, judging from America and England and Western Europe generally.

D: Oh, yes; plenty of life as long as it lasts. We are in no hurry. We are for coexistence and competition. We had to be on the defensive while our modern weapons were inferior to yours; now we can talk as equals.

I: The Chinese, I take it, aren't much taken by "coexistence"—on which they are not even consulted. Are they content with being on the defensive, as you say?

D: Yes—though they are, you will admit, under constant provocation. We are doing our best to keep them quiet.

An awful lot depends on whether Khrushchev can convince them, in the long run, that his "Western" policy is producing results. If there's enough American goodwill—as we hope there is—well and good; if not—

I: Then you'll "go Chinese?"

D: We'll try not to. . . .

I: What do you mean by "goodwill?"

D: Disarmament; Berlin; Germany; recognition of China.

I: I must say that there's something rather tortuous and confusing in the long history of Soviet-Chinese relations. Doesn't some of the trouble go a long way back—to Russian "neutralism" or "isolationism" *vis-à-vis* China after Chiang Kai Shek had licked the Communists in 1927; Stalin's subsequent recognition of the Japanese puppet state of Manchukuo; Stalin's wartime "alliance" with Chiang Kai Shek; the lack of support given by Stalin to the Chinese Communists even after the end of World War II?

D: There's something in what you say; but I think Mao is realistic enough to realize that Stalin didn't have much choice. In 1927 it was "Socialism in one Country"; we just hadn't the strength to carry out collectivization and the first five-year plan inside Russia and, at the same time, foster the Chinese Revolution: that would have been pure Trotskyism. During the war we had, as you know, to be damn careful not to provoke Japan. We had more than enough on our hands without *that.* Perhaps Stalin was over-cautious in 1945 advising Mao to come to some kind of agreement with Chiang Kai Shek; but you must remember that conditions were still extremely difficult; the Americans had a monopoly in atom bombs, and we had to be careful not to get involved in China; but we *did* underrate the Chinese Communists' strength. Of course when, even without our help, the Chinese Communists won in 1949, no one was more delighted than we—and Stalin himself in the first place.

I: Wasn't there some concern in Russia, all the same, that Peking might become a great ideological rival of Moscow? I remember how poor old Anna Louise Strong—who'd been starry-eyed about the Soviet Union for about a hundred years!—was ignominiously kicked out of Russia for having written that the peoples of Asia were now going to look to Peking for guidance, rather than to Moscow.

D: Silly old woman! The Chinese themselves hastened to recognize our leading position in the Socialist camp. For one thing, they needed us desperately in purely economic terms. And Anna Louise Strong was trying to prove to the world that Peking was an ally, not of Moscow, but of Belgrade! The Chinese knew better than anyone that this made no sense. And the Korean war showed what kind of "Titoites" *they* were! Since then, there's never been any question of anyone other than the Soviet Union being "the leader of the Socialist camp"; the Chinese explicitly subscribed to this formula at the Communist Parties' meeting in Moscow in 1957.

I: Was it as simple as all that? Hadn't the Chinese gone much further with their "liberalism" than you did, when they proclaimed the "Hundred Flowers" slogan, or when they seemed, at least for a time, to support Gomulka and Nagy *against you?*

D: That's true; but after Budapest they realized that "liberalism" could be dangerous; and since then they've been much more violent in denouncing "revisionism" and Titoism than we have been.

I: With their Peoples' Communes they even claim to be better Communists than you are, don't they?

D: That's a lot of nonsense, as they soon realized; for it didn't take long before they restored family life in the communes; of course, there have been moments when they were, as old man Stalin once said, "giddy with success." At the Twenty-first Congress Khrushchev made it quite clear you couldn't "skip the Socialist stage"—which is what some of the Chinese were trying to do. And let's face it: economically, the Chinese *need* us; we have, in the last few years, lent them about 2 billion dollars, have helped to set up hundreds of major industrial enterprises in China; without our help, there just couldn't be any proper Chinese industrialization. Of course, they don't like being dependent on us; they are having a hard time, with their austerity campaigns and all that. Also, internationally, they feel isolated and threatened, while we have diplomatic relations with practically everybody, except Franco Spain and the Vatican. To them, America is *the* enemy, while we make a big song and dance of Khrushchev's visit to the USA.

I: I suppose you aren't giving the Chinese A-bombs, let alone H-bombs.

D: Probably not; why tempt providence?

I: But isn't the time approaching when they'll be able to make them themselves?

D: Well, making H-bombs, as the French, for instance, know, isn't all that simple. No doubt the Chinese *know* how to make them; but it'll take years before they are industrially equipped to make them. But, of course, it will be a dangerous moment when China has the H-bomb—dangerous, I mean, for America, above all for America; that's why it's so essential for everybody that the USA establishes normal relations with China long *before* that, and gets the hell out of Formosa. Because it *is* true that, especially since Korea, the Chinese would like to have a really big crack at America.

I: What—a real nuclear war?

D: No; I don't think they'd go that far; but they might go in for some dangerous "brinkmanship" to push the Americans out of Formosa, South Korea and South Vietnam; it would be better if the Americans voluntarily packed up before anything like that happened. . . .

I: You seem a little afraid of China dragging you into a world war, just as you are sitting pretty.

D: "Afraid"—no. Except that we are afraid of *all* lunatics, wherever they are. And there might even be some in China the day she has the H-bomb. But we *can* handle China; without our backing, China wouldn't embark on World War III.

I: Are you sure?

D: Yes, I'm sure, barring lunatics, of course; or unless we again start talking in terms of science fiction.

I: What, for instance? China and America destroying each other, and the Soviet Union remaining neutral?

D: Well, once you start on science fiction, there's no limit to anything. Only remember, on fundamentals, we and the Chinese are in agreement. We are at different phases of development; there's a Mao Tse-Tung "personality cult" in China, while there isn't a Khrushchev "personality cult" here; Mao is a writer and philosopher, a kind of "Chinese Lenin," while Khrushchev is an "ordinary chap"; we are comparatively rich, and the Chinese comparatively poor; we may have different tactics, and ideological differences in our interpretation of Lenin (that is, we quote one bit, and they quote another bit); but both Russians and Chinese realize that if they stick together, they'll win the battle for world Socialism without fail; if they drift apart, they'll only play into the hands of capitalism and imperialism. So all the wishful thinking in the West about our joining the "white race" against the "yellow peril" is utterly unrealistic.

I: Even when there are 1.5 billion Chinese. . . .

D (laughs): One-and-one-half-billion, 2 billion, 10 billion Chinese. The way you people sometimes talk in your hopeless pessimism, one would think that the twenty-first century wasn't going to be the century of the world Socialism, but the century of world cannibalism. . . . I daresay the Rockefellers would sooner be cannibals than Communists; but all the same, you seem to assume that the Chinese will *always* be hungry, and will *always* breed like rabbits. Surely, the example of the Soviet Union is eloquent enough: in 40 years we have become a rich country, with a reasonable birth-rate; what makes you think the Chinese won't be able to do the same?

(c) MIDDLE EAST, HUNGARY AND ALL THAT

The third conversation I shall now record dealt with a variety of subjects, including Germany; but what was said on Germany has in large measure already been dealt with. It is enough to say that the nervousness about Germany being built up as an "aggressive" and *revanchard* power which might well take the law into its own hands one day if it were armed with H-bombs and other nuclear weapons was very genuine. Adenauer was considered "extremely dangerous," the real spokesman of "Dullesism" now that Dulles was dead. Whether those who succeeded him would be better or *even* worse (i.e. actively aggressive) was, to the Russians, one of the mysteries of the future. On no account were they prepared to yield on the Oder-Neisse Frontier, which, among other things, helped to keep the Poles in order. The idea of an eventual Russo-German deal at the expense of the Poles—an idea current among Western diplomats some 10 years ago—was now dismissed as nonsense.

I: Broadly speaking, as I understand it, Khrushchev stands for the *status quo* in the world, which would give the Soviet Union time to finish off quietly her seven-year plan, vastly increase her industrial and economic power, and meantime have as few complications abroad as possible. To achieve this, some kind of agreement with the United States is absolutely essential. Is that right?

B: That's right, but with this qualification: he would like things like CENTO, SEATO and, of course, NATO to be at least watered down in terms of "aggressive power"; if local revolutions like the one in Iraq which smashed up the Bagdad Pact can help in this, then we're all in favor. But as far as *neutral* countries like India, Egypt, Iraq, Burma or Indonesia are concerned, we don't intend to encourage any kind of "anti-capitalist" movements—not that we had anything to do with the Iraq Revolution of July 1958; but it would, of course, be silly for us to deny that we welcomed it—just as we were very upset by the overthrow of Mossadegh in Iran—which was, clearly, a victory for the aggressive and reactionary and pro-Pentagon forces in that country. We are not trying to foist Communist régimes on any of these countries; but you may know that at the time of the Iraq-Jordan-Lebanon crisis in July 1958, Khrushchev made a very important proposal which, I believe, he communicated to Mendès-France, to be passed on to de Gaulle [1]—proposing to turn the whole Middle East into a neutral zone, without any foreign troops or bases in which the Soviet Union would undertake not to interfere with the West's oil interests, and in which all the present frontiers—*including the frontiers of Israel*—would be jointly guaranteed by the Big Four. All four would undertake not to intervene in these countries' internal affairs. Of course, it came to nothing, and the West preferred to set up its ridiculous CENTO, an *ersatz* Bagdad Pact.

I: You keep on saying that you don't want to interfere in the internal affairs of other countries. But what about Yugoslavia? Not to mention Hungary.

B: I knew you'd come to that sooner or later. I remember, back in 1949–50 you had a soft spot for Yugoslavia. We

[1] This is strictly correct, and was confirmed by Mendès-France to the author.

read your articles with some dismay; after all, you had been in the Soviet Union for many years, and we didn't think you would be taken in by Tito.

I: I wasn't taken in by Tito, as you say. I could see all the weaknesses of the Yugoslav case, all this cutting down of heavy industry, the amateurishness of many things the Yugoslavs were doing. In the end, you drove them into such a tight corner that they had no alternative to accepting help from the Americans. But you did write an awful lot of nonsense about the "Tito clique" having been for years in the pay of world capitalism.

B: Khrushchev rushed down in 1955 to apologize for all that. Molotov, I can tell you, was furious. Ideologically, Khrushchev has, of course, followed a very tortuous line; if he had limited his visit to Belgrade to apologizing for the more absurd charges made against the Yugoslav leaders, nobody would have objected (though it did make Suslov out to be rather an ass, when you consider that it was he who did all the blasting of the "Titoite clique" at the 1949 Cominform meeting); but Khrushchev went a lot further, suggesting that each country could choose its own Socialist way. But it was such an infernally confusing time; when the Chinese talked about the "Hundred Flowers," they also were guilty of the grossest kind of revisionism, when you come to think of it. Since then things have been, ideologically, in something of a muddle. The most violent attacks on Yugoslav revisionism have not come from Moscow, but from Peking.

I: Why, some of the Chinese seem to have been treating even Khrushchev as something of a "revisionist," saying that he's been "revising" Lenin!

B: Oh hell, everybody can be accused of revising Lenin. Stalin, too, was said to have revised Lenin. All this is a lot of quibbling. But when the Yugoslavs tell us that they have, with their phoney "workers' councils," discovered real Socialist democracy, and when, at the same time, they live on American charity, we just can't take them seriously. We are sorry it all happened that way, but the main thing at present is still that Yugoslavia should remain neutral. Some day—after Tito—the Yugoslavs will join the Socialist bloc. The fact remains, all the same, that they constituted for us an immense danger in 1948, at the height of the Cold War, when they were spreading their gospel in Czechoslovakia, and Hungary and Rumania and Poland; the whole Socialist bloc was in danger of cracking up. I daresay (and Khrushchev agrees about *that*) we went about it much too crudely; but the situation was desperately dangerous, and any method seemed good enough at the time for discrediting Titoism.

I: That was when I went to Czechoslovakia, and, coming as I did, from Belgrade, I was given a most unpleasant reception. And soon afterwards *Rude Pravo* went for me, calling me a "notorious British spy," and then Krushinsky, that idiot of a *Pravda* correspondent in Prague, also blew his top off calling me a snake-in-the-grass, and what have you. . . .

B: Yes, I remember. Here in Moscow, we didn't take these things too seriously; it was just part of the Cold War game. We knew you weren't a spy, but you did, at that time, defend Tito. We were also annoyed by your blast about what you called "Zhdanovisim."

I: Well, wasn't I right? The Central Committee itself now admits that the "Zhdanov Decree" on music was a bad mistake, saying it was drafted under the influence of the "personality cult."

B: All right, all right; well, you can now consider yourself rehabilitated.

I: I never received any apologies from anybody, the way Anna Louise Strong did, and Konni Zilliacus.

B: You didn't ask for any apologies, did you? Anyway, you got your visa—which amounts to the same thing. It's ancient history, so stop beefing. Lots of people here were in jail, and they don't talk about it. All right then, you're a victim of Beria. But don't you see that we were disconcerted about you. During the war, with your BBC commentaries, the *Sunday Times* and your books, you were in England (and well beyond England) one of the very biggest pro-Soviet opinion-formers; I know you weren't a Communist, but the innate warmth, sympathy and affection with which you spoke of the Soviet people during their hardest years were truly impressive—and very valuable. And then you went off the rails —over Tito, of all people, and over Zhdanov, losing all sense of proportion.

I: I felt you had been unjust to the Yugoslavs; as for Zhdanov, I think his attacks on Prokofiev and the rest were as ridiculous as anything in Saltykov-Shchedrin. And the Czechs who wanted to be more Stalinite than Stalin were a bit revolting.

B: Oh, the Czechs are good people; but they *are* Schweiks; they'll play ball with anybody for a quiet life.

I: No, the Czechs I saw in 1950 in Prague were not Schweiks, they were really vicious NKVD types; if the same people acted as Gestapo informers six or seven years before (and there were plenty of them in Czechoslovakia) I shouldn't be at all surprised. I met some NKVD people in Russia, none was as sinister as these Czech cops were.

B: Well, cops have now been put in their place everywhere, perhaps even in Czechoslovakia. And you mustn't judge people by their cops; cops are, by definition, nasty people. *We* don't like cops either; that's partly why we have the workers' "auxiliary militia" (the *druzhinniki*) and why we are having Comrade Courts; it's all rather less frightening. I don't mean the ordinary *militsioner*—he's usually just a silly ass, more afraid of a violent drunk than a drunk is afraid of him. . . .

I: But to get back to Yugoslavia. . . .

B: Yes, there's one very peculiar thing about the Yugoslavs. They are vindictive. When one of our crack football teams went to play in Yugoslavia, they were beaten; simply lost their nerve because of the really terrible hostility of the Yugoslav crowds; later, they went to Budapest, and the Hugarians were perfectly friendly. It seems to me that the whole unfortunate Hungarian business is now being forgiven and forgotten by everybody—except by Cold War propagandists, of course. It was a tragedy; and we felt it very keenly. The big mistake on our part (and Molotov was a great deal to blame for that) was to have kept Rakosi and Gerö in office for so long; that was really at the root of the trouble. But, of course, there was also plenty of provocation from the West— Radio Free Europe, Mindszenty, and all that. *Everybody* was to blame; but when Imre Nagy caved in to the reactionaries and said Hungary would get out of the Warsaw Pact, what could we do but intervene? We didn't send infantry, we sent tanks; and once they started attacking these tanks, what could we do but hit back? But bad mistakes were made on all sides.

I: But why was it impossible to let Hungary go neutral the way Austria did?

B: It *was* impossible; it would have meant that we had capitulated before an American-inspired rebellion, and that this "neutral" Hungary would have been run by Hungarian Fascists and Nazis from Radio Free Europe. Haven't you a little imagination? Of course, when I say that all is forgiven and forgotten, I don't mean this quite literally. There's still plenty of double-think among the Hungarian intellectuals, and the Catholic Church (as in Poland) is doing its little best to spread hate propaganda against us; but we *have* appeased the working class economically, and remember—in 1956 the Hungarian peasants did *not* budge. They had more plain horse-sense than the wilder people in Budapest. And Kadar is *not* hated the way Rakosi was.

I: Was it really necessary to bump off Imre Nagy?

B: Probably not. Anyway, the Hungarians did it, not we. *I* rather think it was a mistake. Do you think our propaganda on Hungary is too crude?

I: Yes, I do. Lots of things you just don't try to explain —for instance the fact that workers took part in the rebellion.

B: Well, workers aren't *ipso facto* immune against American-inspired chauvinist propaganda. But I daresay the whole case is not being well presented; nor do we properly explain Eastern Germany. Your people go on beefing about "Free Elections"; we've got plenty of good answers to that one; but either we are shamefaced about it, or perhaps just can't be bothered arguing. Why should we? In the end, Eastern Germany will become a genuinely Socialist country; meantime we are perhaps wiser to say nothing. And anyway, if *we* don't want "free elections" in Eastern Germany, *you* don't want them in Korea, Vietnam—or Algeria. So we are quits, if you like to look at it that way! Or, rather, better than quits. After all, the Gomulkas and Kadars we support *do* represent something, and we do not support any equivalent of Syngman Rhee. . . .

I: Ulbricht?

D: Ulbricht, for one thing, isn't quite what Western folklore has made him out to be; and, moreover, as you know, Germany *is* rather a special case. It'll take time to become properly Socialist. And, in any case, it's a matter of the most elementary security not to hand Eastern Germany over to Adenauer and his Nazi generals. You know perfectly well that all the saner people in the West want Germany to remain divided.

Chapter 21

"CULTURAL RELATIONS" AND
IDEOLOGICAL WAR

EVEN AT THE HEIGHT of the "international thaw" that accompanied and followed Khrushchev's visit to the USA the
official Soviet line on "cultural exchanges" continued to be
extremely cautious. Thus on November 7th 1959, David
Zaslavsky wrote in *Pravda*: *"The warmer the international
relations, the more acute the ideological battle.* There is no
contradiction here." He described Khrushchev's visit to
America as an "exceptionally important historic event"—and
not least because "certain reactionary ideologists of the
American bourgeoisie ventured to turn the exchange of
speeches into a dispute between Socialism and Capitalism."
And—"though showing great self-assurance, they suffered a
crushing ideological defeat". Whereupon Zaslavsky proceeded to make hay of Mr. Cabot Lodge who "set against N. S.
Khrushchev's scientific Marxist-Leninist understanding of the
historic process his latest stunt of bourgeois economic thought
—a thing called 'economic humanism.' " And he described
the steelworkers' strike as a battle between half-a-million
second-class "humanists" and a handful of first-class "humanists."

Rather more subtly, Professor Varga, the well-known Soviet economist, wrote in the same issue of *Pravda* that there
was not *one* world, but *two* worlds, and that there was no
getting away from it. Two billion people were still living in
the capitalist countries, but of these less than 500 million
were living in the "rich" industrial countries of North
America and Western Europe, and the rest in the "poor"
countries of Asia, Africa, South America and Southern
Europe. The "aid" to the underdeveloped countries was

ludicrous; the *per capita* production of steel in the USA was 1252.2 pounds. in 1957; in India, it was 19.8 pounds. True, in the "rich" countries, capitalism had won over a "working-class aristocracy"; but "the proletariat still remains the proletariat," and in the USA alone there were nearly 5 million unemployed in 1958. Ideologically, the capitalist world had gone "senile," and was incapable of rejuvenation. Under Socialism, on the other hand, etc. . . .

In the circumstances, "cultural exchanges" with the West had to be handled carefully.

An important statement on these was made by G. A. Zhukov, head of the State Committee for Cultural Relations with Foreign Nations.

No doubt, cultural exchanges could play an important part in reducing international tension (he wrote), "but on condition that, under cover of such exchanges, no alien or hostile ideas are smuggled into the country with which cultural relations have been established." Any "Trojan Horse" tactics should be thoroughly discouraged.[1]

After enumerating the various channels through which cultural exchanges were carried out between the Soviet Union and the Western countries—tourist agencies, British Council, the Cultural Committees attached to the foreign ministries in France and the USA, the special State Committees in the USSR and China, various Friendship Societies, etc.—Zhukov said that all these artistic, scientific, sports and other exchanges had made enormous progress in the last few years, and he "welcomed all those who were aiming at friendly cooperation and healthy competition."

Exchanges with the USA had been severely limited by the "Cold War" for a long time; but lately there had been a great improvement; and in 1958 alone 7,000 American tourists had visited the Soviet Union; the number of Russians, it is true, who had gone to the USA was much smaller, since no privileged ruble exchange rate had been allowed to Soviet visitors.[2]

[1] G. Zhukov in *Mezhdunarodnaya Zhizn,* November 1959.

[2] Here was, obviously, something of a quibble, since the "preferential" tourist rate of 10 rubles to the dollar was still favorable; to expect, as Zhukov did, Soviet tourists to buy dollars at four rubles seemed rather unreasonable.

Zhukov then dealt with the Soviet Exhibition in New York and the American Exhibition in Moscow, declaring that, according to one American critic, the Soviet exhibition was worth "a billion dollars to Soviet propaganda," while (in Zhukov's view) the American exhibition in Moscow, with its "miraculous kitchen," had been a flop. Soviet people had just not been taken in by it. "Both sides had equal possibilities; but if one exhibition was a great success and the other a flop, the reason for this must be deep and fundamental."

"However," he went on, "let's not dwell on this field of ideology, since there are, quite inevitably, irreconcilable contradictions between the Socialist and the capitalist world. Nevertheless, Soviet people are deeply convinced that these contradictions do not exclude the possibility or necessity of peaceful coexistence and economic competition. . . . It is in this spirit that the State Department and the Soviet Cultural Committee are now preparing an exchange program for 1960–1961." [3] This (said Zhukov) was the correct approach to cultural exchanges; but there was also another.

Thus, speaking before the Senate Foreign Affairs Committee, William Benton said it was "more important to get at the Russians than to hit the moon," while the Atlantic Congress, meeting in London in June 1959, stressed the importance of "personal contacts" with Soviet citizens, and of "influencing them." Various attempts were being made, Zhukov wrote, to "convert Soviet citizens to the capitalist faith." An American society called "Arms of Friendship" had worked out a whole system of training American visitors to the Soviet Union for establishing personal contacts with ordinary Russians—and whose addresses it was essential for them to collect. "We shall then find the right Americans to enter into correspondence with them." Instructions were also given to tourists about "giving little presents to Russians" in order to gain their confidence—a pretty naïve way, Zhukov thought, of converting Soviet citizens to capitalism.

And Zhukov quoted *The New York Times* of August 2, 1959, describing an "Information Center for Americans Visit-

---

[3] I attended the signing of this agreement in November 1959. It was an extensive enough agreement, though the Americans complained of the Russians notably rejecting the proposal for an American Reading Room in Moscow.

ing Russia" in East 46th Street—a "non-profit-making organization"—set up by "The Washington Institute for Government Affairs." This organization, Zhukov said, gave prospective tourists instructions similar to those given by the "Arms of Friendship" society. Their aims were clearly American and anti-Soviet propaganda and espionage.

Recalling the snappy remarks made by Khrushchev *à propos* of the cancan he was shown at Hollywood, Zhukov said that this kind of "artistic freedom" just didn't suit the Soviet Union, which had no desire to corrupt the young. Nor was there any excuse for providing pornography for older people.

"We are," wrote Zhukov, "all in favor of the broadest cultural exchanges, including the exchange of truthful information. But we shall oppose any attempt to use such exchanges for carrying out the propaganda of certain rotten conceptions of bourgeois morality which must be alien not only to every Communist, but to every sane human being. . . . We shall not throw our frontiers open to decayed goods and all kinds of filth calculated for the most depraved and degenerate tastes."

In short, no Trojan Horses—and the gentlemen on NATO had better understand this clearly.

At the meeting of the Supreme Soviet on October 31, the same Zhukov went over much the same ground, stressing once again that the Soviet Union would not buy "rotten goods" in the West, and would not allow them to be imported. In short, it was fine for Stokowski and Van Cliburn and Leonard Bernstein and Isaac Stern to come to Moscow, and for Oistrakh and Gillels to go to New York,[1] but cancan films—no.

The obvious criticism of this line among Western residents —and also some Russians—was, of course, that the "rotten goods" not admitted to the Soviet Union included not only cancan films, but also *all* Western newspapers, except Communist papers like the *Daily Worker* and *L'Humanité.*

When I asked Zhukov himself about it—I had known him

---

[1] Amusing crack by Gillels, the pianist, when asked what he thought of American Soviet cultural exchanges. "We send them *our* Jews, and they send us *their* Jews."

well when he was *Pravda* correspondent in Paris—the line he took was that although "much of the stuff" in many English and American papers was harmless, an awful lot of articles on the Soviet Union was written by "pathological types"— mostly refugees from Poland or Hungary; and these "Soviet experts" just stood on their heads most of the time when they wrote about Russia.

Chapter 22

THE LITERARY SCENE

(*a*) LUNCH WITH A SOCIALIST-REALIST BEST-SELLER

I WAS DELIGHTED to see Boris Polevoi again when he asked me to lunch one day in the sumptuous new building of the Writers' Club in Herzen Street. He is a Communist, a highly successful Socialist-Realist writer, and must be one of the happiest men in the world. A native of Tver (he still calls it Tver, rather than Kalinin), he has one of those good open Russian faces, with laughing eyes, and is partly of peasant, partly of working-class origin.

I had first met him in the spring of 1944 during the week we spent together at Uman, in the Ukraine, just after the encirclement and spectacular annihilation of some 40,000 Germans who had clung to their Korsun-Shevchenkovo salient on the right bank of the Dnieper. He was then wearing a very, very grubby captain's uniform and muddy top-boots. After the annihilation of the Korsun group, the rest of the German troops in Central Ukraine hastily fled across the Bug, and from there all the way to Rumania, abandoning in the deep spring mud all their heavy equipment—hundreds of tanks, thousands of trucks and guns. They had never expected Konev to hit out at them in such incredible terrain conditions. Since neither the Russians nor the Germans could move heavy equipment through the deep mud, it was a case of Russian infantry chasing German infantry. The German prisoners we saw then were pretty well demoralized, though one or two SS-men we saw still claimed that Hitler would produce a "secret weapon" one of these days, and this

234

would change everything. A fellow from the Rhineland was full of stories of the "terror-bombers," and of the appalling conditions in which his family were now living and working; he had been impressed by the V-1s and V-2s over London, but wasn't sure that the *Vergeltung* was advancing sufficiently rapidly to enable Germany still to win the war.

The small town of Uman was a fantastic place, with local bearded partisans patrolling the street, still littered with abandoned German tanks and a few German bodies. We talked to two girls who had escaped from the deportation to Germany (one had secured her repatriation by having four of her fingers cut off by a machine), to local partisans, to an *archierei,* an Orthodox bishop who described, with a touch of Dostoevskian buffoonery, how he had collaborated "just a teeny-weeny bit" with the Germans at first, but how he was later locked up for not wanting to pray for the victory of the German Army. And it was the happiest day of his life when "the dear, dear boys of the Red Army" entered the town and he now revered Stalin, but he was—ooh!—so terribly afraid of that great and holy man, the Patriarch of Moscow, for he was such a terribly, terribly strict disciplinarian! Nearly all the young people of Uman had been deported to Germany, and all the Jews in the town had been exterminated.

Polevoi was a real *frontovik,* having spent practically the whole war at the Front. His left eye was half-closed, a result of shell shock at Stalingrad. He was a marvelous *raconteur,* and his conversation lacked that slight stodginess that marked even his best books, such as *The Story of a Real Man,* the story of the Soviet airman who had lost both legs, but still carried on with artificial limbs. This book alone had sold 6 million copies. Shortly before seeing him now I had read his two recent books, his long wartime novel, *In the Deep Rear,* and his *American Journal,* written after a visit to the United States in 1955. Now he had accompanied Khrushchev to the USA, and took a rather more charitable view of the Americans, though, at heart, I thought he still had a good many doubts about them.

Small, dark, stocky, Polevoi at 52 didn't look much more than 40. "You've had a pretty good life, Boris Nikolaevich," I said. "Yes," he said, "it was hard going during the war, as you will remember, but how things have changed since then! Look at us now! You remember our week at Uman; well, I

promise you a spectacle of another order next time you come
to Moscow. We'll go to Siberia; we'll go to the Angara; it's
the most marvelous country in the world. I spent several
weeks there recently. Forty or 50 miles on either side of the
Angara there are villages; but I flew in a helicopter about 100
miles inland from the river across the *taiga*. At the edge of
the forest we saw a bonfire, and we landed on a patch of
open ground; here we found a group of prospectors—young
boys and girls; pretty hefty girls, too. One of them was sitting there with a double-barreled gun between her legs.
'What's that for?' I said. 'It's to drive off the bears,' she
said, 'they often raid our stores, and they've learned the trick
of opening big tins with a sharp blow of their claws and then
eating up the contents.' In these remote parts of Siberia there
are now thousands of hunters, trappers, prospectors of every
kind, coming from near and far. They get big money for the
gold they find. A new pioneering spirit is in full swing in
Russia now; it's the biggest pioneering movement the world
has seen since the great migration from East to West in America. Our task as writers is to encourage this pioneering spirit.
Siberia is developing along two different, but closely allied
lines; on the one hand, there's vast-scale industrialization,
with gigantic hydro-electric stations like Bratsk as its foundation. The mineral wealth in East and Northeast Siberia is
something quite fantastic—diamonds galore—perhaps as
much as in South Africa (from which we now don't have to
import industrial diamonds any more)—bauxite, gold, urani-
um and God knows what else. There's quite a gold and diamond rush there at present; I shouldn't be surprised if thousands of young Americans wanted to join in this rush! Lots
of young people go out there—some are attracted by the good
pay and the good housing conditions in the new industrial
cities; some also like to get away from our stuffier bureaucrats; others still go out there in a spirit of adventure; for
much of the interior is still wholly unexplored. The winters
are tough, but it isn't a horrible country, as some still imagine. It's the most beautiful country in the world; in summer
the vegetation is fantastically beautiful, with millions of wild
orchids, known as cuckoo slippers, and other flowers the like
of which you haven't seen anywhere.

"This mass movement towards the East is the most significant development of recent years, and the great ro-

mance of Siberia is what I am doing my best to put across. The 'unpleasant' side of Siberia—I mean the NKVD camps —is now a thing of the past. Of course, some of our young people prefer soft jobs in Moscow or Leningrad; but more and more are being attracted by the immense possibilities of Siberia. It's really enough to look at the map to want to go out to the Far North—the Siberian Arctic, Kamchatka, the unexplored territories of the Far Northeast. By jet plane you get there in a few hours. . . .

"Things have changed a lot since you were here last," said Polevoi. "The Khrushchev Report on Stalin was, in my view, regrettable; but there was perhaps no other way of making a fresh start. The old man—and he *was* a great man, as anyone knows who was here during the war—became very strange towards the end; I tell you, there was an element of Shakespearean tragedy about it all. His vanity had become a kind of mania. Take those 'war films' that were made after the war—*Stalingrad*, and *The Third Blow*, and *The Fall of Berlin* with omniscient Stalin winning every big battle and making his generals out to be a lot of nitwits. All of us who had fought in the war would squirm at the sight of these films. Moreover, they were so terribly different from the magnificent documentaries made *during* the war."

"You were a great Stalinite in your day, Boris Nikolaevich."

"Yes, I was, and we all were, and it couldn't have been otherwise. But his decline was tragic."

"And Khrushchev?"

"He's a good man, and very, very human. He has a good deal of self-taught culture, even some literary culture, despite his rough exterior. But he doesn't interfere much with writers. He said he was a *lakirovschchik*, a 'varnisher' himself. And why not? Dudintsev, Pasternak—that's all very well, and we know how in the West they went all soppy over them. Pasternak is a man of immense talent; but he's a foreign body in our midst. We are happy people; we are optimistic people; and why shouldn't we be? Look what we've done! In the war—and since the war! The war—you've read my *In the Deep Rear*; well it *was* like that. Our working class was full of heroism. They worked on more or less empty stomachs right through the war, making sacrifices no other people in the world—except perhaps the Chinese—

would have been capable of, and every family losing somebody at the front—sometimes three, four, five sons. Pasternak
vaguely felt the tragedy of it all; but actually it was all rather
remote to him, as he sat there brooding about his 'eternal
values' at his Peredelkino *datcha*. Through a sort of intuition
he wrote half-a-dozen truly admirable war poems, but he
was really outside it all. I suppose he can't help it; but,
let's face it, he is out of sympathy with our whole new
civilization. Of course, the way he was ill-treated by some
people was pretty bad; but the Nobel prize *was* a deliberate
political provocation. *Zhivago* is, in many ways, a very fine
book, but the Nobel Committee wouldn't have made such a
fuss over it if it weren't so alien to all that we stand for. All
right, Pasternak loves Russia, but it's not *our* Russia that he
loves. And his Dr. Zhivago is a rather unattractive character
when you come to think of it; yes, a lofty spiritual life, a
kind of yogi attitude, but mixed up with an awful lot of
rather dreary fornication. . . . That's about the only *action*
he seems capable of. Jars on us a bit. I admit he was treated
roughly—but that's only the fault of the Nobel people. It's
their fault he was expelled from the Writers' Union. Even in
the harshest Stalin days Pasternak was left in peace. It's the
same now, after last year's little storm. Besides, Pasternak
loves being a bit of a martyr, and his vanity has been terribly flattered by all the fuss they've made about him abroad.
. . . However, you probably will never quite understand our
point of view."

Polevoi then talked about other things in his old exuberant
way. I asked what he thought of America.

"America—well, there are lots of nice people there, but an
awful lot of idiots, too, and quite a good number of *svolochi,*
what they call *sonavabitches,* is that it? But I am all in favor
of these new 'cultural exchanges'—let them come and have a
look at what we are doing! But their Exhibition was a
flop. Just like an annex of Macy's. Well, okay, they've got all
these things. But they've had 170 years of continuous and
uninterrupted industrial progress and no wars on their territory. And our people are fully aware of that. . . ."

"And you believe in coexistence?"

"Well, what's the alternative? They won't dare attack us,
and we are not going to attack them. But we'll win this
competition in the end. We've got the 600 million Chinese

with us. And, my God, they are wonderful people! In Shanghai I interviewed that enormous city's Chief Gangster, who has now become a respectable citizen. There's a kind of spontaneous iron discipline in China which even we never knew —except during the worst days of the war. And their population problem isn't a major problem—when they had their birth-control drive, they explained it all over the place with the help of blackboards! I rather think that if the government decided there were to be no children for a whole year—well then, there just wouldn't be any! But this isn't necessary; they've still got immense untapped agricultural resources in the West—in Sinkiang and so on.

"But to get back to literature," I said, "what have been the changes in the last 10 years?"

"We've got a new generation of writers—some of them very, very gifted. I am not saying we have produced a Shakespeare or a Balzac or a Stendhal or a Tolstoy, still less a Dostoevsky. But there was a very sterile period in our literature—from about 1946 to 1953; and that's over now. We are getting away from stereotyped writing. There's variety now—plenty of it. I am all in favor of the 'Hundred Flowers' in literature though, personally——"

"You carry on in the good old Socialist-Realist tradition."

"I certainly do," Polevoi laughed. "And I believe in it. In our particular society, literature has got to be educative and inspiring. We've got to remind the young of the war. And we've got to develop new enthusiasms amongst them—enthusiasm for pioneering, for the Virgin Lands, and so on. Also, we can write quite freely about things which were taboo in the past. All the mess we were in at the beginning of the war—you remember; and about the misdeeds of the NKVD—about the fact" (he pointed to a table at the far end of the dining room) "that that big fellow over there—you know who he is? that's Kovpak, the great Ukrainian partisan chief—was in exile from 1937 to 1940. But this retrospective denunciation shouldn't be overdone. There are more important things to write about, I feel, than these *post-mortems*. Nor do we want to cultivate degenerate art. When I was abroad, I was taken to a Samuel Beckett play—pure *bred sobachi*—a dog's delirium. If that's what you call culture, you can keep it!"

"Have you ever read Kafka?"

"Who's he? Never heard of him . . . I am more interested in the Angara and diamond prospecting in Yakutia. . . ."

(b) OFFICIAL LINES

The work of a gifted writer like Boris Polevoi corresponds almost exactly to the general line laid down on literature by the Party and by Khrushchev himself. His book, *In the Deep Rear,* is not great or profound writing; one would look in it in vain for any very subtle psychology or other literary refinements, but it abounds in "positive" characters—Anna and the other members of the Kalinin "dynasty" of textile workers and good Communists are all people infinitely devoted to the Fatherland and the Cause, and capable of the greatest self-sacrifice and self-denial; so is the old surgeon of the military hospital who dies of a heart attack brought on by sheer physical exhaustion; fine and touching, too, is little Genia Müller, the daughter of a Russian woman and a German Communist—now in a Nazi death camp—who crosses the enemy lines into a German-occupied city to execute a Russian quisling and who, on her return journey, is killed by a German bullet. The only "negative" characters are the loathsome quisling; the faithless husband of Anna, who is ready to abandon his wife and children for a naïve little hospital nurse; and the cheap little Don Juan of a press photographer, whose vulgar advances are rejected with monumental contempt by Galka, another charming little girl working in the half-destroyed textile mill, the chief scene of this wartime novel. The story is unsophisticated; but it makes good reading, and the "positive" characters are all lovable and profoundly edifying people.

Literature in the Soviet Union continues to be a big "industry." In his famous report at the Third Writers' Congress in May 1959, Alexei Surkov, then President of the Writers' Union, proudly announced that the membership of the Writers' Union of the USSR had increased in four years from 3,695 to 4,801. Nearly 5,000 professional writers.

Khrushchev, who also made a speech at the Writers' Congress, seemed less sure that such literary inflation was a good thing. He described, from his own experience, the case of a newly-baked peasant poetess in the Ukraine, whom the local

Writers' Union insisted on giving a flat in Kiev, whereupon her "talent" ran completely dry, and she merely became a burden to the "Litfond"—the financial fund taking care of writers.

Khrushchev had already made a number of speeches on the arts and literature, notably in 1957. Although, on all these occasions, he displayed a certain artificial modesty in saying that it was "not for him" to judge this or that piece of poetry, he nevertheless laid down some general principles, such as:

What our people need is works of literature, art and music properly rendering the pathos of labor, and understandable to the people. The method of Socialist realism provides unlimited possibilities for supplying such works. The Party is waging a relentless struggle against the penetration of alien ideologies into our art and literature, and against hostile attacks on socialist culture. The complexity and peculiarity of the ideological war in the realm of literature and art is further accentuated by the fact that we have to defend them not only against attacks from abroad, but also from those writers and artists in our own midst who are trying to divert literature and art from their main line of development on to wrong roads.

Whereupon Khrushchev sharply attacked Dudintsev whose novel, *Not by Bread Alone,* though containing some "truthful pages," was, nevertheless, "a slanderous book" which had played straight into the hands of the foreign enemies of the Soviet Union. He also argued that some writers had misinterpreted and misunderstood the resolutions of the Twentieth Congress and had been guilty of "revisionism"; in particular, he took to task the "almanac" called *Literary Moscow, 1955* and the woman-poet Margarita Aligher, who had, moreover, persisted in her errors:

The lessons of the Hungarian events (Khrushchev said), in the course of which the counter-revolution made full use of certain writers in the dirty aims it was pursuing, remind us of the harm that can be done when writers become politically careless and lack both principles and character when faced with an onslaught by the anti-Socialist forces.

By 1959 Khrushchev was satisfied that "revisionism" had been defeated inside Russia, and he even gave Dudintsev a pat on the back, saying he had never considered him an enemy; that his book was "ancient history" now; that nobody wanted this book any more, and that he (Khrushchev) was sure that Dudintsev would now mend his ways. He had wanted to have a heart-to-heart talk with him, but had never found the time. In fact, even in writing *Not by Bread Alone,* he probably meant well, tried to "help the Party," but badly overdid it.

The revisionists, Khrushchev now said, had been defeated, and the "rather violent battle" [of 1955–56] was now over, and should be, if not forgotten, at any rate forgiven. The Party itself was quite capable of dealing with, and condemning faults and errors, like those which had arisen from the Stalin "personality cult." Writers, on the other hand, should, without embellishing Soviet reality, still preferably dwell on the "positive" sides:

> I want to take the side of those who, for some reason, have been given the unflattering title of "varnishers," that is, those who make it their aim to demonstrate positive heroes in their books. Such authors do not indiscriminately approve of everything in their heroes; they see these people as they are in real life, in their struggle for asserting what is new in our civilization. . . . It is important that our people be brought up on good examples, since the demonstration of the positive things in life paves the way to the future. Comrades, the power of the example is a great power!

On the face of it, there was very little to choose between this Khrushchev line on literature and the Stalin-Zhdanov line. Similarly, in his inaugural speech at the Third Writers' Congress, Surkov also played safe, in enumerating the following Russian works as *the* most important to have appeared in the last few years—naturally, *hors concours* Sholokhov's *A Man's Destiny*; and after that, Polevoi's *In the Deep Rear,* Kochetov's *The Yershov Brothers,* Katayev's *The Hamlet in the Steppe,* Vera Panova's *Sentimental Novel,* V. Ovechkin's *A Difficult Spring,* Granin's *After the Wedding,* Galina Nikolayeva's *Battle on the Road,* and Panferov's *Meditation,* and novels by Gonchar, Smolich, V. Smirnov, Vadim Kozhevnikov, P. Nilin, and G. Konovalov. He thus concentrated almost entirely on the "better" examples of Socialist-realist literature. The rest of the novels "deserving mention" were by non-Russian writers. Surkov described good books as "schoolbooks of life," said that the best children's books published in the Soviet Union "brought to the mind and heart of a child the most important ideas of our time," said that "family and love relations are not taboo, but cannot be divorced from their social background and be reduced to the mere classical 'triangle,' " referred to Pasternak's "treasonable behavior" which made him "unworthy of being called a Soviet writer," and demonstrated the decay of the West in literary matters by quoting this confession by "the reactionary English writer Colin Wilson": "We've had enough of humanism and scientific progress. They have produced nothing but general solitude, the loss of all hope and the periodic outbreak of wars," and Albert Camus: "The surrounding world has lost all significance, and if life finds any meaning in revolt, it is directed against revolutions in countries where they have already taken place."

This somewhat primitivist approach to literature continues to be the "official line"; but in reality, Russian literature today is a much more complex phenomenon than would appear from either Khrushchev's or Surkov's "book of rules."

(c) UNOFFICIAL LINES—A MAJOR LITERARY REVIVAL?

These "unofficial lines" are numerous, and are not easy to disentangle. The numerous literary discussions I had the good fortune to attend in Moscow both in private homes and at semi-public meetings are often singularly confused and confusing. But a few facts stand out fairly clearly. One is that the more important younger Soviet writers now interpret the Party canons on literature, as propounded by Khrushchev or Surkov, a good deal more broadly than they were able to do in the Stalin-Zhdanov days.

Even those who do not entirely conform are not scared. Those who *do* conform adopt two kinds of attitudes: some are very intolerant to those who don't conform; others are (like Polevoi, for instance) remarkably tolerant.

No doubt, there has been a tightening-up of the Party line on literature since 1955–56—"since Hungary," as one writer put it. When I asked what exactly Khrushchev meant by that "revisionism" in literature which had been "completely and finally" defeated, the answers were seldom very clear. *Who* were the "revisionists?" Usually a few "debunkers" were mentioned: Dudintsev, of course; the poet Yevtushenko; Yashin and a few other contributors to the *Literary Moscow, 1955* Almanac: Margarita Aligher, who is said to have fainted when Khrushchev specifically attacked her at a garden party he gave to prominent writers back in 1957. Now, when I mentioned Khrushchev's attack on her, she made a funny face, and said it was all "very ancient history." All the same, it was clear that, as in Poland and Hungary, so in the Soviet Union, too, there was a certain ferment among young writers, not only after the Twentieth Congress, but also for some time before. After all, Ehrenburg's *Thaw* had appeared as early as 1954, and was a thinly-disguised attack on "ham" painters-laureates of the Alexander Gerasimov school, and a plea for greater freedom in art and literature. A timid little plea, but still a plea.

As for its being timid, one young Soviet writer taunted me rather sharply with having once referred, in a French magazine, to Ehrenburg as "a bogus rebel."

"You shouldn't have used such a phrase," he said. "In our literary sphere, one can only be a rebel within certain limits. If you're an open rebel (like Pasternak) you will soon be out on your ear. Ehrenburg *is* part of the Establishment; all the same, he has been a very salutary influence. He is a man of courage. *The Fall of Paris* may not be a great novel—in fact, it's a rotten novel; but it took some courage to write it at the height of the Soviet-German Pact; it took some courage to denounce the Gerasimov school of painting right and left when Gerasimov was Stalin's pet painter. It took courage at a meeting of the Writers' Union to stand up to one of the bigwigs who in the name of 'us Russians' read out a list of 'rootless cosmopolitans in our midst' and to say: 'Comrade So-and-So, there's one name you omitted from your list—and that's Ehrenburg.' True, he had the great advantage of being personally approved by Stalin, and carrying on him a Stalin letter to prove it. It also took courage to publish *The Thaw* when the Party line on art was still very uncertain. . . . Ehrenburg revived the poetry of Marina Tsvetayeva, who was hounded to suicide by her 'colleagues' in the Writers' Union back in 1941; he has been campaigning for a truly great Soviet painter who was under a cloud for years—Martiros Saryan. No; let's face it: Ehrenburg stands for 'wider horizons' in both art and literature, and he is rightly considered one of the leaders, in fact, *the* leader of the 'liberals' amongst our writers. Who are the others? Fedin, Paustovsky, Vsevolod Ivanov among the old men, and lots and lots of younger writers. At the other extreme, there are the 'hard ones'—Vsevolod Kochetov, of course, Ehrenburg's *bête noire*; Surkov; Safronov; Tvardovsky, too. But, by and large, the sympathies of the younger generation are with the 'liberals.' The Party tried very hard to 'plug' Kochetov's *The Yershov Brothers*; but despite its very large circulation (about 500,000 copies) it is *not* a book that's liked, except, possibly, among the older generation of industrial workers. Not only is it an avowedly 'anti-Dudintsev' book, in which the 'ordinary' worker is pure and disinterested, while the inventor and the chief engineer are crooks, charlatans and profiteers; but there is also, in the book, a mean and scurrilous anti-intellectual streak, and its villain, chief engineer Orleantsev, is a recognizable caricature of——a very well-known Soviet writer, with his little rackets and rather grubby love-life."

To me, *The Yershov Brothers* had a kind of morbid fascination. Its virtuous industrial workers have a sort of anachronistic and posterlike "First five-year plan" quality; the book radiates a passionate malevolence towards the "intellectuals" and smart-alecky industrial careerists; even the strange love of the broken reed of a woman, who had been sterilized by the Germans, for the Yershov brother who had been forced into the Vlassov Army had, for all its improbability, a luridly-tragic quality which pointed to a certain tortuous imagination on the author's part. And in the rather piquant discussions between the opportunists who now said that they had hated Stalin, but had had to keep quiet and those who recalled how, in all sincerity, they went into battle against superior German forces crying "For Stalin and Country!" Kochetov's sympathies are clearly on the side of the latter.

The "hard" writers have, retrospectively, been doing their best to justify their Stalinism of the war years; Tvardovsky, in a poem which was given the widest publicity in *Pravda*, wrote:

... And so he reigned, and so he ruled,
Clasping the reins in his ruthless hand.
Find a man who did not praise him
Or glorify him! ...
Not in vain did this son of the East
Reveal to the end his ruthless and cruel
Unrightness and rightness. ...
Many of us saw him, and before he even spoke
We would rise to our feet, crying Hurray!
And saying "He will be right again."
We made a God of him and why deny it?—
We called him the father of our land.
There's nothing to add, and nothing to subtract.
So it was on earth. ...
For quarter of a century, this man's name,
Coupled with the name of our country
Was like a clarion call summoning our people
To go to work and to go into battle.
We owed him victory,
As he owed victory to us.

And so on, and so on. Here also were to be found passing references to those who "at first, marched in step with him but then descended, one by one, into the shadows" and to the fact that Lenin "had not taught us the art of making gods," and to the fact that "his hands extended to the stars and to the ocean depths" (meaning that Stalin was reputed to know all the mysteries of Science). And yet (the poet added) the great victory over Germany was inseparable from the name of Stalin.

This curious—and rather absurd—semi-apology for having indulged in the "personality cult" is, nevertheless, a *motif* to be found fairly frequently in recent Soviet writing.

But this is chiefly true of the older generation of writers who did overdo their "Stalin cult" in the past.

But Soviet literature, especially during the past few years, has become a good deal more complex than it used to be. One of the keynotes of the Third Writers' Congress in May 1959 was that "in the days of H-bombs, Sputniks and moon rockets, it's high time we stopped being *epigones* of Russian nineteenth-century literature." What this attitude has produced— if one doesn't count some rather amusing, if naïve, science fiction, some of which was recently published in *Komsomolskaya Pravda*—is not quite clear yet. But, broadly speaking, one may divide recent Soviet fiction into three categories; the "functional" literature, of which Polevoi's *In the Deep Rear* is the outstanding example, with *The Yershov Brothers* a bad second; "retrospective" literature touching on all the taboo subjects of the past: the errors of Stalin, the terrible defeats suffered by the Russians in 1941–42; the evils of the "personality cult" and, above all, the misdeeds of the NKVD; and, finally, a rather new type of literature which may, for lack of a better word, be called "Chekhovian." In this Soviet reality is treated in a sort of detached, shoulder-shrugging manner. Among the books of this type, the most remarkable are probably the *contes cruels* of Vladimar Tendryakov, a writer of outstandingly high quality.

The "retrospective" books, with their critical attitude to Stalin and their denunciations of the NKVD, are numerous, and are a particularly interesting new development with their reassessment of old values, and their "Twentieth Congress" *motifs*. The considerable interest in new books is partly due to the readers' curiosity to find new "revelations" about the recent past, and new angles, as it were. A book like Konstantin Simonov's *The Living and the Dead,* a distinctly uninhibited story of not only horrible German cruelty, but also of gross mismanagement and bewilderment amongst the Russians during the German advance on Moscow in October 1941, aroused considerable interest in Russia. The heroic clichés of the wartime and early postwar Simonov were gone. So was the Stalin-worship. Instead, here was a picture of Russian soldiers fighting a chaotic battle against terrible odds, and with the civilians having lost their heads and fleeing from the capital. In the Army itself, there was much chaos and disorder, and some very rough justice—and injustice—was meted out by the little tin gods of the "special department"—the police services attached to the Army.

Many other books touch on what were once taboo subjects —Pavel Nilin's *Cruelty,* for instance, dealing with the tortuous psychology of an NKVD man; Panferov's *Meditation* dealing with the injustice and the mismanagement inside collective farms in the Stalin days; novels by Bondarev and others touching on the tricky and tragic problem of Russian war prisoners who had been forced into Hitler's "Vlassov Army"; [1] and so on.

Perhaps the most outstanding recent novel in this particular category is *The Battle on the Road* by Galina Nikolayeva. It is remarkable in more ways than one. Its opening chapters deal with the days following the death of Stalin, with the hysteria, the bewilderment and murderous stampedes in the Moscow streets; but, soon afterwards, the endless, 700-page novel seems to develop into one of those dreary "industrial" novels revolving round the conflict between two sets of engineers and bureaucrats in a newly-converted tractor plant. But—apart from the extraordinary novelty of the Stalin funeral episodes—the novel contains one of the most candid accounts of how an innocent man is trapped by the NKVD, denounced as an "enemy of the people" and shot; and secondly, it tells the love story of Tina, his only daughter—a woman of flesh and blood—"a Russian with an admixture of Tartar blood which makes her doubly Russian." Nothing banal and conventional in the love story of Tina, the tormented daughter of an "enemy of the people" who marries a nice but unexciting young athlete, and of Dimitri, the married 40-year-old engineer with a dowdy, vulgar, self-satified wife, and with three children to whom he is deeply devoted. The love affair of these two tormented souls is told without any moralizing, and with a proper understanding of the real passion that carries them away. And yet, it is a pathetic sort of love, which has to hide in backyards and backstairs, and in a sordid little room which Dimitri manages to get and about which he bitterly remarks: "Our Socialist era does not lend itself to adultery. . . . In the West, you can go to a hotel; not here." To which she replies: "Do you know why we quarrel so often, why we hurt each other? It's because we have hurt our love. . . . We have hurt it, because we have to hide it in this slum, because we have to hide it as something dirty and shameful." And, in the circumstances, all that is

---

[1] The general line here is that only those Vlassovites were justified who joined this Russian "National Army of Liberation" with the ulterior motive of either escaping at the first opportunity, or of doing sabotage. No excuses are yet made for those who were blackmailed into joining this army by the threat of starvation—which was, in fact, the way in which most Vlassovites were enlisted.

left of their love is the acute physical attraction, and little else. . . .

It is probably true to say that Nikolayeva's love story about Tina and Dimitri is the only full-blooded love story in any Soviet book since Sholokhov's Axinia and Grigori in *Quiet Flows the Don*.

It is unfortunate that this admirably-told love story, as well as the grim NKVD story and the story of Stalin's funeral, should be diluted in the endless and tedious discussions about the faulty counterweights of the tractors produced at the plant where nearly all the characters of the novel are employed! Or rather, this "industrial background" may be essential; only one wishes there weren't quite so much of it. Even so, out of the 700 pages of *The Battle on the Road* about 200 pages come very close to genuinely great writing, which is a good deal nearer to *Anna Karenina* than it is to the insipid and virtuous amours of Simonov's novels.

No doubt, Khrushchev and the Party have laid down certain rules about the kind of literature that is "desirable"; but there is no longer a Kremlin Zeus (as somebody I met in Moscow put it) to hurl thunderbolts at offending writers. All kinds of books get published now, some fairly remote from the rules laid down by the Party. After publication, some such books get severe slatings; but they *have* been published, and nothing more is done about it; and "slatings" often whet the curiosity of the more sophisticated readers.

Not only in a big novel like Nikolayeva's, but, even more so, in the more-or-less short stories written by several younger Soviet writers, can one observe a very marked departure from the conventional type of Soviet fiction. For one thing, the *quality* of the writing is very different from the flat and pedestrian writing of the 1930s, '40s and early '50s, in the midst of which Sholokhov's rich prose constituted one of the few exceptions.

Talk to any literary-minded Russian today, and he will trot out long lists of new names—these are young writers who are finding new ways of expressing themselves, and are not following the beaten track of the straightforward Russuian Pushkin-Turgeniev-Tolstoy narrative tradition. Some of them tend more towards the richer and more complex prose tradition that goes back, *via* certain Soviet writers of the 1920s (like Zamiatin), to Leskov, and (indirectly) Gogol.

These new writers include A. Kuznetsov, A. Volodin, H. Dementyev, V. Ocheretin, V. Moskovkin, L. Ivanov, A. Andreyev and many more. These are still relatively unknown. Those who have already made a mark include writers like Sergei Antonov, Georgi Radov, Yuri Kazakov, Boris Bednyi, Yuri Nagibin, Georgi Bondarev, the Ukrainian writer Stelmakh and Vladimir Tendryakov. Most important among them are perhaps Kazakov, Nagibin and, above all, Tendryakov.

All three of these have, very broadly, been described as "Chekhovian." Kazakov has been sharply attacked in *Literary Gazette* and elsewhere for being decadent, "estheticist," pessimistic, and given to creating absurdly eccentric characters. He, as well as some other new writers, has been used as a peg for starting angry discussions along the following lines: "These people imagine they are in the Chekhov tradition; they assume that Chekhov took a detached, pessimistic, shoulder-shrugging attitude to the world around him, whereas in reality he was a revolutionary writer, full of revolutionary zeal, in fact, a harbinger of the Revolution. See *The Cherry Orchard*. Whatever bourgeois critics may say, Chekhov was not tolerant towards evil."

This is, clearly, a very one-sided interpretation of Chekhov, which could, at a stretch, be applied to some of his stories (like *The Grasshopper*), but not at all to others (like *The Fit* or *A Dull Story*). It will be remembered how in *The Fit* the doctor, who has the last word, shrugs his shoulders over the fit of hysterics the young student throws over the horror of brothels and prostitution, which he had observed on the previous night. What his shrug suggests is: "Well, that's life, and what can you do about it?"

Kazakov, Nagibin and Tendryakov (to take some of the most important new writers) are different from the ordinary run of Soviet writers in that they attach considerable importance to the quality of their writing. They are essentially non-didactic. Tendryakov, moreover, goes in for psychological subtleties and refinements which are unusual in Soviet novels. Nagibin also can tell a straight, but very human and moving story without a moral—for instance his wartime stories contained in the book called *The Man and the Road*, with their simple but very subtle "slices of life," such as *The Road to the Front Line*, telling the story of a shell-shocked soldier and his determination not to be demobbed, not so much out of patriotism as because of his "belongingness" to the Army; his meeting with the girl in the blacked-out train, who gives him a bottle of milk, and whom he fails to see again as he has forgotten her address (for he is in a half-dazed state all the time) is extremely subtly told. Nagibin is, clearly, a writer to watch.

But I do not hesitate to say that there is in Russia today at least one man who has the makings of a great writer, and that is Vladimir Tendryakov. True, he is no youngster; he was born in 1923, but is only now beginning to be more and more widely recognized, though, oddly enough, when I asked one of the official cultural organizations in Moscow to arrange for me a meeting with him, I received the astonishing reply: "Tendryakov? Never heard of him."

Yet among the more sophisticated literary judges, Tendryakov is a major name; my old friend Jean Cathala, one of the best connoisseurs of Soviet literature, referred to him as "the greatest wonder in Soviet literature." Take, for example, this passage about one of Tendryakov's characters traveling in the Moscow Subway and looking at the people around him:

This officer with cold eyes and a sharply-chiseled profile surely starts with physical jerks every morning, is proud of his orderly life, is probably on the mean side, and sees to it that his wife doesn't spend an extra ruble on house-keeping, and goes himself to a commission shop to buy her nightgowns cheaply. And that tired-looking woman with little bags under her eyes must be suffering from an excess of motherly love; through kindness and lack of character she has brought up her son and daughter in such a way that they will go on hanging round her neck, living on her measly earnings. And this fat, imposing man is neither a professor nor an important official; he must either run a mineral-water booth, or serve as a porter in a restaurant. And now, full of his own importance, he is on the way to visit some relatives.

And then there follows the description of a girl the young man also sees in the Subway, and it is a subtly Sartrian, almost Proustian description; in the end, he follows her out of the Metro, but she vanishes in the damp darkness of the Moscow night.

There is some superb writing in *Ukhaby* (Bad Roads), a

selection of stories dealing chiefly with village life. The most famous of these stories include *Bad Roads* and *The Miraculous Icon*. The first tells of a crowded truck which overturns on a very bad and muddy road miles away from anywhere. Only one man is injured, but very severely. After being carried on an improvised stretcher for miles to the nearest village, he is told by a local nurse that only an immediate operation can stop the internal hemorrhage from which he is suffering. But the roads are in such a state that only a tractor can take him to town; and here the man is virtually condemned to death by the president of the *kolkhoz* who, for hours, refuses to "break the law" by providing "for an unauthorized purpose" the only tractor in the neighborhood; when finally he is bullied into releasing the tractor, the injured man dies in acute agony on the way to hospital. It is truly a *conte cruel* told with the utmost economy and mastery, but with a kind of "Chekhovian" shrug; in his own way, the president of the kolkhoz is in his right, so what can you do with such stupid and insensitive people? An equally admirable story is *The Miraculous Icon* in which a village boy fishes out of the river a "miraculous" icon which had disappeared when the village church was dismantled some years before. The boy's grandmother and the older villagers begin to treat the boy as something of a saint, and the bewildered boy becomes the object of a conflict between the religious and superstitious old people in the village on the one hand and the "soviet" schoolmistress and the boy's own schoolmates on the other. Here again, Tendryakov tells the story with the kind of "Chekhovian" detachment which makes it easy to see both the schoolteacher's and the grandmother's respective points of view.

Tendryakov is no escapist; he deals with Soviet reality; but deals with it in his own, wholly unconventional, and genuinely creative way. All his characters are men and women of flesh and blood, subtle and a little unusual; and he is also an exceptionally good storyteller.

For a time all went well, but in March 1960 *Novy Mir* published a short story by Tendryakov, *Three-Seven-Ace* which caused a major uproar in the press. It was described as a libel on Soviet reality. Why? It was a story about lumberjacks in a remote corner of Siberia. To begin with, there was nothing specifically "Soviet" about these people;

they were working in this god-forsaken settlement on the banks of a river, hundreds of miles from anywhere, joined by a rough sort of comradeship, but chiefly interested in making good money, with a little drink and fornication thrown in. And then, one day, Lyosha, one of them, pulled out of the rapids a drowning man, a newly released convict called Bushuyev. And this man promptly proceeds to dominate this group of 20 tough and strong men with the help of—a pack of cards. He wins all the 5,000 rubles saved up by Yegor, the most miserly of the men, and 5,000 more from the others—quite a fortune. Threatening to murder him with an axe, Bushuyev orders his "savior" Lyosha to hide the money for him, and then threaten with murder the most "positive" of all the men in the story, Alexander Dubinin, the "boss" of the settlement, who is in possession of Bushuyev's passport, without which the latter cannot go back to his native Kursk. In self-defense Alexander, after being slightly injured by Bushuyev's axe, knifes the man, and promptly phones the police, who arrive by motor launch the next morning. Alexander is then suspected of having wanted to take the winnings from the dead man. Lyosha, fearing that he would be suspected of complicity with Bushuyev, throws the money into the river; Dubinin is taken away on a charge of murder. The lumberjacks get together and realize that they can save their chief only if they collect the missing money and pretend they have found it; but can this be done without the police smelling a rat? It is on this uncertain note that the story ends. This story, artistically a major masterpiece, is in the manner of Chekhov's more "cruel" tales of life in the raw (such as *The Ravine*); but here all this primeval brutality occurs amongst Soviet citizens living, moreover, in Siberia, the land of hope, optimism and the future. And as if to add insult to injury, Tendryakov puts these dismal thoughts into the head of Alexander Dubinin as he sits there between the militiaman and the dead man's body:

Knifed to death. . . . A story as ancient as life itself—of one man quarreling with another man. A hundred, two hundred, and thousands of years ago, there were Bushuyevs, too, and they would raise their knives and axes over the heads of others, and these would be forced to strike back with their own knives. Is this an eternal curse which will never be lifted?

No doubt it was a sign of great "liberalism" for *Novy Mir* to open its March number with this astonishing Tendryakov story; perhaps it was inevitable that it should have produced some violent protests to the effect that the story was "untrue to life"; the big question is whether such protests are going to discourage editors in future from publishing such "non-conformist" stories, and whether the writers themselves will not become discouraged. The Tendryakov story clearly belongs to that "major revival" in Soviet literature which began in a small but still impressive way about the beginning of 1958, by which time the "Budapest scare" had subsided. . . .

In a writer like Tendryakov we are far removed from the simple "schematism" of the positive-negative characters of the "functional" novel; like Galina Nikolayeva at her best, Tendryakov comes very close in many respects to the classical Russian literary tradition, with a bitter Gorki and a tolerant Chekhov among his literary ancestors.

The question inevitably arises whether there is much written of "unprintable" literature in Russia today. One suspects that a certain amount is written "not for publication"— or, at any rate, not for immediate publication; but, by and large, writers still want to see their work in print. Pasternak could afford to take the extreme step of publishing his *Zhivago* abroad; a few others have done so, too, though anonymously; but the impression I had in Moscow, after speaking to many writers, was that most writers are "good" Soviet citizens, who would much prefer not to have to resort to such subterfuges, but to be able to publish almost anything in Russia, even at the risk of getting it in the neck.

Except for violently denunciatory books, this was, indeed, the position for about a year after the Third Writers' Congress; whether, after the breakdown of the Summit and the revival of various ominously old "vigilance" slogans, the screw will be turned on writers again remains to be seen.

In the relatively "liberal" atmosphere of the winter of 1959–'60 the attitude to Pasternak and *Zhivago* was a singularly mixed one. The "harder" people felt he had behaved badly and even claimed that he constituted a certain danger: if he had not been "put in his place," they said, his *datcha* at Peredelkino would have become a place of pilgrimage "to all kinds of religious cranks the way Yasnaya Polyana had become one in the days of Tolstoy." At a discussion I attended at the Writers' Union one day, with Margarita Aligher, Boris Izakov, Evgeni Dolmatovsky, Sergei Mikhalkov and a few others present, several spoke of Pasternak more in sorrow than in anger; they said they had argued with him no end, but he was "a vain and pigheaded old man" and wouldn't listen to any advice—not even about making minor cuts in *Zhivago*. The main criticism of Pasternak was that he had failed to render the "inner flame that had inspired people during the civil war"; had described those years from a "consumer point of view," and was, if not exactly an "internal émigré," a sort of holy man who was living solely a life of his own. In certain scenes in *Zhivago*—notably the final scene, in which the dying man was trying frantically to open the streetcar window—there was a sort of symbolism which was "deliberately offensive to the Soviet Union." The prevalent opinion seemed, however, to be that a big mistake had been made in making a martyr of Pasternak; it would have been far wiser to let the book be published in a small edition of say, 10,000 copies; there would have been a few nasty articles in the Soviet press about it, and that would have been the end of it. . . . There would have been no Nobel prize and no "international scandal."

Just a few words about children's books—though this is, of course, a subject that *could* be discussed at great length.

The big popular favorites continue to be Chukovsky, Marshak, Agnia Barto, Sergei Mikhalkov—but with old man Chukovsky streets ahead of any of the others. All his children's books come very close to English nonsense verse—he is, indeed, a great admirer of Edward Lear and Lewis Carroll [2]—and there is scarcely a child in the whole of the Soviet Union who doesn't know by heart his *Tarakan* (The Terrible Cockroach)—who frightens with his whiskers the bears, crocodiles, hippopotami, rhinoceroses, sharks and other big animals, until the kangaroo scandalizes them all

[2] Chukovsky, a man of immense literary culture, was well-known even before the Revolution when he popularized Kipling, Oscar Wilde and other English writers in Russia.

by "debunking" the monster and the sparrow swallows him in one mouthful;—or *Doctor Aibolit*—the kind doctor who flies with his thermometer on an eagle's back to Africa to cure the sick little camels, ostriches, hippopotami and other animals of their tummy-aches and headaches with his egg-flip and chocolates—or *Moidodyr*, the story of the dirty boy who won't wash his hands and face, until his bedclothes and breakfast things rebel and fly away from him, and Moidodyr, the irate washstand, stamps his feet at him, and our old friend the Crocodile threatens to swallow him if he doesn't go home at once and wash. This is a "moral" tale, as is also the other tale of Fedora, who kept her kitchen in a filthy state till, one day, all her pots and pans rebelled and fled. The collected poems of Kornei Chukovsky or his single poems (all of them a little naïvely illustrated) have literally been printed in *tens of millions* of copies; "grandpa Kornei" —now 77—is the best-loved children's writer, and, apart from a little moralizing about cleanliness of body and cleanliness of the home, there is nothing didactic, still less political, about his books—unless one sees a symbol in the Russian doctor flying to Africa to cure the baby-hippopotami—or regards *Tarakan* as an early denunciation of the "personality cult!"

So it is quite untrue to assume that Marxism-Leninism is rammed down a child's throat from the age of three! Barto, Mikhalkov and Marshak do more than Chukovsky to exalt the greatness of the *rodina*, the Soviet homeland; and a comparatively recent favorite by Marshak is *Mister Twister*, the terribly important American businessman who blows up at a Leningrad hotel because he sees a Negro among the guests and is finally put in his place.

But Chukovsky remains the great favorite and everybody knows his admirably-chiseled lines, such as in the exuberantly amusing *Telephone*, beginning:

My phone rang.
"Who's speaking?"
"The Elephant."
"Where from?"
"From the Camel's home."
"And what do you want?"
"Chocolate."

"For whom?"
"For my son."
"And how much would you like?"
"Only 200 or 220 pounds.
He won't eat any more. He's still a baby."

After that the Crocodile rings up:

And with tears in his voice he begged:
"Dear, dear Uncle Kornei,
Do send us some galoshes,
For me, and the wife and Toto."
"Oh, but let me see, didn't I send you last week
Three pairs of lovely new galoshes?"
"Oh, those you sent us last week
We ate up long, long ago;
And now we are waiting, and waiting and waiting
To get for our supper
A dozen sweet and tasty galoshes."

And so on, till the final SOS, when Rhino rings up to say
that Hippo has fallen into the bog; and so Kornei has to rush
off in the middle of the night, and with the help of his
various animal friends to save Hippo from drowning:

It's a hard and strenuous job
To drag Hippopotamus out of a bog.

Much of Chukovsky—such as these last two lines—
has passed into the language—like some famous phrases
from Krylov, Griboyedov or Gogol.

And so, Soviet literature remains one of the great un-
knowns of the years to come. Of the nearly 5,000 registered
members of the Writers' Union—from which Pasternak was
expelled—a very high proportion are nothing but hacks, while
others (as even Khrushchev implicitly admitted) are mere
profiteers of a State-patronized racket. It is true that no
country in the world produces great writers by the hundred
or even by the dozen. And yet, one cannot escape the impression that many writers are dissatisfied. Thus, N, one of
the most promising young Soviet writers, said to me one
day:

"Our country is making tremendous progress; we are the equal of America in many ways, and even superior in some respects. But our literature is lagging behind the technical and economic progress of our country. Writers are *beginning* to look for new ways, for new formulae, for new solutions. The quality of our writing is improving; there is greater variety, more imagination, more *style* than there was five or six years ago; but we still have to be reasonably well-behaved. None of us is against the system—except Pasternak; we are on the side of the angels; we have half, two-thirds, three-quarters of humanity more or less on our side; we have even (look at Dolmatovsky!) started writing poems about the Awakening of Africa. We don't, like Chukovsky's Doctor Aibolit, have to give chocolates to sick young camels in Africa; we give chocolates to Sekou Touré. When we write about foreign countries, we can let our hair down, as it were; we can kick the Nazis in the teeth; we can say anything we like about American militarists and monopolists and warmongers; but when we write about Russia, our Russia, many of us are in a bit of a quandary. We are supposed to write 'in the tradition' of Tolstoy, Turgeniev and Chekhov; but the nineteenth-century writers were what's called 'critical realists'; they didn't go in very much for 'positive characters'; they had a skeptical, ironical, often satirical approach to reality; but *we* have to *believe* all the time; we can't be ironical about Soviet reality, and we can't be satirical, except in a very limited and superficial way. In the Stalin days, our literature began to cultivate a special kind of *pathos*; it was becoming positively 'classical,' like Derzhavin's Odes to Catherine the Great—yes, I'm not joking! Several people have remarked on this. Our cult of the heroic, 'positive' character went so far that, *in all seriousness*, Communist journals started boosting—hold tight!—who do you think?—*Corneille!* Yes—*Le Cid*, though admittedly a little archaic, was treated as a kind of ancestor of the Soviet positive hero, with his infallible sense of honor and duty! At that rate, Corneille *should* be much nearer to us than Shakespeare; you remember, perhaps, that in the last years of Stalin, they kept putting off and off and off a revival of *Hamlet* by the Moscow Art Theatre; apparently somebody high-up thought *Hamlet* 'wasn't good for us!'

"This is an extreme case; and all this has changed now.

And yet, we still have doubts about Socialist-Realism. Now, a few young writers are, rather cautiously, getting away from it. No doubt, our age is still heroic, but it hasn't the heroic quality it was given in the days of Stalin. The 'personality cult' did make things a lot easier—especially for the poets; and there was, of course, the genuinely heroic material of the Patriotic War to work on. But the war has become a thing of the past. A certain amount of 'debunking' of the wartime heroics is actually being done now—by Simonov, for instance. We aren't quite as reverent as we used to be. Now, you say you admire writers like Kazakov, Nagibin, Tendryakov. I could mention a dozen more. They don't go in for the Polevoi or Tvardovsky type of 'positive hero' any more. The 'limits' in which a writer can operate have become more flexible. Writing about Soviet reality with what you call a 'Chekhovian' shrug—that's what some of our young writers like Tendryakov are doing—is all very well; but it isn't quite enough. Do you know that we have young writers who are *anti-Chekhov*?"

"You mean the didactic, the dogmatist writers?"

"They, of course—though they've tried to annex Chekhov, too; but not only they. A lot of young writers are anti-Chekhov; they think his writing is flat, anemic, water-colory, something that's not only a trillion miles away from the glaring, blaring revolutionary rhetoric of Mayakovksy, but also a few billion miles away from the verbal pungency of Leskov, Dostoevsky, Gogol."

"Are you, too, hankering for the fantastic, for Gogol's *Nose*?"

"Yes, that sort of thing; something fantastic, expressionist, if you like; back to the 1920s, back to Babel, back to Zamyatin. We want neologisms, eccentric writing, verbal jugglery."

"Surely," I said, "*The Nose* is rather un-Soviet as a subject. Shostakovich tried to render it in musical terms, and got into trouble."

"Maybe Shostakovich got into trouble over *The Nose*, but he *has* been fully accepted now by every authority in the country; and why? Because he's a genuinely *great* composer; and when our authorities are up against real greatness, they accept the artist on his own terms. With one proviso—and that is that he goes through certain 'political motions.' The other classical case is Sholokhov. His *Quiet Flows the*

Don is *not* a Communist novel; it's a kind of anarchist novel; Grigori is immensely human; he is, as somebody said, the last nineteenth-century hero of Russian literature."

"There's Pasternak," I ventured.

"No," said N, "Pasternak won't do. He is a superb poet. But in *Zhivago* he lives in the past. A great piece of writing, no doubt, but not a great book. The characters don't mean anything much. Also, Pasternak never went through even the minimum political motions, and he annoyed *everybody* by beefing about the Soviet system to any Tom, Dick and Harry who came to visit him from abroad. His *datcha* has for years been a sort of Mecca to all anti-Soviet propagandists who managed to get to Russia. Even his best friends—and he has lots of them, for he is a really lovable and fascinating character—began to grumble."

"I saw a lot of Pasternak during and just after the war," I said. "He had a refreshing tongue-in-cheek attitude. He gave me a tiny little book of his, printed in 1945 and wrote:

> To my dear Alexander Werth,
> most eloquent Soviet propagandist
>   With best wishes,
>   Boris Pasternak."

"That's Pasternak all over," N laughed. "He thought there was something slightly funny about Western journalists going all soppy over the Soviet Union in wartime. I suppose he was also rather indiscreet talking to you about things."

"No, not really. He didn't think in political categories, but in human categories. He divided the Russian Communists into two categories, as it were—into what he called the *tolstomordyie*—the 'fat snouts'—and the others. The 'others' were the good, human people, regardless of what they were politically. He liked Fadeyev, for instance, ultra-Stalinite though he was. But, of course, there was one remark he made at least twice to me (and since he seldom repeated himself— for his mind bubbled and improvised in an extraordinary way—he must have felt strongly about it). And that was: 'What *they* are doing in Russia is, socially and economically, probably *quite* admirable. Only why in heaven drag *literature* into it?'

"And then—and this was the last time I saw him; it was in

1947. He was feeling very bitter about Zhdanovism, and all that. Zhdanov, to him, was the perfect 'fat snout.' And, I remember, he then said: 'All right, so I am being treated as a back-number. But there's one thing I can tell you. Before I die, I shall pull off one big stunt yet:—*ya yeshcho odnu shtuku vykinu.*' 'What's that?' I said. 'You'll see!' he smiled with a malicious twinkle.

"Soon afterwards I learned he was working hard on a full-length novel."

"Poor Pasternak," N said. "He was treated pretty roughly. But he behaved rather stupidly. If he hadn't been quite so openly defiant, no doubt *Zhivago* would have been published here; and it wouldn't even have caused much of a furor. Because the Party *is* becoming far more tolerant in literary matters than it used to be. The really big danger is a renewal of the Cold War. If that happens, we may have to sink back into a dreary kind of Zhdanovism; or else we'll go all 'revolutionary' and will start producing dozens of (no doubt very inferior) Mayakovskys, who will write revolutionary poems and stories about China, and Guinea and Ghana and Indonesia. But I doubt whether we really have our hearts in it. We'd much rather be left in peace and cultivate our great big Communist garden and" (N grinned) "plant in it a hundred flowers. Mao Tse-Tung said so; so it must be right."

"Mao changed his line about that, so now you'll be accused of revisionism," I said.

"No," said N, "if we have lasting peace, nobody's going to bother about revisionism. And we'll plant, not a hundred, but a thousand flowers. Hooray for Gogol's *Nose*! And hooray for Fadeyev, too!"

"And for Pasternak?"

"Yes, and for Pasternak, too," N smiled. "For whatever we may think of *Zhivago*, he'll always remain one of our great poets."

And suddenly N began to recite one of Pasternak's earlier poems—the famous one on Brahms, beginning—

> Godàmi kogdà-nibùd v zàle concèrtnoi
> Mne Bràhmsa sygràyut, toskòi izoidù

and ending:

Pod chistyi kak dètstvo nemètski motif . . .
(To a German melody, as pure as childhood)

"Good God," he added, "is there any man in Russia today who knows the Russian language as Pasternak does, with all its infinite wealth, subtlety, flexibility and music? Only, that's not what those Nobel idiots gave him the prize for. All that was *quite* above their heads. And that is what made so many Russian writers so furious. For *we* love Pasternak because he's a great poet; and we resented it when they used him and his political innocence as a vulgar stunt for heating up the Cold War. . . ."

To sum up—insofar as that's possible at all—it seems to me that, at least as far as fiction is concerned, there are three possible lines of escape from the more rigid canons of Socialist-realism—which, when you come to think of it, has produced what is mainly an enormous bulk of essentially *provincial* literature; and this (with the possible exception of the early, "anarchist" Sholokhov, not to mention the wholly different case of *Zhivago*) has really made no impact outside Russia. What, many young Russian writers today wonder, has happened to the *universality* of the old Russian literature, and to its blessed irony? So the lines of escape are (1) "Chekhovianism," i.e. the treatment of Soviet reality in a slightly ironical, undidactic manner; (2) satire—which, however, has only limited possibilities; and (3) a return to the "Leskov" tradition of *writing*—i.e. an escape, as one young writer put it to me, "from anemic Chekhov and flat Tolstoy (the approved Soviet model) to bumpy Leskov, to the *byl'* style, to verbal virtuosity, to Gogol's *Nose*, to the *fantastika* of the 1920s. Only," he added, "there's this: verbal bumpiness often leads to dangerously-bumpy thoughts."

Chapter 23

MUSIC: ALL'S WELL—SHOSTAKOVICH
AND DODECAPHONIC MUSIC

IF SOVIET WRITERS are hopeful, but still at times uncertain about the future of Russian literature, Soviet musicians are in a highly optimistic mood. The bad days of "Zhdanovism" seem definitely over.

On May 28, 1958, the Central Committee issued a Decree (*postanovlevie*) entitled: "On Correcting the Errors made in the Assessment of the Operas *The Great Friendship, Bogdan Khmelnitsky* and *With All Your Heart,*" the first of which, as we know, had been the peg on which the famous "Zhdanov Decree" of February 10, 1948, was hung—a Decree in which a savage attack was made on the "formalist" and "anti-people" music of Shostakovich, Prokofiev, Khachaturian, Miaskovsky and other leading composers.

This new Decree started by noting the "positive" value of the 1948 Decree:

The Central Committee of the CPSU notes that the Decree of February 10, 1948, concerning Muradeli's opera, *The Great Friendship,* played, on the whole, a positive role in the subsequent development of Soviet musical art. This Decree defined the aims of musical art based on the principles of Socialist realism, and stressed the importance of the links between art and the life of the Soviet people, the best democratic traditions of the classics and folk-music. The formalist tendencies in music were rightly condemned, as well as those alleged "innovations" which created a gulf between art and the people, and turned music into something that could interest only a narrow circle of "arty" *gourmets.* The development of music in the last few years confirmed the rightness and timeliness of these instructions.

And now came the apology:

At the same time the assessment of the work of certain composers was in several cases unfounded and unjust. There were faults in Muradeli's opera which deserved sober criticism, but which did not justify its being denounced as a formalist work. Gifted composers, such as Shostakovich, Prokofiev, Khachaturian, Shebalin, G. Popov, Miaskovsky and others, whose works sometimes revealed the wrong tendencies, were simply denounced as the representatives of a formalist, anti-people tendency. . . . Certain wrong appreciations in the Decree reflected a subjective attitude to certain works of art by J. V. Stalin personally.

Similarly, Stalin was now made responsible for subsequent attacks on Dankevich's opera, *Bogdan Khmelnitsky* and on V. Zhukovsky's opera, *With All Your Heart*, as well as for certain *Pravda* editorials published in 1951 "on his instructions."

As we know [the new Decree went on] a very adverse influence was exercised on Stalin in these matters by Molotov, Malenkov and Beria. . . .

Just like that!
Whereupon the Decree noted that:

While the Decree of February 10, 1948, directed correctly the development of Soviet music . . . it contained, at the same time, many unjust and undeservedly sharp criticisms of the work of many highly gifted Soviet composers; such a negative attitude was characteristic of the personality cult period.

It therefore gave the following instructions:

(*a*) The editorial of *Pravda* (editor, Comrade Satyukov) should, on the strength of the present Decree, publish a leading article containing an all-round and profound analysis of the main problems concerning the development of Soviet musical art;
(*b*) The Regional Committees, the Central Committees of the Communist Parties of the various Soviet Republics, and the Min-

istry of Culture of the USSR should conduct the necessary explanatory work in artistic unions, art schools, etc., in connection with the present Decree, bearing in mind the necessity of raising still further the artistic and ideological level of Soviet musical art and the further consolidation, amongst creative intellectuals, of Communist ideology and of the bonds uniting art and the life of the people.

Leading Russian composers could not help laughing a little angrily at some features of this Decree; why blame Molotov, Malenkov and Beria for what had happened in 1948 when everybody knew that the real villain was the late Andrei Alexandrovich Zhdanov? Recalling the incredible three-day conference of composers and musicians, presided over by the said Zhdanov, one prominent composer, who had also been attacked as a "formalist," screwed up his face and said: "I can tell you, that was really by far the nastiest and most humilating experience in all my life."

At the same time, these same composers were delighted with the new Decree—with its explicit (if belated) "rehabilitation" of men like Prokofiev and Miaskovsky—both of whom had died in the interval, Miaskovsky's death having been hastened by the deep sense of injury he had felt as a result of the 1948 Decree.

Just as there are nearly 5,000 writers in the Soviet Union, so there are about 2,000 composers. Needless to say, only a small proportion of these are of any importance *as* composers: the rest. apart from writing casual bits of (mostly light) music, teach in various music schools; some others make a living by composing incidental music for the cinema; nevertheless, there are at least a few dowen composers who "matter."

Apart from "big" names both in light music—Blanter, Soloviev-Sedoi, Zakharov, Novikov, etc.—and in serious music—Shostakovich, Shebalin, Shaporin, Kabalevsky, Khachaturian, etc.—and at least one "big" name in the next generation—Sviridov—everybody in the Moscow musical world in the winter of 1959–60 was now talking about the particularly brilliant "third" generation of young composers, now in their twenties.

At the *première* of Sviridov's very exciting new work, the *Pathetic Oratorio,* I had in the interval a long conversation with Yuri Shaporin, the composer of *The Field of Kulikovo,*

The Song of the Russian Land oratorios and of *The Decembrists* opera, now running at the Bolshoi Theater, a true successor of the Rimsky-Korsakov–Mussorgski tradition,[1] and now one of the Grand Old Men of Russian music. He did not conceal his delight at the "revocation" of the 1948 Decree, and spoke with real enthusiasm of the new young composers now cropping up all over the place, among them many of his own pupils at the Moscow Conservatory.

Who then, according to Shaporin, were the highly promising new composers? He mentioned Sidelnikov, author of an oratorio in the grand Russian style called *The Lament of Boris over the Dead Gleb*; Artemiev, the author of a poignant musical poem, I *Was Killed at Rzhev*—the story of a dead soldier watching the further victorious progress of the Red Army; Shchedrin, the brilliant young composer of a new *Hump-Backed Horse* ballet and much else; and a young (Prince) Andrei Volkonsky, who had only a few years ago come to Russia, having been born and educated in France, where he received his first lessons from Rachmaninov. Volkonsky, Shaporin said, was an exceptionally brilliant and original composer—the author of an *Eluard Cantata* "with a quite heavenly aria"; of incidental music to Shaw's *St. Joan*; and of some admirable chamber music including a Trio, a Quintet and much else—"polyphonic, lapidary, classical and rather chromatic music"; I gathered, however, that Volkonsky was proving a little "too original" to some orthodox tastes, and had lately been expelled from the Conservatory, where something of a dog-fight was still continuing amongst the "progressives" and the "traditionalists." Shaporin also said that "an immense amount of interesting stuff" was now coming from the non-Russian parts of the Soviet Union, particularly from Azerbaijan and some of the Central-Asian republics.

Later I heard many other new names mentioned: among them Galynin (piano concerto), Kara Karayev, and a young composer of symphonic music, Ovchinninov, a pupil of Bogatyrev's, who was described as "a major genius"—even though he, too, had recently got into serious trouble at the Conservatory.

---

[1] This did not save him from being badly mauled as a "formalist" by Zhdanov back in 1948.

The big Lenin Prize work of 1959 in the field of music was Sviridov's *Pathetic Oratorio*, an enormously dynamic, vigorous and inventive "poem" of the Revolution and Civil War, all of it written to the incisive but "unmusical" words of Mayakovsky. The most striking part was perhaps Part II, describing the rout of the Wrangel army, with Mayakovsky's mocking lines being not sung, but recited against the background of the *Eternal Memory* music of the Orthodox funeral service.

As Shaporin remarked: "Until not so long ago, Sviridov was a faithful pupil of Shostakovich's; but, like Skriabin, Shostakovich cannot be 'followed,' he can only be 'imitated' —and his *Essenin Oratorio* was, a little too obviously, inspired by Shostakovich's *Song of the Forests*. But now Sviridov has developed a very original style of his own."

Which way is Russian music going? There is no doubt that musical culture is more widespread in Russia than in almost any other country. The popular composers are numerous and an enormous amount of good, bad and indifferent music is produced by them. As for "high-brow" music, this is no longer discouraged as it was in the Zhdanov days. Prokofiev and Shostakovich are both treated as great national composers of world fame, and the influence of Shostakovich, though by no means a Socialist-realist in the accepted sense, is sufficiently strong, and his authority sufficiently great to encourage a great deal of new experimentalism in music. Partly, one suspects, in self-defense, and in defense of the "new school," Shostakovich goes, however, out of his way to keep this "modernism" within reasonable limits.

Significant in this respect was the interview given in Warsaw in the autumn of 1959 to a Polish paper and reprinted in *Soviet Music* of November 1959. In reply to the question whether any attempts were made in the Soviet Union to depart from the major-minor system, Shostakovich said:

The major-minor system is not typical of the Russian folk song. This has a richness and variety of natural intonations of its own which were already well utilized by Glinka, Rimsky-Korsakov, Mussorgski, Skriabin and other composers, who all had a great influence on music abroad, particularly on the French impressionists.

Equally rich in new melodic (*lad*) resources are the musical cultures of the non-Russian nationalities of the Soviet Union. We do not have to experiment in atonal music, since we have the vast and still almost untapped resources of the non-Russian folk songs of our country at our disposal. Take, for example, the various pentatonic patterns of the Tartars and other nations, the peculiar systems of Georgian, Azerbaijan or Tadjik music, or the "unrolling" system of Yakut music. All this is far removed from the major-minor music of Western Europe, and lends great freshness to such Soviet masters as Prokofiev, Khachaturian, Sviridov, Kara Karayev, etc.

And then came this "apology" for his own past "modernism":

In the early 1920s we also went in for all sorts of supersophisticated experiments; fortunately, we soon realized that all this was pretty fruitless. . . . Our composers are not judged according to whether or not they keep within the limits of tonal music; the only criteria are whether their music is good, i.e. full of meaning and artistically valid.

Asked whether Shostakovich believed in the future of dodecaphonic music, he replied:

I am convinced that in music, as in all other fields of human endeavor, new ways should be sought. But I am certain that dodecaphonic music can get us nowhere. The narrow dogmatism of this purely artificial system can only paralyze the composer's creative imagination and wipe out whatever individuality he has. It is understandable that there isn't a single work by Schoenberg, the inventor of this system, to have gained general recognition. The same is true of Webern. At the Warsaw Festival we heard a very early (1910) work by Webern; it made a bigger impression than anything he has written since; it seems to me that his talent was dried up by the dodecaphonic dogma. The means of expression in this kind of music are, indeed, extremely limited. At its best, dodecaphonic music can only express depression, prostration and deadly fear—i.e. moods contrary to the normal human being, especially in a Socialist society. . . . Dodecaphonic music belongs to the old world; it has been invented by people who are afraid of the present and do not believe in the future. . . . It is nothing but a passing fashion. The even newer tendencies to which it has given rise, such as pointillism, are altogether contrary to what we mean by music. The Belgian pianist and Italian flutist who performed one such work were quite incapable of memorizing it and had to play from the score. . . . If even professionals cannot memorize a work, it shows that it's completely meaningless. The Western *avant-garde* music demonstrated at the Warsaw Festival is contrary to common sense and human nature.

Similarly, Shostakovich dismissed as "complete nonsense" both "concrete" and "electronic" music; a lot of these noises had been used ages ago in the cinema and radio as "background noises"; but to ask people to sit down in a concert hall and to listen to them in all seriousness as though they were music was just ridiculous.

In conclusion, he rather sharply criticized the Warsaw Festival where dodecaphonic and "experimental" Western music predominated; also, he regretted that so many young Polish composers—and even an eminent musician like Boleslaw Szabelski—seemed to be interested in these tricks, instead of following in the tradition of Chopin and Szymanowski; he also regretted that an outstanding young Polish composer like W. Lutoslawski should not have been performed at the Festival. He hoped that, at the next Warsaw Festival, "the true correlation of the musical forces in the world" would be more faithfully represented. It was no use giving the impression that the world was producing nothing but dodecaphonic music. He wanted to hear more music which appealed to the wide masses, and not just to a handful of sophisticated "specialists."

This attack by Shostakovich, himself denounced in the past as an "anti-people formalist," on ultra-modern music cannot, however, be dismissed as a mere tactical move, or as a political demonstration. Although Shostakovich is very far from conforming to the more primitive canons of Socialist realism (least of all in his chamber music or in his Twenty-Four Preludes and Fugues), and while fully conscious of being a bold "innovator" in Russian music (with him and Prokofiev as the two great models to very many young composers) he has, nevertheless, more or less forced himself to meet the official doctrines at least halfway. His music is tonal; and there is certainly more melody even in highly complex and sophisticated works like his tenth and eleventh Symphonies than there is in his very early works. And, like Sholokhov in literature, he is now accepted as being sufficiently "big" to be immune against "fundamental" criticism.

The Soviet Union continues to be a land of music-lovers. It has its low-brows (who buy up by the million gramophone records like Solovyov-Sedoi's latest hits), its middle-brows, who rush, as before, to the usual Beethoven-Tchaikovsky-Rachmaninov type of concerts, and its highbrows, who are interested in Shostakovich and Sviridov and other *new* Soviet composers. As distinct from 1948, the Party seems to have agreed at last that new musical works are not necessarily "anti-people" even if they do not "catch on" after a first hearing. But, in the view of Shostakovich, even the more complex forms of musical composition should have a melodic content—a view which was, in fact, fully endorsed by Prokofiev who considered melody the first essential of *any* musical work.

The output of new compositions in all the fifteen Soviet Republics is, of course, enormous. In search of new material, many composers (for instance B. Arapov of Leningrad) go and spend months and even years in China or in outlying areas of the Soviet Union; others follow, more or less, in the footsteps of Prokofiev or Shostakovich (e.g. the Leningrad composer of piano music, N. Chervinsky); much of such music is performed on a local level, or else included in Uzbek, Estonian, Latvian, Kazakh or other "festivals" in Moscow and other big cities; needless to say, only a very small proportion of this music "survives," and, in all the arts, the composer of serious music fights against heavier odds than any other artist to gain at least partial recognition. As in all other countries, it is infinitely more difficult for a composer than for a writer to become "well-known"; also, there are many "famous" composers in Russia—Miaskovsky, Shaporin, Shebalin, etc.—who have still made no impression on the outside world. Still, as one of Shostakovich's pupils—a young man in his twenties—put it to me: "We turn out an awful lot of rubbish. But we have a very widespread musical culture. An awful lot of music is being sung or played on an amateur level; look at all our *samodeyatelnost*! In some respects the situation is comparable to eighteenth- and nineteenth-century Germany; everybody (at least among the bourgeoisie) *musizierte*, as they say in German; in countless homes people would get together to play chamber music, no matter how badly; yet it was against this background of mediocre *musizieren* that Germany produced the big names— all the way from Bach to Wagner. It's when you have an *active* musical culture (and radio and gramophone records are passive, and therefore insufficient) that you get results; the Mozarts and Beethovens suddenly start popping up. Prokofiev and Shostakovich have already become world classics. There'll be more yet . . . I don't think the Party will do anything so deadening again as that 1948 Decree. It's learned its lesson."

Chapter 24

BETWEEN WASHINGTON AND
THE SUMMIT

(a) A WINTER OF EUPHORIA

SUCH WERE SOME of the aspects of Soviet life as it was shaping during the winter of 1959–60. Russia seemed contented and happy. Khrushchev's visit to the United States had created a feeling of euphoria, a feeling that the world was moving in the right direction—towards "a diminution in international tension," as the phrase went. Not all was well, of course, but as both Khrushchev and Gromyko said at the famous meeting of the Supreme Soviet of October 31, 1959: "The hand of the barometer is moving towards 'fair'—though not as quickly as we should like it to."

Khrushchev himself, in his long review of the international situation, was both optimistic and conciliatory. I attended that meeting and all Western observers in Moscow then said that this was "the most conciliatory speech he had ever made."

The "positions of strength" and "roll-back" policies had proved completely futile, he said. Lenin (Khrushchev argued) was "profoundly right when he spoke of the necessity of peaceful coexistence." Some people in the West were still arguing for and against "accepting" this Soviet proposal; the truth was that peaceful coexistence was not so much a proposal as "an objective necessity." Perhaps for the benefit of certain Chinese leaders, Khrushchev recalled Lenin's "wise and flexible policy" which aimed at the survival of the young Soviet State, and which was so different from Trotsky's adventurous "leftist" policy of "neither peace nor war," which

272

could only play into the hands of the German imperialists of those days.

After stressing once again the importance of his visit to the United States and the "great value" of his conversations with President Eisenhower—notably on general disarmament, the peace treaty with Germany and the Berlin problem—Khrushchev recalled the important contribution to an improvement in the international atmosphere made by his earlier talks with Mr. Macmillan, whereupon he paid some specially warm compliments to France. Although he regretted that France was a member of "military blocs directed against us," there were in fact no real conflicting interests between France and the Soviet Union:

We warmly appreciate the realistic utterances of President de Gaulle and Prime Minister Debré on the finality of the Oder-Neisse frontier. These are an important contribution to the consolidation of peace in Europe.

Even in his statement on Algeria Khrushchev sounded extremely friendly to France:

Naturally, like all peace-loving people, we are worried about the war that has been going on in Algeria during the last five years; but General de Gaulle's recent self-determination proposals may play a very important role in settling the Algerian problem, provided they do not remain mere figures of speech, but are followed up by realistic steps which would safeguard everybody's interests. We know that there are close historical bonds between France and Algeria. . . . We do not deny that our sympathies are with the oppressed people fighting against colonialism and for their independence and national freedom. Therefore, the peaceful settlement of the Algerian problem would, in our view, greatly enhance the international authority of France and her rôle as a Great Power.

Although the "ice of the Cold War had cracked," it was, however, still too early to say that all danger of war had passed. There was still considerable cause for alarm in Europe. Western Europe was dotted with bases and, despite countless protests, "the West-German Army is being equipped with nuclear arms and rockets."

Next on Khrushchev's list of "danger points" were Turkey and Iran, both of which had entered into anti-Soviet alliances, while Turkey had become a stronghold for American rocket bases, instead of following the wise neutral policy of Kemal Ataturk.

Khrushchev then called on both Turkey and Iran to revise their foreign policy.

After that, Khrushchev dwelt on other danger points, in the first place China. He described the conception of the "two Chinas" as complete nonsense. Both Roosevelt and Truman had recognized that Formosa constituted part of China, and Chiang Kai Shek was no more qualified to speak in the name of China than Kerensky would be to speak in the name of the Soviet Union!

The Taiwan (Formosa) "problem" was therefore an internal Chinese problem and the Soviet Union would continue to support China in her endeavor to reunite the country.

Khrushchev did not, however, give the impression that he favored any attempt by Peking to restore "Chinese unity" by military means.

Next "danger point": Korea. Syngman Rhee, Khrushchev said, was completely discredited; and if only foreign troops were moved out of Southern Korea, the two lots of Koreans would soon achieve unification of the country.

Khrushchev further deplored "foreign interference" in the internal affairs of Laos, which, as a result, had become a minor danger point, but still a danger point; the fault lay with the organizers of SEATO.

Finally, Khrushchev "deeply regretted" the frontier incidents that had recently occurred, with loss of life on both sides, between China and India. Brotherly bonds united the Soviet Union with China, and the Soviet Union was also developing the friendliest relations with India. He therefore urged both countries to settle their differences in a friendly and peaceful manner.

The rest of Khrushchev's speech was devoted to disarmament.

Here he outlined once again the proposals he had submitted to UN; explained again why the priority given by the West to control could only be a form of espionage, but denied that the Soviet Union had presented its plan on a "take-it-or-leave-it" basis. Even a partial agreement would be acceptable to the Soviet Union: for instance, one providing for the prohibition of nuclear weapons and, in the first place, the banning of nuclear tests; the creation of a European area of control, inspection and the limitation of foreign forces; the creation of an atom-free zone in Central Europe; the liquidation of military bases on foreign territories and a non-aggression pact between the NATO and the Warsaw Pact Powers.

At the Summit Conference, he concluded, priority should be given to (*a*) disarmament, (*b*) peace treaty with Germany, (*c*) Berlin.

Meantime, he appealed to all the Powers to do nothing which would create new difficulties before the Summit meeting, and create distrust and suspicion. For its own part, the Soviet Union would do everything to improve the international atmosphere between now and the Summit.

There was something prophetic in this appeal; *and was it not, in effect, an appeal to the USA to stop its "spy flights," of which Khrushchev was fully aware?*

Gromyko, who spoke at the same meeting of the Supreme Soviet, dealt chiefly with disarmament. He expressed satisfaction at the fact that "at present" nobody was making any nuclear tests, and repeated, in a slightly different form, what Khrushchev had already said about control:

Those who want control first and disarmament later are more concerned with espionage than with disarmament.

The Khrushchev and Gromyko speeches of October 31 set, as it were, the tone for the Soviet press during the months that were to follow. The tone was, generally, optimistic, except that little was left unsaid about the "danger points."

On the one hand, Khrushchev's visit to the USA continued to be treated as the beginning of a "new era." In *Literary Gazette* of November 21 even the fire-eating David Zaslavsky, in an article called "From Friendliness to Friendship"— prophesied that "historians would start the story of complete disarmament from Khrushchev's visit to the USA."

Even some rather fancy schemes were being played up as possible future examples of large-scale Soviet-American co-operation—for instance the project by a Soviet engineer, P. M. Borisov, for the building of a "climate-changing" dam across the Bering Straits between Siberia and Alaska. Much was also made of a statement in *Pravda,* by Adlai Stevenson criticizing American foreign policy as "obsolete."

On the other hand, however, the "adverse influences" in the USA were not altogether being neglected:

Whereas Herter was treated with marked reserve (the Russians seemed to have strong suspicions about him), attacks continued to be frequent against Allen Dulles, Nelson Rockefeller, Acheson and Truman as the principal political enemies of better Soviet-American relations. Eisenhower continued to be treated with great politeness, though his announcement that the nuclear tests moratorium would end on December 31—whether in practice the USA resumed tests after that date or not—was taken badly. A certain disquiet about things being not "all-well" in America was to be reflected in Khrushchev's next major international review—that before the Supreme Soviet on January 14, 1960.

Also, alongside reports like that of a Carnegie Hall meeting, where a Columbia professor said that the Khrushchev visit had "opened a new historical era," there were reports of the Cold War campaign conducted in various countries by the Moral Rearmament Buchmanites; as well as stories of the grubbier sides of "American civilization," such as the Van Doren quiz-show scandal.

Throughout the four months following Khrushchev's return from the USA the Soviet press continued an almost constant artillery barrage against Adenauer.

In the case of de Gaulle, the Soviet press had, however, been instructed to pull its punches. His press conference of November 10 was given in only an expurgated form; the remarks on the danger of "world Communism" and on "the yellow multitudes of China" (which, he implied, were also a menace to Russia) were omitted; but there was some sharp criticism of the French Government for having exploded its A-bomb in the Sahara and, under a banner headline of "THE SAHARA MUST NOT BECOME A TESTING GROUND FOR NUCLEAR WEAPONS, *Komsomolskaya Pravda* and other papers proceeded to report the extreme annoyance caused by the first French A-bomb test in the various African and Arab countries.

But while, on the one hand, the Soviet press reported, almost day after day, the great joy and enthusiasm with which France was "awaiting its eminent guest (Khrushchev), "and although nothing continued to be said about Algeria beyond what Khrushchev himself had said on October 31, a fairly strong and consistent anti-colonialist line continued to be maintained throughout. The greatest prominence was given to the visit to the Soviet Union of Sekou Touré, the President of Guinea, who was flown down to Gagry, where he dined with Khrushchev and had long conversations with him. Also, Guinea was given a Russian credit of 140 million rubles.[1]

Guinea's "positive neutrality" was praised in the Soviet press as a wise policy, and in the farewell broadcast he gave on Moscow TV, Sekou Touré not only dwelt on the progress in independent Guinea (emancipation of women, etc.), but spoke with special enthusiasm of the Soviet Union, where the entire people were "united round the Party and government"; where culture was not a privilege of the few, and where there was no racial discrimination, but a genuine feeling of friendship for the colonial peoples now breaking their chains.

Much attention was given, altogether, to the "general awakening" of Africa; frequent reports from Accra, Conakry and other African capitals were published by O. Orestov (who had now become the quasi-permanent *Pravda* correspondent in Africa) and others.

[1] Although the "Western bloc" was still far ahead of the "Communist bloc" in the amount of aid given to the underdeveloped countries between 1954 and 1959, the figures published in Washington in August 1960—nearly 18 billion dollars of Western aid, as against nearly 4 billion dollars Eastern aid for that period—were rather misleading. It was not clear how much of Russian aid to China was included in this second figure; the first figure, moreover, comprised various forms of aid—not all strictly economic—given by the USA to South America and by France to the "Community" countries. According to Washington sources, the Soviet Union was trying, in particular since 1959, to "establish bridgeheads in certain parts of the Free World," notably in Africa and in Latin America. The most significant recent moves were Soviet loans to Ethiopia and Guinea, *as well as a 100-million-dollar loan to Cuba.* In 1959 the Soviet Union had also given considerable aid to two Arab countries— the UAR and Iraq—while the biggest single loan (375 million dollars) had been granted to India for her third (1961–66) five-year Plan. Further substantial credits had been granted to Afghanistan (besides a gift of 30 million dollars for building a major road of 500 miles linking Kushka with the Soviet frontier), and 250 million dollars to Indonesia, besides other smaller loans or gifts to Burma and other countries.

The Russian approval of "positive neutrality" also applied to Nasser; much was made of the aid Russia had supplied to Egypt for building the first part of the High Aswan Dam, of the medal Nasser presented to Khrushchev, and of Nasser's big speech on January 10 in which he warmly thanked the Soviet Union for its "disinterested aid." As usual, no mention was made of Nasser's persecution of the Egyptian Communists—a point on which Peking felt very strongly.

Considerable interest was shown during those months in certain "danger zones" (Laos, in particular) and in places where the Western Powers were beginning to meet with difficulties, notably Cuba and Japan. The greatest prominence was given to all opposition in Japan to Kishi, "the American puppet"—who shared with Adenauer the privilege of being more viciously and frequently cartooned in the Soviet press than any other foreign leader. The succession of enthusiastic reports from Japan began with a *Pravda* dispatch from Tokyo on November 27 describing the gigantic mass demonstrations against the new "security" pact with the USA and in favor of Japanese neutrality.

Oddly enough, extremely little was said in the Soviet press during those months about China, apart from Chou En-Lai's letter to Nehru (*Pravda*, November 11), whereas a tremendous amount of space was given to India, with whole pages devoted to the Bhilai steel works set up with Russian help, complete with articles by Indians like a Mr. Chakravarti, on "Two Approaches, Two Results"—tending to prove that Soviet aid to India was more disinterested and more effective than Western aid. Not only was Voroshilov sent to open the Soviet pavilion at the Agricultural Exhibition in Delhi in January, but Khrushchev himself was going to visit India a month later on his way to Indonesia. Meantime, Mikoyan had been sent on a similar mission to Mexico and Cuba. This visit to Cuba was a major landmark.

In short, there is no doubt that, whereas the establishment of better relations with the United States and an agreement on disarmament, Germany and Berlin were in the center of Khrushchev's preoccupations, *the Russians were, even during the post-Washington euphoria, extremely interested in the changes that were taking place in Africa, were "competing" rather energetically with the West in the "uncommitted" countries (India, Egypt, Guinea), were watching with great*

*eagerness the signs of any Western setbacks (Cuba, Japan),
and with some alarm the "American intrigues in neutral
countries (Laos)."*

Thus, Soviet foreign policy was conducted, as it were, along
two parallel lines: agreement with America and her allies on
certain specific points (disarmament, Germany, Berlin) which
was primarily required for immediate security reasons; and,
secondly, "peaceful competition" with the West in Asia,
Africa, etc., containing a certain "missionary" element which
could, historically, be traced back to the Comintern. Only, the
methods (economic aid) and tactics (no revolutionary verbi-
age) used were just as different as were the territories on
which this Russian influence was now being exercised. Interest
in the Communist parties of France and Italy was slight, and
in those of Britain or the USA non-existent; nor was Russia
interested in the Communist Parties of the underdeveloped
countries. Instead, it was keenly interested in their govern-
ments, insofar as these were "anti-imperialist."

Neutralism, though frowned upon by Peking, was considered a good thing and the old maxim "Those not with us
are against us" did not apply.

At the meeting of the Supreme Soviet on January 14
Khrushchev gave what might be called an interim report on
the international situation—roughly, halfway between his
visit to the USA and the Summit Conference. After dealing
in the usual self-congratulatory style with the internal and
economic situation in the Soviet Union, he dealt at great
length with the general international outlook, and sounded, if
anything, rather *less* optimistic than on October 31. While
saying that the world was gradually moving away from the
Cold War, he warned his audience not to be overoptimistic,
since the "warming-up process" went, as it were, in zigzags.
All the same—

We may expect a great deal from President Eisenhower's return visit to our country in June. The Soviet Government hopes
that the noble work of creating confidence in the relations between our two countries which we started at Camp David, will
continue in Moscow.

It was all the more regrettable, he said, that influential
people in America, such as "the unholy Rockefeller-Acheson-

Truman trinity," were still speaking from positions very far removed from that of Camp David. It was also regrettable that President Eisenhower should have declared, on December 29, that the nuclear test moratorium was about to end.

He then dealt once again with disarmament and with the Bill put before the Supreme Soviet *for the reduction of the Soviet Armed Forces by one-third—i.e. by 1,200,000 men.* This would be of the greatest benefit to the economy of the country; but, considering the development of new types of weapons, the Soviet people could be certain that this cut in their Armed Forces "did not diminish the impregnability of their country."

In the course of his long speech Khrushchev also sharply attacked Adenauer, adding—and here he used the familiar wartime vocabulary—that "if the West-German reptile ever tried to crawl out of its lair, it would not, this time, be allowed to crawl all the way to Moscow or Stalingrad, but would be crushed in its own territory."

Khrushchev further announced the coming visit to Moscow of President Gronchi of Italy, and his own journey to Indonesia, India, Burma and Afghanistan. After paying a particularly warm tribute to President Sukarno of Indonesia, he ended with a long harangue against colonialism.

(b) THE INDONESIAN TOUR

There was a striking contrast between the frigid reception given in Moscow at the beginning of February to President Gronchi—who left Russia without, apparently, asking Khrushchev to pay a return visit to Rome,[2] and the all-round good-fellowship and cordiality that marked Khrush-

---

[2] For instance, in his speech at the Italian Embassy reception, Khrushchev went out of his way to recall that Italy had been an ally of Nazi Germany, and that Italian soldiers had taken part in the invasion of the Soviet Union. Also, he alluded to the close relations between the Italian Government and Adenauer, and altogether made no secret of his hostility to the Vatican. With a touch of rather heavy irony he complimented Gronchi on the courage he had shown in coming to the Soviet Union at all. Some acid words were also used by the Russians, in the course of the Gronchi visit, about American bases in Italy.

chev's visit to Indonesia, with calls, on the way or on the return journey, to India, Burma and Afghanistan.

This visit to India and to the other "uncommitted" countries of South-East Asia had a multiple purpose. One was to secure the full support from Nehru, Sukarno and other Asian leaders for Khrushchev's disarmament proposals and to demonstrate the great solidarity between the Soviet Union and the countries Khrushchev was visiting in this and other matters of general policy. Nehru, at the public meeting in Calcutta on March 1, referred to Khrushchev as *"a real friend"* and as *"the man who was carrying the banner of peace for all people."* Disarmament, he also said, was particularly valuable to the underdeveloped countries, and he stressed the fact that India had, throughout her history, been a fervent believer in peace and non-violence.

Khrushchev paid, in the course of his numerous speeches, various tributes to the "peace philosophy" of India. (Gone were the days of Russian snarling at Gandhi.)

Secondly, Khrushchev was extremely anxious to bring about a settlement between India and China; and his visit to India helped to pave the way for Chou En-Lai's subsequent (though disappointing) talks with Nehru.

Thirdly, Khrushchev made a point of visiting the Bhilai steel works and other industrial and agricultural enterprises set up with Soviet technical and financial aid. At Bhilai he attended a lively meeting, in which he not only reminisced about his early days as a "common worker," but also spoke with considerable technical knowledge of the various aspects of steel and pig-iron production and of the saving in metal in the actual building of the plant that the use of reinforced concrete represented, as against the use of steel—"which a country like India should use as sparingly as possible."

He foreshadowed the time when—especially if disarmament made any substantial progress—the Soviet Union would play an overwhelmingly important part in the economic development of the underdeveloped countries.

In the Soviet-Indian communiqué it was stated that Khrushchev and Nehru had noted with satisfaction, not only the fullest agreement on disarmament, but also the successful development of economic and cultural relations between the two countries: it enumerated the various enterprises set up in India with Soviet aid (Bhilai steel works, maching-tool works at Ranchi, an electric power station, a state farm, an oil refinery, etc.). In addition to earlier credits, the Soviet Union was now granting India a further credit of 1.5 billion rubles.

All went off very well in Burma, too, where Khrushchev visited the technological institute and a hotel in Rangoon which the Soviet Union had presented as a gift to the people of Burma. Similarly, on his return journey, Khrushchev exalted the active friendship between the Soviet Union and Afghanistan. On his return to Moscow, he expressed great satisfaction at the modernization that was in full progress in Afghanistan: during his (and the unmentioned Bulganin's) visit there in 1955, most of the women in Afghanistan were still veiled; now they had dropped the veil. Both at Kabul (where he visited the Soviet-built airfield and other enterprises built with Soviet aid), as well as on his return to Moscow, Khrushchev delivered a little side-kick at American-controlled Pakistan and supported the Afghan proposal in favor of a referendum in Pushtanistan. The Pushtanis should determine themselves whether they wished to form part of Pakistan, become independent, or join up with Afghanistan.

But if Khrushchev still pulled his punches in India and Burma, both of which were "positively neutral" without any strong anti-Western bias, in Indonesia—where he spent fully twelve days—he missed no opportunity of attacking colonialism vociferously, making the most of the fact that the Dutch were still clinging to Western New Guinea. If Nehru was still slightly reserved in relation to the Soviet Union, President Sukarno of Indonesia suffered from no such inhibitions. (It was not surprising when, a few weeks later, one of the Lenin Peace Prizes was awarded in Moscow to the Indonesian President.) Both in his address before the Indonesian Parliament on February 26 and at his Djakarta press conference on February 29 Khrushchev touched more squarely on a number of points than he had done in either India or Burma.

Thus, before the Indonesian Parliament, he said that colonialism had today adopted new tactics and that no ex-colonial country, though now nominally independent, could consider itself safe. The collective colonialism, represented by an aggressive force like SEATO, was constantly plotting against the unity of countries like Indonesia.

After saying that Soviet help to the underdeveloped countries was wholly disinterested, Khrushchev made an extremely important point when he agreed with President Sukarno that *the four-power Summit meeting in May could not be considered as "representative."*

Why then are we taking part in this meeting? You will remember, members of the Indonesian Parliament, that we asked in the past for a more extensive Summit meeting. We then argued that both camps should be more adequately represented, and that certain neutral countries like India should also be included. But we met with no response from our Western partners. Apparently conditions are not yet ripe in which they would see the light. Meantime, it would, in my view, be a mistake to reject a small thing because we can't get anything bigger, since, at even such a limited Summit, we may still achieve many things which would improve the international atmosphere.

And then:

And yet, what constitutes a Great Power these days? By "great" powers "strong" powers are meant. We are against this definition. At the Summit there should certainly be room for countries like China, India, Indonesia and Japan. The fact that certain powers—which by both their area and population, are much smaller than the great Asian powers—should be represented at the Summit, and these Asian powers should not be, is an absurd anachronism—which hits every thinking person in the eye.

And Khrushchev said *the time was not far off when these great Asian countries would take part in any "Summit" meetings.* He also indicated that much smaller countries should be given better protection than they had been, up till now, by the UN.

He then attacked the Kishi government in Japan.

At the Djakarta press conference on February 29, in reply to a remark to the effect that Kishi had described Khrushchev's earlier statement as "interference in internal Japanese affairs," Khrushchev now let fly: He declared the Japanese-American "security" Pact was one directed against the Soviet Union, asked whether the Kishi Government wasn't planning to resurrect, with American aid, the old Tanaka Plan for the conquest of Asia—a plan which Indonesia had certainly not forgotten.

And then came another lecture on what the Soviet Union meant by aid to the underdeveloped countries:

The Soviet people gladly share their experience with all peoples, and gladly help young independent countries to build their own national economy. I am glad to say that for a number of years now economic and technical co-operation has been developing between the Soviet Union and numerous Asian and African countries. In 1960 alone the Soviet Union will help in setting up 383 industrial enterprises in 22 different countries. . . . Our aid aims, above all, at helping countries to develop their own means of production, which, in turn, would increase these countries' economic and political independence. . . . The Soviet people earnestly hope that, with the completion of their gigantic seven-year plan, and with a reduction in military expenditure, they will be able to supply more and more and more equipment and technical aid to the countries of Asia and Africa, and so contribute to the development of their national economies. Our interest rates are very favorable, and are merely intended to cover the costs of the operation; and our loans are not accompanied by any conditions which would be contrary, in any way, to the sovereignty and dignity of the countries concerned. We Communists aim not only at our own countries having better living conditions; we want *all* countries to have better living conditions.

As against this:

If I want to be quite candid, I must say that the Western Powers, which, over the centuries, have pumped untold wealth out of their colonies, and are continuing to do so in various ways, even after these colonies have conquered their political independence, might surely, in the name of justice, give them back some of the stolen property. . . . But they still work along the old principle: "You can't sell without cheating." Western aid is calculated to create a strangle-hold over the country "benefiting" from this aid.

All this was a far cry to the friendly Washington exchanges.

The joint Soviet-Indonesian communique of February 28, signed by Khrushchev and Sukarno, was of considerable interest:

In it the Soviet Union reaffirmed its support for the principles laid down by the Bandung Conference of 1955; [3]
It supported the Indonesian claim on Western Irian (New Guinea);
It approved the calling of the May "Summit," but added that, in future, other countries, including "uncommitted" countries, should, if possible, take part in such major international conferences;
Both countries agreed that Indonesia's "active, neutral and independent foreign policy" was a valuable contribution to the preservation of peace in the world;
Both countries noted that the general agreement of economic and technical co-operation between the two countries of September 15, 1956, was working satisfactorily; the two signatories had also discussed further Soviet credits for setting up steel, engineering, chemical, textile and other works in Indonesia; an agreement had been reached for a further credit of $250,-000,000.
As a gift to Indonesia, the Soviet Government had decided to build at Djakarta a hospital with 200 beds, and a polyclinic attached. Two libraries (partly scientific) were presented by Khrushchev to two Indonesian universities, and the Soviet Union was also contributing to the building of a Technological Institute for training Indonesian specialists in shipbuilding and oceanography.

For nearly four weeks did the Soviet press and radio concentrate on describing in the most rapturous terms the Khrushchev visit to Southeast Asia. Two or three pages a day were devoted to descriptions of the enthusiastic crowds and to the countless speeches made by Khrushchev, Sukarno, Nehru, etc.

The full significance of the visit, especially from the "cultural" angle, was discussed at great length in *Pravda* of March 15, by G. A. Zhukov, head of the Soviet Cultural Committee, who had accompanied Khrushchev on the trip. He dwelt on the fact that Asia had good reason to distrust "white men"; *the Russians were the first "white men" who*

---

[3] Whether China was fully supporting these now was far from clear.

could be trusted. With a few exceptions like Dr. Albert Schweitzer, "white" men from the West, in going to these countries, went there merely with the idea of amassing a little fortune as quickly as possible and of going home after that. Also, there were still only too many Western scouts who roved about the underdeveloped countries these days, dressed up as *kulturträger* with their various "information offices" and the like. These were very different from people like "that modest Russian woman doctor, Makeyeva, who had wandered from one Indian village to another to relieve suffering, and who had become a legendary figure in Indian folklore." Brave Russian men were now building roads in the jungles of Borneo to new centers of industrial development. And so on, and so on.

Actually, the cultural exchanges were still rather limited. There were, said Zhukov, seventy Indonesian student studying in the Soviet Union, including the son of Mr. Priyomo, the Indonesian minister of education. And he recalled that when an audience of Indonesian students said to Khrushchev: "Will you take fifty of our students to Russia?" he replied: "Fifty-one, if you like!" (Fifty-one, not five hundred!)

A big impression had, all the same, been made by his announcement that a "Friendship of Nations University" would be set up in Russia—where "gifted young people from poorer families in countries which had newly won their independence" could go.[4]

What counted above all, Zhukov said, was not the exchange of films and artists, but the establishment of human contracts between the peoples of Russia and Asia; and wherever Russians and Asians met—for instance at Bhilai— and worked together, the results were good.

In all this Russian presentation of Soviet-Indian and Soviet-Indonesian relations, there was no doubt an element of oversimplification; for one thing, no comparisons were ever made between the quantity of Russian versus Western aid given to these countries; or the respective number of, say, Indian students studying in Russia or the West; and yet one could see how the "peaceful competiton" with the West was going to develop in the coming years; and why, psychologically,

---

[4] Later, after the murder of the Congolese leader, this was to be given the name of the "Lumumba University."

the Russian "anti-colonialist" propaganda was bound to be effective.

In this seemingly fruitful establishment of friendly relations between the Soviet Union and a country like Indonesia, there was one unknown factor: and that was China. Was not Indonesia, potentially, a Chinese "sphere of influence?" Was not Russia trying to forestall China, while the latter was still too busy at home? The question was put by many Western commentators. It is hard to say what the answer is. There seemed, in February 1960, some fairly strong ideological differences between China and Russia on this very question of countries like India and Indonesia. And at any rate, one thing is certain: while in Indonesia, Khrushchev very seldom mentioned China, and certainly did not give the impression that he was, in any way, acting as the representative of some kind of Soviet-Chinese economic or ideological bloc. . . .[5]

(c) KHRUSHCHEV'S PARADOXICAL VISIT TO FRANCE

The change of scenery from Indonesia to France was very striking. It was not only a change of scenery, but also of political temperature—though, oddly enough, the Russians, and indeed Khrushchev himself had gone to France, as we shall see, with a number of preconceived notions, which lent the Russian visit to France a curiously paradoxical aspect, a certain unreality, and many touches of more or less unconscious comedy.

There was going to be an interval of only a few days between Khrushchev's return from Indonesia and his arrival in France; but suddenly he developed flu and the visit was postponed for about ten days. Needless to say, there was some inevitable talk of a "diplomatic illness," which was attributed to all kinds of causes: Russian resentment at Adenauer's "growing influence" on de Gaulle; various reports to the effect that the West—and de Gaulle in the first place—were not going to budge one inch on the question of Berlin; and, finally, the attempts by the French to include in Khrush-

---

[5] As in the case of Egypt and some other countries, the Russians turned a blind eye to the official Indonesian attitude to the local Communists, whose papers, in particular, had been prohibited.

chev's program a visit to the Sahara oilfields—a visit which Khrushchev would have considered extremely tactless *vis-à-vis* the Algerians and, indeed, the whole Arab world.

As it turned out, Khrushchev's illness was not a diplomatic one. Whether he had flu or not, he was certainly extremely tired after his fortnight in the tropical heat of Indonesia. When finally he arrived in Paris on March 23 he was not at the top of his form.

When, a fortnight later, he made a big speech at the Luzhniki Sports Palace in Moscow to report on his *Tour de France*, the tone was rather different from that of the enthusiastic speech he delivered to the Moscow public after his return from the USA. He seemed slightly embarrassed and inhibited. He said nothing at all about the French régime; nor was he very precise about de Gaulle; he no longer went out of his way to pay de Gaulle the compliments he had paid him in the two big speeches he had made in the last few months before the Supreme Soviet. Now he said that the net result of the visit to France was "rather good," and suggested even that he had got on better with de Gaulle than he had expected:

In Paris, as well as at Rambouillet, we talked at table, or during walks in the park. These conversations were good and candid, warm and, I might even say, friendly. Certain bourgeois journalists had prophesied that de Galle and I were such different types that we would certainly quarrel. One of them even said he wished he could have hidden under the table to hear the awful row. Fortunately for him, he wasn't there; he might have died or rage listening to the perfectly peaceful way in which we talked.

But there was something halfhearted about this bit of badinage.

Without going into any details as to what was said, Khrushchev merely declared that he and de Gaulle were, by and large, in agreement on the problem of disarmament:

I might say that on this fundamental question our points of view coincide. (*Prolonged applause.*) And even if the journey to France had done no more than clarify our positions on this question, it would have been worth while. That is why we can say that the results of the journey were positive.

And yet, there was, it was felt, something "not quite right" about Khrushchev's speech on his French visit.

What then was wrong about the Khrushchev visit to France? I was able, during that visit, to speak to a great many Soviet journalists and diplomats, and this is the impression I got:

For one thing, Khrushchev was not in very good health when he arrived in Paris, and, therefore, not in very good form. Besides, like most of the persons who accompanied him, he seemed to have some preconceived notions on France. It is true, that, since September 1958 (the first de Gaulle-Adenauer meeting) the Russians no longer had any very great illusions on de Gaulle. But lots of Soviet people were still, as regards France, full of a few naïve ideas they had picked up at school. France to them was "the Mother of Revolutions, the mother of generous ideas," the land of Voltaire, Balzac, Stendhal, Victor Hugo, the country of the Great French Revolution, of the Commune of 1871, of the Resistance during the last war. The "people of France" were something rather special.

The Soviet press had, indeed, for months, been describing the tremendous enthusiasm with which the people of France were looking forward to the Khrushchev visit. And during the visit itself, the whole tone of the Soviet press was positively rapturous. *Literary Gazette* would print in French right across the top of its front page: C'EST MAGNIFIQUE! or VIVE L'UNION SOVIETIQUE! The rapturous tone of the Soviet reporting is hard to imagine without a few quotations taken at random. Thus, in *Literary Gazette* of April 2 my friend Boris Polevoi wrote:

We always knew that France was a hospitable country. It receives kings, presidents, heads of government with the greatest courtesy. But with N. S. Khrushchev it was different. True French politeness quickly turned into genuine cordiality, and official courtesy into that marvelous hospitality which is reserved for only the dearest and most beloved guests. We Soviet people—even those of us who had never been in France before

—know well these cities—Paris, Brodeaux, Marseille, Nimes, Metz, Verdun, Reims, Lille, Rouen—ancient cities full of glory which we know since our earliest youth, and which we love with a sort of tender affection thanks to the great French writers and the great French painters.

It is not very clear why any Russian should tenderly love Metz—but never mind. And Polevoi went on:

Many of the foreign correspondents who prophesied that the journey would be a failure have now learned their lesson: every day they witnessed the meetings at which the official personages of France—the President of the Republic, ministers, prefects, mayors and deputies—and, above all, the people of France—the peasants, workers and intellectuals—paid tribute to their Soviet guest with so much solemnity and with so much affectionate cordiality. . . . Yes, anti-Soviet propaganda had proved a washout: the descendants of those who had captured the Bastille, who had danced in the streets to the tune of the *Carmagnole*, of those who had died on the barricades of the Commune could not but welcome with all their heart the head of the government of our great Soviet Union.

The *équivoque* cannot but hit you in the eye. On the one hand the Commune, on the other hand—M. Debré! The Soviet visit took place, as it were, on two levels: on the one hand, it was politically opportune for Khrushchev to meet de Gaulle, and to agree with him as far as possible; on the other hand it was a sort of sentimental pilgrimage, And yet, as it turned out, the *real* French people, corresponding most closely to the Soviet conception of the French people, were, in spite of everything, the Communists. The photos of cheering crowds published in the Soviet press were mostly photos of French working-class (i.e. largely Communist) crowds. Officially, however, this was called "the French people."

As for the others—i.e. the official personages—one had the impression that the Russians found them almost too good to be true. Practically *all* the French were extremely polite, though only too often in a *protocolaire* kind of way. Nobody went out of his way to say anything unpleasant to Khrushchev. In his Moscow report on the visit, all that Khrushchev found to criticize was the "Kir incident" at Dijon where the

Church hierarchy forcibly prevented the 84-year-old Canon Kir, mayor of Dijon and a hero of the Resistance, from receiving Khrushchev at the town hall or from even meeting him privately.

But apart from that, everybody was perfectly "correct" and even nice, including some of the high-ups of the régime like M. Chaban-Delmas at Bordeaux, or a Socialist leader like M. Defferre, Mayor of Marseille.

At times, Khrushchev almost seemed bored, and he might even have liked to have a bit of a dog-fight with M. Defferre, as he had had one with the Labor leaders in London or with the labor union leaders in San Francisco. But nobody had the slightest intention of "provoking" him. So, feeling he needed a change, he went into the press carriage on the train between Lille and Rouen just for the pleasure, one rather felt, of saying a few home truths to some of the American journalists there. There he pounced on one of them: "Go on, write on the Soviet Union all the swinish nonsense you want." And then he added:

You remind me of a drunk who went to see a doctor. "What shall I do, doctor, about my red nose?" "You drink a lot?" said the doctor. "Well, yes, rather." "Then," said the doctor, "drink still more till your nose goes blue."

On the following day the entire Soviet press carried this story. It was as if the French trip wasn't, without this kind of thing, providing enough entertainment to the Soviet readers; and Khrushchev liked to keep his public amused. Yet in France, everybody was so damned "correct"; if only Defferre or, better still, Guy Mollet had wanted to provoke Khrushchev! But that again would have been awkward: he couldn't very well attack Mollet without saying some rude things about de Gaulle and his system.

In fact, apart from the artificially-created incident with the American newspaper man, there was only one occasion on which Khrushchev lost his temper, and that was when, at Verdun, he attacked M. Jacquinot (one of de Gaulle's Ministers accompanying him) for not being more aware of the German danger.

Here was really something fundamental.

What, indeed, puzzled Khrushchev and all the Russians

accompanying him was the kind of indifference with which the French seemed to react to his violent diatribes against German militarism—a question on which Khrushchev, like all Russians, felt very strongly. True, there were stories in the Soviet press of an old French veteran of Verdun shaking hands with Khrushchev, with tears trickling down his wrinkled face; but, as a Soviet correspondent later remarked to me:

The thing that has bothered us most during this visit to France is that the French seem to have forgotten the German invasions. Can it be that Verdun—which was, after all, their Stalingrad—no longer rings a bell? Makes one wonder whether Ehrenburg and all our other "French experts" have not grossly exaggerated the anti-Boche sentiment existing in France.

"But, after all," he added bitterly, "the French did come to terms with the Germans in 1940; and isn't Vichyism playing a certain part inside the de Gaulle government?"

And then he said: "Also, we have always been taught that there's a great revolutionary tradition in France; but does it really exist—apart from the Communists?"

And then there was Algeria. Soviet correspondents I saw were rather puzzled about that, too. As one of them said to me:

No doubt it would have been awkward for Khrushchev to say anything about Algeria. But we were all much impressed by de Gaulle's self-determination offer of September 16 last and, even more so, by his handling of the Fascist rebellion of January 24. But now we can't make head or tail of it any longer. During his last meeting with de Gaulle, Khrushchev wanted to declare himself in full agreement with de Gaulle's self-determination offer in exchange for a de Gaulle statement confirming his earlier stand on the Oder-Neisse frontier. De Gaulle turned it down.

And then there were the French Communists. In his Moscow speech, Khrushchev said practically nothing about them, apart from having "warmly shaken hands with comrades Thorez and Duclos" when they met in Lenin's little flat in the 14 arrondissement. (There had been no "kissing on the mouth in Russian style," as *L'Aurore* had reported.)

Privately, Khrushchev had also told Thorez that Russia attached very great importance to a settlement of the Algerian problem; but that was all.

As for de Gaulle himself, Khrushchev seemed puzzled by the man.

Despite the assurance he gave his Moscow audience that his talks with de Gaulle had been satisfactory, there seemed some doubts about it among the Soviet correspondents accompanying him. Had there been *full* agreement on disarmament (later Khrushchev claimed that de Gaulle had gone back on the assurances he had given him)? And Berlin? Apparently de Gaulle had been wholly uncompromising. Even so, at the time of the last Rambouillet meeting, Soviet correspondents were saying that "the two old men were getting on like a house on fire." How could this be true? And, at the press conference he gave soon afterwards Khrushchev mumbled and stumbled, and seemed rather tired, and not too delighted. And his prefabricated speech on TV where, for the first time since his arrival in France, he went out of his way to boost the Communist régime in Russia, was delivered in a flat, tired voice, and did not make a particularly good impression in France. Not that this prevented French radio from paying a remarkable farewell compliment to Khrushchev who was described by the professionally anti-Soviet M. Maurice Ferro (of all people!) as *"un très grand homme d'état"*—a phrase quite obviously used on de Gaulle's personal instructions.

It is quite true that very many people in France—and not only Communists—who saw Khrushchev and Mrs. Khrushchev thought they were *sympathiques*; "Krou-Krou" had, on the whole, made quite a nice impression, and, apart from some snarling in the *Figaro*, *L'Aurore* and the *Parisien Libéré*, the trip had been covered in the French press very fully and, on the whole, sympathetically. But this didn't mean very much; and the impression among Soviet correspondents towards the end of the visit was that, nicely though everything—or nearly everything—had gone off, the whole visit had proved singularly inconclusive, and that Khrushchev had perhaps even been a little too gushing and had wasted a lot of breath for no very "positive" purpose. Had the chances of the Summit improved? There was very little to show that they had.

(d) COLD WAR CURRENTS BEFORE THE SUMMIT

The short period between the end of the inconclusive visit to France and the American spy plane incident was marked —and this is very important to remember—by a serious deterioration in Soviet-Western relations.

The Soviet press continued to publish rapturous retrospective articles about the reception given to Khrushchev by "the French people," even ten or twelve days after the end of the visit, but very little was now being said about de Gaulle, except that some of his utterances during his London visit were given a very unfavorable reception. "It was particularly regrettable (said *Pravda* of April 11) that, after recalling our joint battle against Nazi Germany, de Gaulle should have added in his London speech that the alliance with Bonn was essential for both France and Britain." Even before that, *Literary Gazette* of April 9 said that while it continued to be optimistic about the prospects of the Summit meeting, there was no doubt that a lot of dirty work was going on, especially in the USA and in Western Germany. Significantly, too, the Soviet press began to be acid about the French atom bombs in the Sahara, the second of which had been exploded at the time of Khrushchev's visit to France. Now, on April 11, *Pravda* published a glowing article on the opening of the Afro-Asian Solidarity Conference at Conakry; this was illustrated by a large photograph showing a huge crowd of Africans carrying a banner: PAS DE BOMBES ATOMIQUES AU SAHARA!; and the enthusiastic story of the "free people of Guinea" ended with some more melancholy reflections on the fact that the great mineral wealth of Guinea "was still being exploited by French, English and American companies which were paying Guinea only a small fraction of their profits."

All these were straws in the wind. But many more were to come. Another was the extreme dissatisfaction shown over Mr. Herter's Chicago speech of April 4. How seriously this was taken in Moscow may be judged from the fact that *Pravda* of April 14 devoted to it an interminable blast of four complete columns, from which it became only too clear that Herter was not interested in the Soviet disarmament proposals, despite his earlier (and much more favorable) comments on the Khrushchev Plan; and that on NATO, the future of Germany and Berlin, he held views very like those of Dr. Adenauer. Herter, *Pravda* said, was now trying to tie up Berlin once more in the "all-German packet"; instead of clearing away obstacles on the way to the Summit, the Secretary of State was, much to Adenauer's delight, building up new obstacles; and the whole article was entitled "HERTER OUT OF STEP WITH THE TIMES."

Highly significant in the light of what happened at the Summit a month later was the fact that the article on Herter was followed by the report of a statement by Adlai Stevenson sharply criticizing the United States government for its "policy of fruitless anti-Communism and stupid self-deception." In the same speech Stevenson spoke of the "Dynamic and purposeful" policy of the Soviet Union, and, moreover, dwelt on the absurdity of not recognizing the existence of China with its 650 million people. Instead, the United States Government continued to hobnob with dictators, while bleating about freedom.

It is clear from this that, *already in the middle of April (if not before) Khrushchev had some very grave doubts about the Eisenhower Administration wanting to get anywhere with the Summit meeting.* That this was so was to be confirmed by the violent attack on Nixon and Dillon in *Pravda* on May 27, two days after Khrushchev's famous speech at Baku. From both the attitude of the Soviet press during the greater part of April and Khrushchev's Baku speech it seems obvious that, in the Russian view, Eisenhower—whatever he himself felt about it—was surrounded by Cold War men. If the Russians were not so convinced of this, would they have built the U-2 incident into quite so decisive a test case as they did? Did the thought not cross Khrushchev's mind at the time of the Baku speech—i.e. even before the U-2 incident—that it might be better to wait till somebody else replaced the Herters, Nixons and Dillons—unless Eisenhower took a line very different from theirs?

True, Khrushchev began his review of the international situation in his speech at Baku by sounding an optimistic note:

We consider that the international situation is good. The meetings we have had with foreign leaders, and in the first place our visit to the USA, our talks with Mr. Macmillan, our visit to India, Burma, Afghanistan and Indonesia, and our recent visit to France all point to a reduction in international tension. . . . We have the impression that all the leaders we met understand the necessity of settling international disputes by means of negotiations, and not by military means. I believe that this favorable process will continue. But, at the same time, I consider it my duty to point to certain highly unfavorable factors in international life which call for a certain vigilance and caution.

After dealing with the thorny problem of nuclear tests, Khrushchev then said:

As regards the questions which will have to be considered in Paris, I must say that, as the day of the Summit meeting approaches, the more one-sided is the approach to these problems on the part of certain Western statesmen. . . . We don't have to look far for examples. Mr. Dillion's pre-Summit speech simply stinks of the Cold War. . . . He keeps on talking about the "constant Communist threat to peace," wants to throw overboard the whole concept of peaceful coexistence, and grossly distorts the Soviet proposals on disarmament, on the peace treaty with Germany and the turning of West Berlin into a free city. Dillon is trying to bring in an element of malevolence and distrust on the very eve of the Summit conference—that is, at a time when it is essential to create an atmosphere of mutual confidence.

Khrushchev complained that all that Dillon had said was wholly contrary to the Camp David spirit (suggesting thereby that Eisenhower was *perhaps* in disagreement with this *new* line—at least he hoped so), but then promptly added (*a*) that Mr. Dillon was, after all, "no outsider in American government circles" and (*b*) that even if one assumed, in spite of this, that he was only speaking for himself, his words could not be ignored, since there were many other things which made one "sit up with a start."

And Khrushchev ended his speech by saying that if all else failed, the Soviet Union would sign a peace treaty with the German Democratic Republic, and then the West would have no right to enter West Berlin by land, water, or air.

The importance of the Baku speech of April 25 should not

be underrated; while still giving Eisenhower the benefit of the doubt, Khrushchev said in it, in effect, that all the important American leaders were against the Summit meeting —or at least against its achieving any positive results:

> There are some who think that this Summit meeting can be merely a place where a few opinions will be exchanged, and where nobody will be committed to anything.

It is also significant that both during the days preceding, and during the days following the Baku speech, the Soviet press was nothing but a series of blasts against the would-be wreckers of the Summit—Adenauer in the first place, but also Dillon and Nixon. *Pravda* was particularly annoyed by Nixon for not only failing to disavow Dillon's "pure Cold War" outlook, but also for repeating Adenauer's "ideas" on Berlin, and for treating the East-German republic as "a myth of Soviet propaganda." "Some myth!" *Pravda* of April 27 exclaimed. "A myth which in terms of industrial development is well ahead of Sweden and Italy, and in terms of electric power is bigger than Belgium, Holland, Denmark and Finland taken together!"

On the same page as this three-column blast against Nixon and Dillon in *Pravda* of April 27 was also a three-column dispatch from Pyongyang under the title:

SYNGMAN RHEE'S BLOODY RÉGIME CRUMBLING
Hundreds of Thousands of Insurgents in the Streets of Seoul.
Demonstrations Throughout South Korea.
Syngman Rhee Announces His Resignation.
The Rebellion Is Spreading.

And three days later, *Pravda* devoted three more columns to the "incredible economic mess" that had been made of South Korea, that "bloodstained show-window of the Free World." And it ended with a call to American troops to get out of Korea. "Perhaps the whole of America will realize at last that this is the rotten régime for the maintenance of which 160,000 young Americans were killed or maimed."

Thus, only a few days before the U-2 incident, the Soviet Government and its press were pretty sure of two things: leading American statesmen (Dillon, Herter, Nixon—*perhaps*

Eisenhower himself, but that remained to be seen) were being thoroughly obstructive about the forthcoming Summit meeting, and, secondly, the "Free World" was creaking in several places: Japan, Korea, Africa, Cuba.

Chapter 25

COLLAPSE OF THE SUMMIT

ON THAT MAY 1, the May-Day parades in Moscow, Leningrad and other cities were much the same as they had been in previous years. A rather routine speech was made to the troops by Marshal Malinovsky, the Minister of Defense, who said, among other things:

> The peoples of the whole world are expecting from the coming Summit meeting a just and urgent settlement of the most essential problems of our time: complete and general disarmament, the liquidation of the remnants of World War II [i.e. peace treaty with Germany and the Berlin problem]. . . . But while we note that international relations are warmer than they used to be, we must not forget that, in a number of countries, there are some influential forces still . . . striving to take the world back to the dark days of the Cold War. This compels us to be extremely vigilant and to maintain our defenses at a high level. . . . We shall deliver a smashing blow at any aggressor who would attempt to attack our great country. . . .

It is just possible that the moment this speech was delivered, Marshal Malinovsky already knew about the spy plane that had been brought down at Sverdlovsk that morning. . . .

During the next few days nothing very striking happened. On May 1, *Pravda* had run a rather optimistic international survey by Ehrenburg, in which he had gone all lyrical about the month of May being a good month, a month of hope. During the next two days the spotlight in the Soviet press was chiefly turned on South Korea and the downfall of

Syngman Rhee. On May 4, the Lenin Peace Prizes were announced; these were conferred on President Sukarno of Indonesia; on Cyrus Eaton, the "friendly capitalist" of Ohio; on Laurent Casanova, the French Communist leader; Alexander Korneichuk, the Ukrainian playwright; and Aziz Sherif of Iraq. Mr. Novotny and other Czechoslovak leaders arrived in Moscow to open a Czechoslovak Exhibition, and Khrushchev made a long speech in which he demonstrated that, although Socialist Czechoslovakia had inherited more from the capitalist order than most other Socialist countries, prewar Czechoslovakia was still an unhappy country suffering from periodic slumps and unemployment. The papers continued to publish angry articles about Western Germany and Adenauer.

Significantly, *Pravda* of May 5 reproduced in full Walter Lippmann's article on Berlin and other "Summit" subjects, "even though disagreeing," as it said in an editorial note, "with some of Lippmann's views."

Lippmann's main points were these:

Although the rest of the world was in a state of ferment, things in Europe had, more or less, settled down. Neither East nor West had any serious intention of reuniting Germany; nor was the West challenging the Oder-Neisse Frontier. The only serious bone of contention between East and West in Europe was West Berlin; and this was, above all, a matter of prestige. But West Berlin had no solid juridical or political basis; nor was there any hope, in a foreseeable future, of Berlin becoming the capital of Germany. It was therefore in the interests of the West to negotiate with Khrushchev a new statute for West Berlin, a statute of a permanent international kind, supported by all sorts of international guarantees. Otherwise, without a political future as the capital of Germany, the Berliners themselves would gradually lose interest in their city, and it would wither away.

May 2, May 3, May 4—still nothing was said about the U-2 spy plane. Instead, on May 5, the papers were full of the rather startling news of the new appointments and dismissals made at the Plenary Meeting of the Central Committee of the CPSU on the previous day.

A. N. Kosygin, N. V. Podgornyi and D. S. Polyansky were appointed full members of the Presidium of the Central Committee; A. B. Aristov, though remaining a member of the Presidium and P. N. Pospelov remaining a candidate-member, were relieved of their posts of Secretaries of the C.C.; same with N. G. Ignatov and E. A. Furtseva, all of whom were given other appointments (Furtseva, for example, being appointed Minister of Culture). F. R. Kozlov was appointed Secretary of the C.C., while remaining a Member of the Presidium. As against this, N. I. Beliayev and A. I. Kirichenko were excluded from the Presidium of the Central Committee.

The demotion of Beliayev was attributed to the fact that something had gone seriously wrong in Kazakhstan and particularly in the Virgin Lands there; the further demotion of Kirichenko, who had for so long been Khrushchev's right-hand man, was something the man-in-the-street in Moscow found no easier to figure out than the Soviet expert in America or Western Europe. Nor was it at all clear to any outsider why, for example, Furtseva had been appointed Minister of Culture, rather than G. A. Zhukov, who was thought in Moscow to be the most likely candidate for the post.

But all this was still relatively unimportant. The first Khrushchev bombshell came towards the end of his long speech at the meeting of the Supreme Soviet on the afternoon of May 5. He started his speech with a routine discussion of the new law that had been proposed abolishing income tax in the case of lower salaries and wages, the proposed new currency reform and other economic matters. And it was not till he had spoken on these questions for nearly two hours that he came to his international survey. He started by giving an even more pessimistic view of the Summit than he had done at Baku some ten days before; he again attacked Adenauer, Herter, Dillon, and Nixon, saying, in particular, how regrettable it would be if President Eisenhower cut his visit to Paris short and handed over to Mr. Nixon: it would be like "asking the goat to guard the cabbages." He (Khrushchev) did not doubt Eisenhower's sincere desire for peace; but, unfortunately, his powers were "being limited by certain circles," and Nixon certainly belonged to these.

And Khrushchev then, "on instructions from the Soviet Government," solemnly announced the violations of Soviet sovereignty by the United States that had taken place "in recent weeks." First, there was the spy plane of April 9 which had, with impunity, penetrated into Soviet air space; the question of sending a protest to the USA had arisen, but, since the plane had not been brought down, this was considered useless; instead, a severe warning had been given to the Soviet anti-aircraft defenses to see to it that this did not happen again. Sure enough, encouraged by their impunity, the American military decided to repeat their exploit on May 1. This time the plane was shot down (*loud cheers*). After giving a warning to "our good neighbours," Turkey, Iran and Pakistan, and saying that the Soviet Government intended to submit the matter to the Security Council, Khrushchev hastened to give Eisenhower the benefit of the doubt:

Had this flight been authorized by President Eisenhower, or had this act of aggression been committed by the militarists from the Pentagon without the President's knowledge? It would be very disquieting if military juntas could, after the model of General Franco, take the law into their own hands. . . .

While asking the outside world not to underrate the strength of the Soviet Union, Khrushchev still ended by appealing to the United States Government to "stop the cold war and stop all provocations" and by saying that he would still go to Paris "with a pure heart and the best of intentions." Only it was no use trying to talk to the Soviet Union from "positions of strength" or to extract one-sided concessions from her.

On the following day the Soviet press reported from New York and Washington the "bewilderment" caused in the USA by Khrushchev's revelations, but also the "hysteria" with which certain American papers were now calling on the United States Government to "sink the Summit—once and for all."

On May 7, speaking again before the Supreme Soviet, Khrushchev, with a great display of malicious glee, showed up all the lies the American authorities had thought up since his first speech by revealing that the U-2 plane had been shot down near Sverdlovsk, and that the airman, Francis Gary Powers was alive and in Russian hands. And there followed all the various snappy details about the "poison needle" and about the gold rings with which Powers "was perhaps hoping to seduce lady-Martians."

But again, as in his first speech, Khrushchev was determined to give Eisenhower the benefit of the doubt:

> Having received a report of my last speech, Mr. Hagerty declared that, in his view, President Eisenhower knew nothing about the plane incident. I think it quite possible that the President knew nothing about this plane having been sent over Soviet territory and not having returned. . . . But, as I said last time, such impudence on the part of the military, acting on their own responsibility, may well lead to the most disastrous consequences.

In conclusion Khrushchev said that what had happened would not cause the Soviet Union to increase its military expenditure, or reconsider its peaceful international policy; but it had already led to certain organizational changes in the Soviet armed forces: a "general command for rocket troops" had been established, and its commander-in-chief was "a wonderful gunner, who had already distinguished himself during the war against Nazi Germany, Chief Marshal of Artillery Nedelin."

But things went from bad to worse. Whether Khrushchev was willing, or not, to look upon the U-2 flight as an unfortunate isolated incident, the explanations that now came from Washington no longer made it possible for him to do so. At a reception at the Czechoslovak Embassy on May 9, Khrushchev still tried to be jocular about the affair, making hay of the "extreme embarrassment" shown by the United States government; it was, according to Khrushchev, Allen Dulles who had put the United States Government in such a spot. But the Russian tune changed from this kind of jocular *badinage* to real anger on May 11 as a result of the Christian Herter statement: this was the third official American statement on the subject.

Near the new "American Exhibition" in Gorki Park, where the remnants of the spy plane were shown to an angry Moscow public, Gromyko gave a press conference to 500 journalists. First, he recalled the "completely mendacious" American statement of May 5, then the further statement by the State Department of May 7 which no longer tried to deny the flight deep into Soviet territory, but still claimed that the United

States Government had not been informed. But on the day before, May 11, came the third official American statement, this being made by Herter in person; to describe this statement as "cynical," Gromyko said, was to put it much too mildly. Herter had proclaimed these spy flights as part of a set American policy, which had been approved by the President of the United States; in fact, the State Department (and the President) had given the military a completely free hand in this matter. The line Herter had taken was that these flights were "necessary for the national defence of the USA." All this, Gromyko said, was an incredible violation of international law, and of those very principles of national sovereignty to which the American Congress had subscribed on several occasions in the past. In answering questions, Gromyko said that Khrushchev had made it plain that if anything like this happened again, the Soviet Union would strike at the bases harboring the American spy planes.

This press conference with Gromyko was followed by an impromptu press conference, in the same Gorki Park, with Khrushchev, who just "happened" to turn up there.

He started by being extremely angry, referring to Herter's "impudence, real impudence." Herter, he significantly added, had "put President Eisenhower in a very awkward spot. I should not like to be in Mr. Eisenhower's place, when he comes to the Soviet Union, because questions *are* going to be put to him. But I can say this: the Soviet people are polite people, and there will be no excesses of any kind; but the questions certainly will be put to him." Significantly, too, Khrushchev repeated twice in the course of this press conference that, if the matter were properly handled by the American side, "the incident would be digested in the end." He even said that the "incident" would not necessarily be put on the agenda of the Summit Conference. He thought America's other Western partners—de Gaulle and Macmillan —were not at all pleased with what the Americans had done. And, in conclusion, he again appealed to the Western press to say nothing which would increase the tension still further:

For our own part we shall do everything so that the present tension could be "digested"; we want international relations to return to their normal rut, and we want good relations to

be restored between the Soviet Union and the United States—
but the USA will have to help in this.

But, as against this, he used some very threatening phrases
from which he hoped countries with United States bases would
draw the right conclusions.

Again (on May 13) *Pravda* quoted at great length another
Lippmann article sharply attacking the State Department for
having, after it had been caught telling childish lies, thought
up a new and unprecedented policy of "justifying espionage,"
espionage being something which "should never be admitted."
This, among other things, was putting countries like Turkey,
Pakistan and Norway in an extremely awkward position.

It is curious how the Soviet press should have reported
Eisenhower's own press conference, in which he endorsed
the Herter statement, only indirectly—for example by quoting some sharp criticism of Eisenhower in some Greek
papers. But in reality, it was this endorsement by Eisenhower
himself of the Herter statement, which in Khrushchev's view,
almost finally ruined the chances of the Summit. During the
next few days more and more mass meetings were being held
all over the Soviet Union to condemn "the aggressors and
the warmongers."

Though looking glum, Khrushchev, nevertheless, in arriving at Orly, paid the appropriate compliments to the French
people and to General de Gaulle, and expressed the hope that
the Summit meeting would be successful, despite the attempts
made by the supporters of the Cold War to wreck it.

After shaking hands with M. Roger Frey and a few other
official personages, he then drove straight to the Soviet Embassy; then went for a walk through the Paris streets; after
that he drove to St. Germain—where he had himself photographed on the famous terrace—and, from there, to the
Soviet Embassy *datcha*—formerly a royal hunting lodge—
near Brunoy. Here he spent the night. In the morning, seeing
a neighbor mowing his lawn, Khrushchev went up to talk to
him, took the scythe from him and showed that he, too,
could handle a scythe very competently.

It was during that night that the Russians launched Sputnik
IV weighing 4.5 tons.

After a big breakfast and his morning exercise with the

neighbor's scythe, Khrushchev, accompanied by Marshal Malinovsky and Mr. Gromyko, and escorted by a dozen motorcyclists, drove back to Paris. The night before, he had asked to be seen by General de Gaulle and Mr. Macmillan—but not by President Eisenhower. At 11.30 A.M. he arrived at the Elysée, still accompanied by his two ministers. In the afternoon he saw Mr. Macmillan.

It was clear from the start to both the French and the British that Khrushchev was in an uncompromising mood and was unwilling to discuss anything with Eisenhower, least of all the U-2 incident, unless he received a formal and public apology for this violation of Soviet sovereignty, a promise to punish those guilty of what had happened, and a firm undertaking not to continue these flights over the Soviet Union. De Gaulle tried to minimize the importance of the U-2 flights, saying that Sputnik IV was, after all, going to fly over France hundreds of times, to which Khrushchev is said to have replied: "I swear by God Almighty that there is no photographic equipment on Sputnik IV"; as for Macmillan, he pleaded rather plaintively with Khrushchev, begging him not to wreck the good work that had been begun. Khrushchev stuck to his guns; international law had been violated; the U-2 flights showed that America was threatening the Soviet Union with war and that, in such conditions, no honest and sincere discussions could take place. In the afternoon, Khrushchev returned to the Soviet Embassy in an angry and morose mood; there he worked on the "declaration" he was going to make on the following morning at the preliminary meeting of the "Summit."

The coverage of the Summit by the Soviet press was a curious mixture of angry polemics and sentimental idyllic descriptions of Khrushchev's casual meetings with "ordinary French people"—such as a little girl called Annie Laporte whom Khrushchev met in a small food shop in the rue de Grenelle, and "whose head he stroked paternally."

This was followed by an angry polemical article on the preliminary meeting at the Elysée at which Khrushchev not only put again his demands to Eisenhower, but also declared that, in present circumstances, his visit to the Soviet Union would be untimely and inopportune.

Most significant of all, however, was the reproduction in full, on the front page of *Pravda* of May 18, of Walter

Lippmann's article on just why, in his view, Khrushchev had decided not to go on with the Summit Conference. Lippmann's main points were these:

The Summit meeting had broken down because of the U-2 plane or rather, because of the position taken up by the United States Government and the President. Khrushchev had done his best to leave the door open for Eisenhower by saying he did not believe the President knew anything about this flight. Instead of taking advantage of this opening, Eisenhower had openly challenged the sovereignty of the Soviet Union. When on Monday Eisenhower told Khrushchev that the flights would be "suspended," this came too late. If Ike had said this a week earlier, it might have made all the difference. For during the past week, the Soviet Union had managed to put the fear of death into America's allies with bases round the Soviet Union. Against the Soviet demands that their territory be no longer used for American spy bases, countries like Japan, Pakistan, Iran, Turkey or Norway hadn't a legal or moral leg to stand on. The Soviet Government would not miss this opportunity of weakening, if not destroying, the system of bases surrounding the Soviet Union. Russia's aim was to neutralize these countries, and she would not miss this opportunity of pushing them a long way towards such neutrality. Moreover, it had become clear to the Russians during the past few weeks that the United States Government—or France, for that matter—was determined not to budge an inch on the question of Berlin, despite the assurances given to Khrushchev by Eisenhower at Camp David; there had been a very marked hardening in the American position since about the middle of March.

The fact that *Pravda* should have reproduced this article in full is highly suggestive. It shows that, in the main, it agreed with Lippmann. Short of a major diplomatic victory for the Soviet Union in Paris (an unequivocal and public apology from Eisenhower—which would also have the appropriate repercussions in Japan, Turkey, etc.), the Summit no longer made any sense. Without such an apology, the "Camp David" spirit could no longer be kept alive, and there was nothing "positive" that Khrushchev could bring back to Moscow.

And Lippmann certainly put his finger on the sorest point of all: which was the fact that the United States had "challenged" the very concept of Soviet sovereignty, which implied a breakdown of the system of "international legality" on which Khrushchev was hoping to build up "coexistence." In this sense, the breakdown truly marked the end of an "optimistic epoch."

For let us remember this. For several years past, and especially since 1955, Soviet foreign policy—culminating in the Khrushchev visit to the USA—had been moving in a certain, fairly definite, direction; now the direction had clearly changed, except that "ultimately," as Khrushchev was to say, the doctrine, indeed the "objective fact," of coexistence would have to be recognized by the West; but the Soviet Union could "wait." This fact that the Soviet Union could "wait"— and not only six or eight months, but much, much longer— was new; so was also Khrushchev's announcement to the effect that Soviet Russia had managed to live for 42 years without any Summits, and could live without them for another hundred years. What had happened to all the "urgency" which Khrushchev had never ceased stressing?

This was new—and a little grim; it meant the breakdown of *the* Khrushchev policy, and its replacement by something new and uncertain—except that he never ceased reiterating that a world war was still inconceivable and out of the question—short of somebody going crazy on the American side. But that there would now be a return to the Cold War was, unfortunately, sufficiently clear. But a Cold War of a kind that again was different from the Cold War of the late 1940s and early 1950s, with Russia remaining in the main on the defensive, and the West indulging in containment, roll-back and brinkmanship tactics.

Although a large part of the Western press went out of its way to show that Khrushchev had "wrecked" the Summit, it is extremely difficult to see how Khrushchev could have taken part in the Summit in view of the position taken up by the United States Government and Eisenhower. Even as a purely psychological demonstration of mutual goodwill (i.e. without any concrete results of any kind) the Summit could, in the circumstances, have made no sense. Khrushchev had no illusions about anything being achieved either in the field of disarmament or in the German field; and, as a "psychological success" it would have been possible only if there had been a real Soviet-American reconciliation (in effect a Soviet diplomatic victory) over the spy-plane "problem." There is little doubt that Khrushchev was desperately anxious to secure such a reconciliation—which would have, to some extent, marked *a continuation of his previous policy;* his failure to obtain satisfaction explains the extreme exasperation with which he spoke at that final press conference at the Palais Chaillot. And, at the back of his mind there must well have been the idea (already suggested by Lippmann) that if the West wanted their spell of Cold War, then the Russians had a number of cards to play which they hadn't had before: Japan, Turkey, and other countries with American bases were restive, while the upheaval in Africa was taking on unprecedented proportions—or so at least the Russians thought.

Much was, of course, made in the Western press of disagreements inside the Soviet Central Committee where, it was alleged, Khrushchev's "Western" policy was being severely criticized; even more was made of the great ideological row on revolutionary tactics which, it was claimed, had broken out between Moscow and Peking. Peking had certainly made a great song and dance over the U-2 plane as a demonstration of the perfidiousness of Khrushchev's "friend," President Eisenhower, and of the fallaciousness of Khrushchev's "Western" policy. All this may well have had *some* effect on Khrushchev's whole attitude in Paris; but even if there had been no pressures from inside the Central Committee or from China, it is *still* difficult to see how Khrushchev could have adopted a more "conciliatory" line in Paris; Russian anger had genuinely been aroused both by the U-2 and the subsequent American statements; and Khrushchev himself felt personally insulted and betrayed: after all the raptures he had gone into over his visit to the United States during the previous autumn he had now been made to look a fool and a simpleton. This personal frustration accounted for a great deal both in Paris and after—particularly for his personal anger against the "feeble and gutless" behavior of Eisenhower.

Little need be said on the last two days of Khrushchev's stay in Paris. Pointedly he went on the Tuesday morning with Malinovsky to a village in the Marne department where, back in 1917, the Marshal had been billeted as a soldier of the Russian Expeditionary Corps fighting together with the French against the Germans on the Western Front; summoned back to Paris by de Gaulle—the message was carried by a motorcyclist—Khrushchev inquired whether the meeting called at the Elysée was to be a "preliminary" meeting or a regular meeting of the Summit; since it was meant to be a regular Summit meeting, Khrushchev refused to attend, in the absence of the apology he had demanded from Eisenhower. Then, on the Wednesday, Khrushchev gave his farewell press conference, at which he was angry and abusive and which was even more chaotic than it might have been if the interpreters had been a little more competent.

He started with a brief "historical survey" of what had happened since May 1; then dealt with Eisenhower's promise to "suspend" the flights over Soviet territory—an assurance which, Khrushchev indicated, was wholly insufficient and did not imply any apology for what had happened before.

Then he thanked de Gaulle and Macmillan for the efforts they had made to make the Summit meeting possible; but regretted that they had not taken a sufficiently "objective" view of what had happened, and had not, therefore, been sufficiently firm with Eisenhower. And then came the rather chaotic questions and answers; here Khrushchev likened America to cats that were eating the cream or were getting into the pigeon-house, and explained what one had to do with such cats; he threatened again the countries that were harboring American spy planes; said he would sign a peace treaty with Eastern Germany "whenever he thought fit"; said he had had some doubts about "my friend" Ike even at the time of the Camp David talks; and that was why he had not raised with him the question of the spy planes which (he already then knew) had been flying over the Soviet Union; he patted the Latin-American countries on the back for having shown Nixon where he got off, and gave a tremendous boost to "the heroic people of Cuba"; he fumed against the "Nazi hecklers" whom, he said, Adenauer's agents had sent to this conference; but ended, all the same, on a conciliatory note; he still believed that the Soviet Union and the United States would be friends, and that if not the next government, then the government "after that" would realize the absolute necessity of coexistence and Soviet-American friendship. Asked about the American election, Khrushchev made this singular remark:

I believe the American people will have the wisdom to elect a worthy president. But if they elect an unworthy man with whom it will be difficult for us to agree, and who will not have understood the necessity of living in peace with all countries, including the Socialist countries, well, we'll just have to wait for the next election; if then again a man is elected who doesn't understand the necessity of peaceful coexistence, we shall just have to be patient again. We are not in a hurry! Our road—the road to Communism—is clearly mapped out before us, so we know where we are going. Sooner or later, I am sure, you will follow us.

There was something rather desperate in Khrushchev's manner when he said: *"We are not in a hurry!"* It meant that he was ready to postpone an agreement with America for ten, fifteen, twenty years. But what would happen meantime to the armaments race which, Khrushchev had so often said in the past, could *not* be allowed to drift? The very suggestion that disarmament was *not* urgent, that Russia could wait indefinitely, pointed to a kind of desperate and irresponsible mood on Khrushchev's part. And to all of those who saw him that day, he was, clearly, an unhappy man.

There was some nervousness about the visit he was going to pay to Ulbricht and Grotewohl in Berlin on his return journey to Moscow. But it soon became apparent that he was not going to do anything very rash and dangerous. No peace treaty with East Germany was going to be signed yet—much to the disappointment, one might add, of the East-German leaders. It is even said that Grotewohl was so disgusted that he failed to see Khrushchev off at the airfield when the Soviet premier left for Moscow.

Chapter 26

FROM SUMMIT TO UN ASSEMBLY—
ENTER AFRICA

IT WAS A very strange summer indeed, that summer of 1960. Perhaps the two most striking things about it were (*a*) that Soviet foreign policy continued, even more than before, to be very much a one-man show, with Khrushchev holding, seemingly quite unassisted, the center of the stage, and (*b*) that after the fiasco of the Paris Summit in May he seemed—whatever his private views on the subject were—to have lost interest in resuming important conversations with the United States, Britain and France—at least in the immediate future. True, soon after the Paris breakdown, he put forward new disarmament proposals, and although he said that, of all the problems pending, disarmament was the one which could *not* wait, his whole tone suggested that he had no great illusions about meeting with any constructive response.

Instead of persisting with any idea of coming to an early agreement on anything with the USA and her partners, Khrushchev—and, indeed, the Soviet press—made it quite clear during the months that followed the abortive Summit, that Soviet foreign policy had shifted its ground. A variety of new factors had entered into the world situation which could no longer be ignored or treated as being of only secondary importance now that the prospect of an agreement with the Big Three of the West had gone for the present. To exploit these factors now *might* greatly strengthen the Soviet Union's hand if and when there *was* another Summit.

The most striking proof of a new stage in Soviet foreign policy having begun was to be seen from the sudden interest the Russians were now showing for the GPRA—the "Provisional Government of the Algerian Republic." So long as the Russians had hoped to come to terms with de Gaulle, they had deliberately cold-shouldered Ferhat Abbas and his colleagues, even though these had been treated with regal honors in Peking. Not that Moscow had now decided to follow in the footsteps of Peking; as Khrushchev's famous speech at Bucharest in June was to show, there were still some sharp ideological differences between Moscow and Peking, notably on the question of the "inevitability of war"; what is more, Khrushchev seemed genuinely piqued and irritated by some of the comments made in China about the Paris Summit having finally demonstrated the fallacy of his "Western" policy.

It would be rash to conclude that Khrushchev had completely shifted his ground from his "Stalinist" "Socialism in one country" (or rather, bloc) position—which was, in a sense, the true basis of his "peaceful competition" and "*rapprochement* with America" policy—to a "Trotskyite" or "Comintern" policy of "world revolution." It wasn't as simple as that. Where Khrushchev differed from some of the Chinese ideologists and other "Leninist purists" was in the great value he attached to the crystallization in the world of a Third, Neutral Force. And this tied up with two relatively new phenomena—(*a*) the development of "neutralist" tendencies among several of Russia's neighbors—not least among those who had started scratching their heads after the ominous warnings given them by Moscow as a result of the U-2 incident—notably Norway, Turkey, Iran and Japan—and (*b*) the spectacular speed with which the "colonialist order" was breaking down, not only in Africa, but also in Latin America, and in the first place in Cuba. No single country received more space in the Soviet press during that summer of 1960 than Cuba; a great deal of space was also given to all the various new independent countries of Africa, with top priority first, for Sekou Touré's Guinea as the least suspect of being still under "neo-colonialist" domination, and, later, for the Congo, which was in the gravest danger of being run by so many "imperialist puppets." In the Russian view, Lumumba was not perhaps the ideal leader, but he was the only one representing something like an anti-colonialist central government.

It would, indeed, be a mistake to think, as has been suggested, that the Russians, with little or no experience of Africa, were extremely naïve about the "national-liberation movements" there; time and again, the Soviet press stressed that there was practically no élite in the Congo—no technicians, doctors, or administrators; and that, in their absence, a new state like the Congo was severely handicapped in making a start. One Soviet diplomat even complained to me on one occasion that the Congolese were "pretty impossible people"; the Belgians had left them in such a state of ignorance that they didn't know a Russian from an American—that was why, at the height of the trouble in July, a Soviet press correspondent—"just because he was a white man"—was beaten up! In many ex-French colonies, the situation was bad, too (with only 6 per cent of children in the Gabon going to school) but nowhere was the situation as bad as in the Congo. And the Russians were also aware of the fact that in some countries the new native leaders had been "bought up by the imperialists"—for instance it was openly alleged that practically the whole government of Togo were, if not exactly pro-British, at any rate fanatically pro-Unilever. But so long as these countries were reasonably "neutral," there was not only hope of "peaceful competition" between the two blocs developing there, but also of these countries becoming part of a very important neutral bloc at the UN and elsewhere. Needless to say, the expulsion of the Soviet and Czechoslovak Embassies from Leopoldville was something that the Russians took extremely badly, and contributed to their resentment against Mr. Hammarskjöld. But, in reality, the Russian onslaught on Hammarskjöld had deeper and more far-reaching motives than appeared at first sight.

And so, on May 28, before a meeting of Shock Workers in the Kremlin, Khrushchev made his first big speech since the collapse of the Summit. And he now also angrily related how the Security Council had failed to condemn the spy-plane's flight over the Soviet Union. World opinion had, at any rate, been informed of the Soviet complaint to the Security Council; and that was something; as for the Security Council's "verdict," nothing much could have been expected even with such a foolproof case, since the majority of the Security Council were America's allies or flunkeys.

But the matter would be put before the General Assembly.

And again he spoke with great bitterness of Eisenhower, and of that Camp David meeting at which the President had addressed him as "my friend." "May the Lord preserve me from such friends, and I can take care of my enemies," Khrushchev said.

He went on for a long time. He said he was gratified to learn that the Norwegian Government had protested to the USA against attempts to use Norwegian bases for spy planes; the attitude of the Pakistan Government was more ambiguous; and Khrushchev therefore warned Pakistan once again that the Soviet Union would take "appropriate measures" if any more provocative flights took place from Pakistan bases. He further expressed the hope that better relations would be established with Turkey, now that the pro-American government had been overthrown there. Further, he warned Italy and Japan that the Soviet Union would take "the most resolute action" against any further spy flights.

But Khrushchev ended on an optimistic note: Syngman Rhee had been overthrown; Batista in Cuba had been overthrown; there was an important change of government in Turkey; Kishi would soon be overthrown; things were on the move.

Malinovsky also made a speech at the Shock Workers' meeting at the Kremlin; his main theme was that "we must keep our powder dry." Significant was the manner in which he went out of his way to praise Khrushchev—it was like an answer to the rather far-fetched stories in the Western press about an alleged conflict between Khrushchev and "the Army." He, too, gave a "stern warning" to Japan and other countries with United States bases. A few days later the Soviet press reported that this warning had had "a very salutary effect" in Japan.

Although Khrushchev had said that the Soviet Union was "not in a hurry" and could "wait," he nevertheless called a press conference only a few days after his Kremlin speech, and produced another three-stage disarmament plan which, he said, should be examined by the 10-Power Committee at Geneva; the first stage was to comprise the elimination of the "means of delivery" of nuclear weapons, in accordance with the French proposals to that effect, and the setting up of an appropriate control machinery once this "elimination" had been agreed upon. As we know, this Plan was not accepted at Geneva, and the Soviet press ironically quoted the French press describing M. Moch's embarrassment at the difficulties that were being created by Britain and the USA over this "French-inspired" proposal.

Further *post-mortems* on the Paris Summit continued to be made, and the Soviet press gladly lapped up anything damaging to the USA—Drew Pearson's description of Macmillan's fury when he first heard of the U-2; Nehru's remarks to the effect that the USA had violated international law.

The attitude to France was becoming increasingly critical; not only was more and more space given to the war in Algeria, but—with a delay of two-and-one-half years— *Pravda* gave a tremendous display to Henri Alleg's book, *La Question*, describing how he had been tortured by General Massu's paratroopers.

About the middle of June, the Soviet press was jubilant over Mr. Hagerty's unfortunate experiences in Tokyo and the subsequent cancellation of Ike's visit to Japan. "One Fiasco after Another" was the title of *Pravda's* editorial on June 18, while the inside pages were devoted to gloating reports of the consternation caused in the USA by this "diplomatic Pearl Harbor." Yet despite several nights of rioting in Tokyo, the new American-Japanese Pact was ratified, all the same— a fact which was only briefly noted. In spite of this, it was argued, Japan was moving in the right direction.

There was a significant interlude in the midst of all this sniping at the USA. At the meeting of the WFTU in Peking, which opened in the second week in June, some sharp ideological differences were revealed between Moscow and Peking; at least according to Western sources, some of the Chinese went so far as to treat Khrushchev as a "right-wing revisionist," little better than Tito!

Be that as it may, Khrushchev decided that it was high time things were put straight with the Chinese. On June 12, *Pravda* went out of its way to attack "leftist deviationism" in an article on the fortieth anniversary of the publication of Lenin's *Leftism, an Infantile Disease of Communism*. A week later, Khrushchev left for Bucharest to attend the Congress of the Rumanian Communist Party, and here, on June 21, he went a great deal further than Kuusinen had already done in April to show that it was no use approaching Lenin from a purely "scholastic" point of view, without reference to the new conditions in the world:

The general line of our foreign policy was laid down by the Twentieth Congress and confirmed by the Declaration of the Communist Parties in November 1957 [signed also by the Chinese Communists]. . . . This policy is the policy of coexistence, of the consolidation of peace, of the reduction in international tension and of the liquidation of the "Cold War." Similarly, the Twentieth and Twenty-first Congress agreed that, in our time, war is not inevitable. What Lenin said about imperialism remains in force and will continue to be our guiding star both in our theory and our practice. But we must not forget that Lenin's arguments were put forward several decades ago when several elements, which are decisive in the historical development today, were still absent. . . . Some of Lenin's theses on imperialism related to a time when there was no Soviet Union yet, and no other Socialist countries. . . . There are now over a billion people in the Socialist Camp. . . . Now there are more and more countries favoring peace amongst nations. Moreover, imperialism no longer has the colonial *hinterland* it had before.

Also, comrades, it is no use repeating mechanically what Lenin said several decades ago, and to go on maintaining that imperialist wars are inevitable, so long as Socialism has not won throughout the world. . . . The time may come when capitalism will be maintained in only a small number of countries —some of them maybe not much larger than a coat button. Are we even then still to go on looking up what Lenin said about the "inevitability of imperialist wars"?

And he concluded with a further attack on "scholasticism," saying that if Marx, Engels and Lenin could rise from the dead, they would pull the ears of those who were being so stupid as not to take account of "the real co-relation of forces and the concrete realities of the present time."

Not that Khrushchev absolutely excluded the possibility of an "imperialist attack" on the Soviet Union or on the Socialist Camp; but he thought it extremely improbable in view of the Soviet Union's military might—not to mention Hitler's sad experiences in that field.

This Khrushchev pronouncement was important and generally reassuring; it showed that, whatever capital he was planning to make of the "neutralist" forces that were taking shape in the world, he had not abandoned the principle of coexistence with the West. But the various changes that were taking place in Africa and elsewhere were, at the same time, providing the Soviet Union with new opportunities which it would be wrong to miss altogether. . . . Hence a certain "dualism" in Soviet foreign policy which had not yet been fully apparent in the heyday of the Soviet-American *rapprochement*—a *rapprochement* the reality of which Khrushchev had clearly overrated. Both Khrushchev and, with him, Soviet opinion had been somewhat carried away by the overoptimistic Soviet propaganda drive that had followed Khrushchev's visit to the USA.

The Bucharest Communiqué, signed by the Communist and Workers' parties present (including those of China, Korea and Vietnam) reaffirmed the Declaration and Peace Manifesto drawn up by the same parties in Moscow in November 1957. They reiterated (much to Khrushchev's satisfaction) that it was "possible to prevent war in present conditions," and while repeating what had been said in 1957 about the working class in capitalist countries being able to establish Socialism "by peaceful means," they now added that, in some countries, it might be possible to achieve a Socialist revolution only by "*unpeaceful means.*" Was this a concession to Peking? But if so, it was mainly a verbal concession, and, below the surface, some serious differences continued between Peking and Moscow.

And now, at the end of June, there began a confused period—which was to last right up to the UN Assembly, and which was marked by growing friction between the Soviet Union and the West, and by Cuba, the Congo and the rest of Africa taking up more and more space in the Soviet press. The Geneva disarmament talks were, in Khrushchev's view, getting nowhere, and he informed Macmillan, de Gaulle and Eisenhower that the Russians were withdrawing from the talks; the whole matter, he said, could be more usefully discussed by the UN Assembly.

Soon after his return from Bucharest, Khrushchev went on his visit to Austria; the whole atmosphere of this trip was on the chilly side, and was marked by a few angry explosions from Khrushchev at various press conferences—above all about Adenauer and the Bonn Nazis who, he said, were already dreaming of another Anschluss.

editorials or furious dispatches from O. Orestov, the *Pravda* correspondent in the Congo. On August 6, he reported that, encouraged by Mr. Bunche, "Tshombe was becoming more and more insolent"; on the 7th, he spoke of the "collapse of Hammarskjöld's mission"; adding: "The traitor Tshombe is triumphant after Hammarskjöld had decided not to send UN troops to Katanga." A few days later Orestov was equally angry because Hammarskjöld had gone to Elisabethville with 300 Swedish soldiers; Ghana, he reported, was "reacting sharply against Tshombe," while Lumumba "had lost all confidence in Hammarskjöld."

On the face of it, one might argue that the Russians were taking an oversimple view of the Congo situation; in reality, they knew how great the difficulties were for a man like Lumumba; thus, on August 29 *Pravda* reported that "only a very small number of Congolese have any higher education at all; and of the 36,000 school-teachers who are to start teaching this year, 26,000 have not even completed their elementary education." Clearly the Soviet Union could not embark on sending thousands of her own people to the Congo; even apart from the language difficulties, it seemed a hopeless venture. But the anger against Hammarskjöld continued to be kept up—if only because he had not given any support to Lumumba.

In reality, however, Hammarskjöld's admittedly not very brilliant handling of the Congo situation was little more than a pretext for starting a campaign in favor of reorganizing the UN on different lines. No doubt, Khrushchev's attack on Hammarskjöld misfired at first; but that did not mean that the campaign in favor of a "trinity" or "troika," comprising the Neutral Bloc, would be abandoned. The "trinity" principle could, at any rate, be applied to disarmament, if not to the UN as a whole.

It seems at any rate, that after the various new complications that had arisen in the Congo and the expulsion from Leopoldville of the Soviet and Czechoslovak Embassies—a pill not easy for Khrushchev to swallow—the Russians decided to rely much less on their direct intervention in the Congo than on the growing anger the developments there had arouse in Ghana, Guinea and other African countries.

Cuba was the other country to which an enormous amount of attention continued to be given in Moscow during the two months preceding the famous General Assembly meeting. On July 21 a communiqué was published after Raul Castro's visit to Moscow; there was a mass meeting, in Moscow, too, at which "We are with you, Heroes of Cuba!" and similar slogans were displayed. An official TASS statement and learned articles by Soviet historians were published to prove that the Monroe Doctrine was "a rotting corpse."

Chapter 27

THE SOVIET UNION ENTERS THE
DECISIVE (?) SIXTIES:
REVOLUTIONS, COEXISTENCE—OR
BOTH?—LAST WORDS ON GERMANY

IT SEEMS UNNECESSARY here to describe in full detail that
memorable "all-star" General Assembly of the United Nations to which Khrushchev sailed on board the *Baltika*, taking
with him Gomulka, Georgiu Dej, Kadar and other Communist leaders. This journey to the United States was very
different from Khrushchev's visit in September 1959. He
was scarcely on speaking terms with the Americans now, and
his whole manner—complete with the shoe-banging episode
at the UN—was truculent and defiant throughout. He was
determined to make friends with as many African leaders as
possible or, at any rate, to make on them a very big impression as the defender of Congolese unity and independence
and number one friend of the underdeveloped countries
and number one enemy of both colonialism and neo-co-
lonialism.

Pages and pages in the Soviet papers were devoted not
only to Khrushchev's own speeches, but also to speeches by
the more "trusted" African leaders like Nasser, Nkrumah
and Sekou Touré. More spectacular still was Khrushchev's
overwhelming cordiality to Fidel Castro, whom, much to the
dismay of United States authorities, he went to visit at his
third-rate hotel at Harlem—to whose Negro population all
this was fantastically new and exciting.

The attacks on Hammarkjöld scarcely abated for a moment, though Krushchev persisted in saying that these attacks were not directed against the Secretary-General personally, but only against Hammarskjöld as the representative of the capitalist bloc, as the defender of American and

Belgian colonialist interests in the Congo. For although Sweden ranked as a country of the Neutral group of powers, Hammarskjöld represented the capitalist bloc, and it was therefore more essential than ever to replace the chief of the UN by three chiefs representing the three groups of Powers. This was important both with reference to disarmament and to the correct use to be made in future of any armed intervention by the UN. On how exactly this "trinity" was going to work, Khrushchev was not, however, very explicit; in particular, did he imply, or not, that each of the three members of the "trinity" would be armed with the veto? [1] But from what he was to say later—notably to Walter Lippmann in April 1961—it was fairly clear that the veto principle may have been at the back of his mind from the start. He also said to Lippmann that there could be neutral *countries,* but that no *man*—no matter to what country he belonged— could ever be considered neutral. Hence the fundamental Russian objection to Hammarskjöld and to the excessive powers he wielded.

Among the other high lights of Khrushchev's activities at the UN Assembly were—apart from his non-stop campaign for disarmament—his official *de facto* recognition of the Algerian Government, and his proposal that the headquarters of the UN be moved from New York to Switzerland, Austria or—the Soviet Union. The desirability of this, he said,

---

[1] There was at first some confusion on whether he even implied this; one argument used against his plan was that, under a "trinity," the Soviet Union would "control two-thirds of the executive power at UN." At the luncheon given in Khrushchev's honor by Mr. Cyrus Eaton on September 27, the Soviet Premier said: "If these people think that the Neutral representative of the 'trinity' will always support the position of the Socialist countries, then I can only say that it doesn't say much for the capitalist position. It merely shows that the present policy of the Western powers is not meeting with much sympathy in the Neutral countries." (*Pravda,* Sept. 29, 1960.) This rather suggested that Khrushchev was thinking at that time more in terms of a majority vote, rather than in terms of a veto.

As for Hammarskjöld himself, as Sir William Hayter wrote in *The Observer* of April 9, 1961: "Vicious and repellent as this vendetta is, it is easy to understand. . . . Hammarskjöld is not a lackey of Western imperialism, but he is a Westerner all the same. However real his opposition to Belgian policy in the Congo, the Russians can be excused for feeling that he is not quite their kind of man."

had been made apparent by the insulting way in which he himself, Fidel Castro and, above all, a number of African delegates had been treated in "this so-called democracy, where racialism is still rampant."

But this bad-tempered explosion against the United States was perhaps merely a momentary impulse, produced by a good deal of bad humor and bad manners on all sides, rather than the cornerstone of a long-term plan—which the attack on Hammarskjöld was certainly intended to be.

Since Eisenhower was still President, the question of the future of Soviet-American relations hardly arose in the course of Khrushchev's stay in New York, apart from his usual reiterations about the necessity of disarmament, peace, coexistence, and so on. He also repeatedly stressed the fact that his chief aim in coming to the UN at all was to demonstrate to the world the absolute necessity of disarmament; but the real significance of his UN activities was in the public stand he took in relation to Africa, Cuba, etc.

Throughout, as already said, his truculence was much greater than it had been even during the most unpleasant moments of his visit to the United States in 1959. Something had, clearly, changed in the international atmosphere. The "revolutionary" tendencies in Soviet foreign policy were becoming more apparent, the "*status quo*" tendencies less apparent. The quarrel with Eisenhower had made it more difficult than ever to resist the temptation to make political capital out of the capitalist world's difficulties and embarrassments in the Congo, in Algeria, in Africa generally, and in countries like Cuba.

Khrushchev left the UN after three truly hectic weeks; he had left a very bad impression with the Western delegations, but he had enormously interested and intrigued most of the Africans and a certain number of Latin-Americans—which is, after all, what he had set out to do.

But the months that were to follow Khrushchev's UN fireworks and stink-bombs were to be singularly flat and inconclusive. True, there was the long meeting of the 81 Communist Parties in Moscow in December, and this ended in a somewhat uneasy compromise between the Russians and the Chinese, with the Russians admitting more openly than before the principle of recognizing and supporting the "just wars" of peoples for their liberation.

But fundamentally, even now the dualism of Soviet foreign policy continued. On the one hand, peaceful coexistence remained an essential part of this policy, with Khrushchev patiently waiting for the opportunity of reaffirming it together with Kennedy[2]—the new President whom he continued to treat with a marked show of politeness—at least up to the time of the CIA's Cuban fiasco. And even then, the tendency in the Russian press was to blame the CIA and the Pentagon, rather than Kennedy himself, for what had happened—but rather with the suggestion that *Kennedy was, unfortunately, a prisoner of "these people."* Could he, therefore, be taken any more seriously than Khrushchev had —erroneously—taken Eisenhower?

Needless to say, there was an explosion of rage—genuine rage—in Russia over the attempt to invade Cuba, just as there had been over the revolting murder of Lumumba.

But, as distinct from Laos, where the Patet Lao forces had been, more or less, openly encouraged by Russia, it was not practical for her to intervene in the Congo, except that Soviet diplomacy missed no opportunity of supporting the "most independent" of the African states in their sharp opposition to Western activities in the Congo.

Whether, or not, Russia was (apart from the rather special case of Laos) going to intervene in any "just wars" was to remain one of the great questionmarks. The general impression of Western observers in Moscow in May 1961 was that even if America herself invaded Cuba, the Soviet Union would *not* risk a nuclear war for Castro's sake; but she would certainly make things diplomatically so hot for the USA that the whole thing could only end in a vast international fiasco for Washington. This time, it was thought, Russia would certainly manage to mobilize practically the whole of world opinion against the USA.

As for fighting "small wars," however "just" these might be, Khrushchev had repeatedly asserted that small wars might easily lead to a big war, and therefore the utmost cau-

---

[2] He had disliked Nixon so much that he seemed relieved when Kennedy was elected, even though, on one occasion, he had remarked that there wasn't much too choose between them: "Two boots," he said, "make a pair."

tion had to be exercised: and small wars as such (for example, another invasion of South Korea by the North Koreans) were not to be encouraged. But "civil wars" could be different; if, for example, a major guerrilla war broke out in South Vietnam against the Diem régime, it might be possible, within reasonable limits, to support the "rebels." In this context, a significant admission was made by Khrushchev in his famous statement to Walter Lippmann in April 1961.

> Speaking of Iran (Lippmann wrote) . . . he said that she had a very weak Communist Party but that, nevertheless, the misery of the masses and the corruption of the government were surely producing a revolution. *"You will assert,* Khrushchev said, *"that the Shah has been overthrown by the Communists, and we shall be . glad to have it thought that all the progressive people in Iran recognize that we are the leaders of the progress of mankind."* . . . It would be fair to conclude (Lippmann commented) that he is not contemplating military intervention and occupation . . . but that he will do all he can by propaganda and indirect intervention to bring down the Shah. In his mind, Iran is the most immediate example of the inevitable movement of history in which he believes so completely.

In 1959, at the height of the Khrushchev–Ike honeymoon, Khrushchev did not speak in these terms; and it was certainly an odd new way of talking of a country with which the Soviet Union has diplomatic and, at least nominally, good-neighborly relations. Nominally—because, after all, what Khrushchev said about Iran and "the misery of its masses" he could just as easily also have said of India; but he just didn't. So it is clear that what was at the back of his mind were strategic, rather than "revolutionary" considerations, and that what worried him was not Iranian misery, but American bases.

In other words, what worries Khrushchev is Russian security, much more than "the inevitable movement of history" which, for all he cares, may be very slow indeed in places where it does not directly affect the Soviet Union.

Therefore, if Lippmann is probably wrong to attach great importance to Khrushchev's more outrageous remarks about the Shah of Persia, except insofar as the Shah is an American stooge (and the Russians still feel bitter about the fall of Mossadegh brought about by the CIA), he is a thousand times

right in saying that, to Khrushchev, the real key problem is
Germany and, above all, the question whether the West
Germany Army will be supplied with nuclear weapons or
not. Here, and perhaps here alone, will Russia ultimately
take very great risks—even the risk of a head-on collision
with the United States—if she thinks that the West German
Army will become an immediate menace to Russian security.

Lippmann's impression was that Khrushchev was "firmly
resolved, perhaps irretrievably committed, to a showdown on
the German question." We need not dwell here on the
various solutions that might be considered, including the
pis-aller solution of simply "freezing" the German problem
for two or three years, in the hope that some loose kind of
confederation could be agreed upon by the two Germanies
before this period was up. But, as Lippmann said, Khrushchev
was unlikely to call for a showdown in Germany—at least
until he had had an opportunity of discussing the matter
face-to-face with Kennedy.

There seems very little doubt that not only Khrushchev
himself, but Soviet opinion generally would be prepared to
take great risks to destroy the danger of a German provocation; the memories of World War II, as we have seen from
the foregoing narrative, are still very fresh in Russia. The very
genuine nation-wide enthusiasm for Sputnik or Gagarin
springs primarily from the thought that all these great scientific
achievements—not matter how infernally costly to a country
like the Soviet Union—are sure to act as a kind of warning
to America and, more important still, to Germany.

Whether the Soviet people are *vitally* interested in the
overthrow of the Shah by the hungry multitudes of Iran, or in
the liberation of Western New Guinea by Indonesia, or even
in the ultimate fate of Cuba or the Congo is much more
doubtful. Certainly, they are less vitally interested in them
than in Western Germany. The prospect of actively supporting liberation movements and revolutions all over the world
entails not only a variety of risks, but also involves considerable expenditure. There is still an enormous amount of
work to be done inside the Soviet Union. She can afford to
buy Cuba's sugar; but she cannot materially support dozens
of big and small revolutions all over the world; these will
very largely have to rely on their own resources—as indeed,

the Chinese Revolution did. Similarly, in the 1930s, even the Spanish Republicans had to pay cash for what little help they received from Russia; and, in this respect, the situation has not perhaps radically changed.

No doubt, Russia is a going concern, with enormous prestige in the underdeveloped countries, but her resources, only 15 years after the most devastating of wars, and with a vast arms expenditure, are not unlimited. Industrially, she has made stupendous progress; agriculturally, things are still very far from perfect. It is significant that during several weeks in the early months of 1961 Khrushchev should have put aside foreign affairs altogether, and should have toured the country to make angry and endless speeches to denounce all the mismanagement that was still going on on the agricultural—i.e. food-producing—front. There were grave doubts whether the Soviet Union would soon catch up with the USA in the *per capita* production of food.

Also, the feeling of security, prosperity and continuous progress, and that sense of euphoria and self-satisfaction which marked, in Russia, the period that followed Khrushchev's "epoch-making" visit to the United States, no longer appeared to be there any longer after the breakdown of the Summit—and ever since. No doubt, having quarreled with the USA, the Russians were feeling, more and more, on the side of the angels; and yet, one may well wonder whether, deep down, most of them would not prefer to count Uncle Sam among their principal friends, rather than men like Sekou Touré and Fidel Castro. For all this has a bearing on the internal situation.

With America as her friend—or at least as a truly "peaceful competitor"—Russia could afford, to some extent, to relax—even while on her "way to Communism." The new kind of Cold War, which began in May 1960, brought with it, as was to be expected, new austerities and new severities; the extension of the death penalty and the fierce campaign against "parasites," complete with the opening of deportation camps (which, in 1959, seemed a thing of the past) suggested that the new Cold War—if it continued much longer— might well turn the "liberal" Khrushchev Phase into a much sterner kind of system, under which essentially *un-Communist* coercion would once again take the place of sweet and comradely Communist persuasion. Would not this in itself slow down the "transition to Communism?"

Perhaps, in actual practice, these "camps for parasites" are intended to be no more than a severe warning to those blatantly violating the rules of "Communist morality"—even though they may do so, as said before, for "objective" economic reasons for which certain chronic weaknesses in the government and administrative machinery are responsible. It is these which create black-market possibilities and temptations. It is more than doubtful that Khrushchev wants to return to the old "NKVD system," though he probably thinks that a *threat* of a return to it may have a disciplining effect on the more unruly members of Soviet society. So the whip may be cracked from time to time.

Even so, there is something familiarly unpleasant in the whole idea, just as there is in the sporadic revival of McCarthyism in a variety of forms in the USA during the past year. The two beastly things—both, in a way, by-products of the Cold War—somehow tend to go together. An intensification of the Cold War would have inevitable repercussions inside both countries.

K AND K IN VIENNA

As we have seen, Khrushchev decided, almost immediately after the breakdown of the Paris "Summit" in May 1960, to "wait for Kennedy," rather than provoke any major international crisis anywhere. His eagerness to meet Kennedy, after the latter had been elected President, was very great, and it was something of an achievement of Soviet diplomacy to have brought about the "K & K" meeting in Vienna in June 1961, despite Kennedy's obvious reluctance at first to agree to it. During the two days in Vienna, the two K's had several meetings and, in the end, a very brief communiqué was published which, above all, pointed to some real agreement with regard to an "effective cease-fire" in Laos, and to the desirability of setting up there "a neutral and independent" government. Also, the two K's, having reviewed a variety of world and Soviet-American problems, had agreed to "remain in contact." On the face of it, it wasn't much, but it was something. Curiously, in Vienna, as well as during the days that followed, the Russians made the meeting sound much

more important than the Americans did—so much so that
even in the Russian version of the communiqué the English "useful meetings" was translated as "fruitful (*plodot-
vornyie*) meetings"; and Khrushchev seemed at first anxious
to produce the impression that the ice had been broken, and
that there had been a return to something like the "Camp
David spirit."

At the same time, it was quite clear that no real progress
had been made on any major problem: on Germany the
two K's seemed to talk at cross-purposes, one insisting on the
necessity of a German peace treaty implying a *de facto* recognition of Eastern Germany, the other insisting on the West's
inalienable rights in West Berlin—rights which, if necessary, it would defend by armed force. But in reality, there
were some indications of a possible compromise here as, indeed, there had already been in the last few months of
Dulles: one possibility mentioned was a maintenance of the
status quo in West Berlin against the—at least *de facto*—
recognition of East Germany by the West. But this was still
only a hope, and a separate Russian peace with East Germany remained a possibility.

No progress was made on disarmament either, even though
the Russians are extremely anxious about it—with an eye not
only on Germany, but also on China. But on the question of
stopping nuclear tests they now, curiously enough, seemed
in no desperate hurry,[3] and preferred to link the treaty on
the stopping of nuclear tests to at least a preliminary treaty
on general disarmament—a singular adoption by them of
Dulles's fruitless "package-deal" formula. This Russian switch
was largely attributed to their increased reluctance to submit to inspection, after the U-2 incident which had sharply
intensified their "espionitis." The CIA's exploits in Cuba had
not made things any easier. Moreover, they were still very
uncertain about the Kennedy Administration's attitude to
disarmament generally, but, at the same time, did not anti-
cipate any immediate resumption of nuclear tests by the
USA. So they could wait for a while.

On the reform of the UN Secretariat and, indeed, the extension of the "troika" principle, complete with the veto, to

[3] This, of course, was written before the Russians broke the
moratorium themselves and resumed nuclear testing in October.

disarmament and much else, Khrushchev seemed more determined than ever; one important card, Russians in his entourage asserted, which he had up his sleeve was this: after Hammarskjöld had gone in 1962, the *de facto* Secretary-General of the UN would, in the absence of any agreement about the "troika," be one of the Indian representatives, wholly unwelcome from the American point of view. In any case, Khrushchev obviously intends to persist with his "troika" idea. So it was till Hammarskjöld's death.

An "optimistic" story current in Vienna was that Khrushchev would, by seemingly unilateral concessions (peaceful settlement in Laos, no showdown over Berlin) appease certain Western countries, such as Britain and the Scandinavian countries, which are particularly worried about the rearmament of Western Germany. In this way he could play on fundamental Western differences. Was this wishful thinking?

And although, after Vienna, the Russians were all smiles, they seemed, deep down, worried about Kennedy. There had not only been the crazy Cuban adventure, but the USA had very nearly sent troops to Laos; and there were only too many people around Kennedy who were again thinking in terms of "containing" Communism with the help of small, non-nuclear wars, or at least with a constant threat of these. (A counterpart of the "just war" theory?)

"The trouble with Kennedy," one Russian observer remarked to me soon after Vienna, "is that, feeling America slipping in the world, he is calling on 'all the energies' in America to rally against Communism. That being so, it is extremely difficult for him to give a favorable interpretation to the Vienna meeting, since this might discourage the anti-Communist crusaders in America. When the *New York Post* talks about 'institutionalizing the Cold War,' and says that this is the new Administration's policy, it doesn't sound too good, does it? Perhaps Kennedy would like a genuine settlement with us, but no doubt he has to reckon, from the standpoint of his re-election, with the three most reactionary forces in the country (I mean in the international field): the Catholic hierarchy, the labor unions and the Southern Democrats. And then, of course, there are, as before, the Pentagon and the CIA. The truth is that we have a clear, cautious long-term policy, whereas with America, headed by a young, inexperienced and emotional President, we just don't know—and neither do you—where we stand, what with Truman's cold-warriors like Harriman and Acheson again getting busy."

"In fact," I said, "you are beginning to regret Eisenhower?"

"I wonder," my friend smiled. "Perhaps there's something in this idea that the Republicans are the peace party, and the Democrats the war party. What a pity," he added jokingly, "that they couldn't make Mr. Macmillan President of the United States! Anyway, we are rather anxiously expecting England to see that the USA—and Germany—don't do anything crazy. The English—look at their attitude to China, for instance—have a far better sense of history than the Americans have."

"Have *you* got a good sense of history?" I said.

"Not too bad, though occasionally we do oversimplify things a little. . . . But believe me, there is *no* oversimplification on our part where Germany is concerned. We understand Germany better than the West does. And we are not going to take any chances with the Fritzes. They've cost us 20 million people—the equivalent, let me remind you, of *17 million* American dead or *5 million* British dead. I wonder to how many in the West this has *ever* occurred. *You* saw the Leningrad blockade; *you* saw Stalingrad in 1943. So you remember."

"Yes, I remember," I said.

"And that's why we want the German and Berlin problems settled once and for all. Once that's done, we shall be able to breathe more freely."

"But after that," I said, "there'll still be Cuba, and the Congo, and all that. You'll still be interested in *them* . . ."

"Well, yes—up to a point; but only insofar as they will still be part of a natural and inexorable historical process . . ."

"In which you will want to have your say."

"Yes—and why not?"

Chapter 28

EPILOGUE: THE TWENTY-SECOND
CONGRESS AND AFTER

THE MOST SURPRISING THING about the Twenty-second Congress of the Soviet Communist Party was that it *was* surprising—perhaps quite as much, in its own way, as the Twentieth Congress of 1956, which ended with that famous "secret" report on Stalin. The publication in July 1961 of the party's Draft Program—that blueprint for the "transition to communism"—had led the uninitiated to suppose that this Twenty-second Congress would be a sort of apotheosis of the Khrushchev regime, a solemn consecration of ideas which had, in fact, been current over the last three or four years (i.e., since the defeat of the "anti-party group") in all theoretical party journals. These never ceased to suggest (as we have seen) that if, in the eyes of Marx and Lenin "full communism" was still a very distant ideal, the establishment of a Communist society had now, under Khrushchev, become an "immediate and tangible reality." It seems that Khrushchev himself took a very special pride in having made a world-shaking contribution to Marxist doctrine with his Draft Program (a large part of his twelve-hour speech at the recent Congress was, in fact, very largely a rehash of that interminable document). He and other Soviet leaders responsible for the document were proud of having brought forward some new formulas, such as the early replacement of the dictatorship of the proletariat by an "All People's State," and also of having laid down the lines for a much greater "democratization" of the whole hierarchy of Soviets, starting with the Supreme Soviet itself. Their plan for rotation of leaders promised a salutary blow at "bureaucracy" and would

334

enable "the people" to take a more direct and active part in running the country. Also, elections would be more democratic; there might even be two or more candidates for voters to choose from.

No doubt, there was still a lot in the Draft Program—and in Khrushchev's speech—which left many points obscure. Was it the party's intention, for example, to abolish gradually the *kolkhoz* system and replace it by uniformly wage-earning *sovkhozes*, i.e., state farms (which were, moreover, to be progressively "urbanized")? As we know, the Soviet peasant today still very largely thrives on being able to sell the produce grown on his private plot; and it is still very far from certain how valid the party's claim is that in "a growing number of *kolkhozes*" the peasants are finding it more profitable to surrender their private plots to the *kolkhoz* and to let the latter be turned into something increasingly like a state farm. If one follows the reports of the Congress, one finds that there still seems considerable uncertainty in the minds of the leaders themselves about what exactly to do in this matter.

The Draft Program was interesting in other respects, too. It contained, for example, a number of curious admissions about the peasants, who enjoy no automatic sickness benefits, no old-age pensions, no paid holidays; they still benefit far less than the "other" 50 per cent of the nation from that "welfare state" which the Soviet Union so greatly prides itself on being.

Over all these fairly awkward problems Khrushchev was to skate rather lightly; and, though he repeated, over and over again, the spectacular figures of industrial and agricultural production in 1980, the "ordinary" people in Russia were still rather uncertain as to how "communism" was really going to work in practice, especially in respect of food. Would agriculture progress as rapidly as industry? This was something on which Khrushchev himself seemed to have some doubts; for he kept on threatening that he would "pull the ears" of those responsible for agricultural production. And, as we know, the Virgin Lands are *not* producing as much as Khrushchev had hoped.

One could not but wonder whether these doubts about the success of Khrushchev's agricultural policy had not at least something to do with one of the big surprises provided by

this Congress—the obsessive harping on the crimes and misdeeds of the "anti-party group"—Molotov, Malenkov, Kaganovich and others—including the 80-year-old Marshal Voroshilov. Molotov, in particular, was being charged with all kinds
of sins—especially with wanting to cut down free public
services, to increase rents and fares; in fact, with having been
against *all* the more popular features of the Khrushchev
"welfare state." The trouble with all these doctrinal quar-
rels was that we heard only one side of the story: what,
in the secret councils of the Kremlin, Molotov had *really*
proposed, we just don't know, and he was not given a chance
to reply.

But one cannot escape the suspicion that all this non-
stop harping on the misdeeds of the long liquidated "anti-
party" group would have been totally unnecessary if there
were not, inside the party, some secret but genuine opposition to Khrushchev on vital doctrinal grounds, on the actual
methods to be employed in the "transition to communism"
and, last but not least, on foreign policy.

The whole problem of "peaceful coexistence and peaceful
competition" with the capitalist world was in the very center
of this Congress. Mikoyan declared:

Molotov altogether rejects the line of peaceful coexistence, reducing this concept merely to the state of peace or rather, the
absence of war at a given moment, and to a denial of the possibility of averting a world war. His views, in fact, coincide with
those of foreign enemies of peaceful coexistence, who look upon
it merely as a variant of the "cold war" or of an "armed peace."

One could not help wondering whether Molotov and the
rest of the "anti-party group" were not being used as China's
whipping-boys by Khrushchev and his faithful followers. For
something, clearly, had gone very, very seriously wrong in
Soviet-Chinese relations, which were never easy, and had now
deteriorated worse than ever.

The effect of Chou En-Lai's clash with Khrushchev, together with the everlasting attacks on Molotov & Co., had
shifted the whole attention of the world, including that of
the Soviet people, from the "epoch-making" 20-year program
to the present Soviet-Chinese conflict. Not only, as we know,

did Chou En-Lai publicly treat Khrushchev's attack on Albania as "something that we cannot consider as a serious Marxist-Leninist approach" to the problem (i.e., as something thoroughly dictatorial and "undemocratic"), but the Albanian leaders went out of their way to be openly abusive to Khrushchev, calling him a liar, a bully, and so on. It was extremely doubtful that the handful of Albanians who call themselves Communists could have done this without the direct approval of their Chinese friends. The big question was whether, in the name of a restored Chinese-Soviet solidarity, the Chinese would choose to persuade the Albanians to present their humble apologies to Khrushchev—or get rid of Enver Hoxa. These seemed about the only two ways in which the "unhappy incident" could now be closed.

But Albania was merely a symptom of a real *malaise* between China and Russia. There were other symptoms. Khrushchev, for all his bombastic prophecies about the inevitable decay of capitalism, was genuinely favorable to "peaceful coexistence" and wanted, above all, the Berlin and German problems to be settled peacefully; he knew that he was never more popular than at the time of the Russo-American "honeymoon" of 1959. But it seems that pressures against him were coming from somewhere—in the first place from China, but perhaps also from that "China Lobby" which, I had been assured in Moscow nearly two years before, exists on the quiet inside the party. To these people, solidarity and unity with China should be the real basis of Russia's future policy. And the Chinese, as the Albanian incident showed, had strong suspicions that Khrushchev was anxious to secure a "shameful" peace with the West. The fact that China (which is obsessed by Formosa—to Khrushchev a very small matter) should have been supported (up to a point) by North Korea and North Vietnam was highly indicative. And one could not but wonder whether Marshal Malinovsky, who was blowing hot and cold, exalting peace but also almost openly considering the possibility of preventive war against the West, wasn't trying to keep the Chinese quiet. And this brings us inevitably to the 50-megaton bomb. Was not this dropped primarily in order to "appease" the Chinese—especially after Khrushchev's "humiliating" surrender to the West in canceling the German peace-treaty deadline of December 31?

What did it all add up to? Indications are that Khrushchev (and, with him, the bulk of the Soviet people) favor peaceful coexistence and (with the exception of Berlin) the maintenance of at least a relative *status quo* in the world. The Chinese, North Vietnamese and North Koreans, on the other hand, feel that, militarily, Russia is strong enough to support them in the "just wars of liberation" they would like to embark on before long: with China attacking Formosa and the North Koreans and North Vietnamese liberating the southern half of their respective countries.

Perhaps, by the end of the Congress Khrushchev was in a more difficult position than any since 1957, when the "anti-party group" nearly liquidated him. He seemed strong enough inside the party to cope with any internal opposition; but if he was up against China's crusading spirit in world affairs, he was going to be faced with the most agonizing choice in his life. Support China? No. Break with China? Infernally difficult and perhaps disastrous. Or would he merely try, by all kinds of dangerous concessions, to persuade China to be patient?

In a way the end of the Twenty-second Congress of the Communist Party proved just as surprising and unexpected as its beginning, with the throwing out of Stalin's body from the Lenin Mausoleum as the grand finale. The Congress, which was to be essentially economic, giving its blessing to Khrushchev's plan for "laying the technical-material base" for the transition to Communism which would "in the main" be achieved by 1980, became more and more, as the days went by, like a direct sequel of the Twentieth Congress of 1956.

The "world-shaking" economic blueprint for the establishment of Communism in the Soviet Union was, as it were, being taken as read, and the whole emphasis was now being placed on the evils of Stalinism. What had been parts of Mr. Khrushchev's "secret report" in 1956 were now brought into the open—the cynicism and inhumanity of Stalin, the liquidation of Tukhachevsky and other top-ranking generals, and of "thousands" of innocent men.

It was no longer a case of denouncing the crimes and errors committed by Stalin "in his old age, under the influence of Beria," but of accusing him of crimes committed long before senile decay had set in. Most significant in this

respect was the almost open indictment of Stalin, by Khrushchev himself, as the murderer of Kirov in 1934—a murder
which was to let loose the whole machinery of the super-
purges of 1936-38 with their tortures and other monstrous
violations of "Socialist legality."

In the same breath, Molotov, Malenkov and Kaganovich,
in particular, were directly accused of having had numerous
people arbitrarily murdered by the N.K.V.D.

However, there was still nothing to indicate that there was
going to be anything in the nature of a public trial of these
men. It was quite obvious that if there were such a trial
without the horrible tricks of the 1936-38 purge trials, and
Molotov & Co. were to be given a fair hearing, in strict con-
formity with "Socialist legality," they would not only bring
forward a reasoned defense of their policies and criticism of
Khrushchev's, but they might even in counter-attacking, try
to show that Khrushchev's own record, as one of Stalin's
henchmen (particularly in the Ukraine after the war) was not
as impeccable as one was now led to assume. Had not the
Ukraine, too, suffered from arbitrary deportations and execu-
tions like the rest of the country?

On the face of it, this defense of "Socialist legality" and
the ever-repeated assurance that there would never, never
be a return to the monstrous methods practiced under Stalin
was calculated to make an excellent impression in the country at large, as was also the violent attack made by one
speaker on Vyshinsky, with his own "personality cult" and
his monstrous theory that "confession" was sufficient as evidence (a theory which, this speaker indicated, had not yet
been entirely discarded by Soviet jurists).

But all the news from Moscow suggested that a large part
of the public, and particularly the intellectuals, were extremely puzzled and rather bothered by the way the Congress developed, especially during its later stages. The most
striking thing at it was, of course, that 100 per cent
unanimity with which, officially, all these attacks on Stalin,
Molotov and the "personality cult" were approved and endorsed.

When the head of the Agitation and Propaganda Department of the Central Committee, L. F. Ilyichev, now promoted to the rank of secretary of the Central Committee,
thundered away, like the rest, about the "personality cult,"

people could not but help smiling quietly to themselves, for
Ilyichev had been one of the hardest and most fanatical of
Stalin men, and even quite recently, at a gathering of foreign
correspondents, he had angrily denounced all that "hee-
hawing" at Stalin that was going on abroad, Stalin being a
very, very great man, whose memory "every Russian will always cherish," he said.

To the Russian intellectuals, the most disturbing aspect
of the Congress was, indeed, the fact *there was not even the
remotest suggestion of anything in the nature of a free discussion of the Stalin issue.* Alexander Tvardovsky had, only
a year ago, been allowed to publish a poem in *Pravda* which
was a kind of semi-apology for his former Stalinism. (I quote
it in an earlier chapter.)

Now Tvardovsky, like the rest of the speakers at the Congress, joined in the chorus about the evils of the "personality
cult," and in the collective effort to build up a marzipan Lenin
under whom no innocent people were ever killed!

Everybody in Moscow knows that the attitude to Stalin
among the rank-and-file party men (so many of whom had
risen under the Stalin regime while many others still associate victory over Germany with Stalin's name) is an extremely mixed one, and the unanimous adoption, without
even the slightest suggestion of disagreement, of the resolution ordering his body to be thrown out of the Mausoleum
seems to have made a rather unpleasant impression: at this
"monolithic" Congress there was no more scope for any
sort of free discussion than there had been under Stalin.
As for the decision made "at the demand of the working
organizations of Stalingrad themselves" to change the proud
and cherished name of Stalingrad to "Volgagrad," this caused
the most widespread, though more or less tacit, annoyance,
and suggested to many something almost "pathological" in
Khrushchev's hatred for his former "dearly beloved leader."
But publicly, nobody appears to have protested.

In short, there was something singularly artificial about the
"debate"; on this, as on other questions (apart from minor
economic details) there was a distressing unanimity; everybody was toeing the party line laid down by Khrushchev.

There was, however, something even more artificial: after
Chou En-Lai had made his rather spectacular departure, after
accusing Khrushchev of an "un-Marxist, un-Leninist" atti-

tude to Albania, speaker after speaker continued to deplore the behavior of the Albanian "Stalinites," but not a single word was said about China.

It was quite obvious that strict instructions had been given by the leadership not to raise this awkward and fundamental question. At the same time, it was becoming increasingly clear to everybody that the "chuck-his-body-out" resolution was intended as an anti-Chinese demonstration.

Chou En-Lai had gone out of his way to lay an enormous wreath on Stalin's coffin, which (so the story went) had prompted Mr. Khrushchev to remark acidly: "If that's how you feel, why can't you take him away to China?"

For if the Albanians were "Stalinites," were not the Chinese "Stalinites," too—in all kinds of senses: not only was Mao the "Chinese Stalin" as Hoxa was the "Albanian Stalin," but, like Molotov, the Chinese would not subscribe to Khrushchev's basic doctrine of peaceful coexistence.[1]

It may seem paradoxical still to think of Khrushchev as the "man of peace," after the more-than-50-megaton bomb.

But it seems fairly clear what Khrushchev is aiming at. He, like most Russians, is obsessed by the "German problem"; to him, West Germany, rather than America, is the most "aggressive" element in the world. By creating further nervousness with his super-bomb, by trying to scare the Scandinavian countries into frantically appealing to the United States to get some sort of German settlement, he seemed, on the eve of 1962, to be aiming at the solution which was in the center of Gromyko's speech at the Congress. Stretching points mercilessly, Gromyko kept referring in the most glowing and extravagant terms to the Khrushchev-Kennedy meeting in Vienna as an event of immense historical significance, tremendous promise, and so on.

In short, what Khrushchev obviously wanted (though he left it primarily to Gromyko to say so) was a Soviet-American tête-à-tête, a Khrushchev-Kennedy meeting which would "save peace" *in extremis,* by producing some kind of general agreement about Berlin and Germany: for this alone would put an end to the present Russian military bluster-

---

[1] Here also, there is something of a quibble. It could very reasonably be argued that Stalin (who had invented Socialism in one country) was a "peaceful coexistence" man, and that China was being internationally "Trotskyite" rather than Stalinite.

ing, the insane shelter-mania in the United States and the growing war hysteria (the growing belief that "it's inevitable") which, as Khrushchev now knew, was by no means confined to the United States any longer, but was already spreading to Britain and, to a lesser extent, to the rest of Western Europe.

To Khrushchev, the rift with China (capable, it was thought in Moscow, of "starting something" in the present international situation) was making a settlement with the West not less urgent, but even more urgent.

For let us, in conclusion, hand it to Khrushchev; bluster or not bluster, he knows at heart (just as any responsible American must know it) that there can be no victory *for anybody* in an all-out thermonuclear war, and that virtually total annihilation of not only America and Russia, but probably of the rest of humanity, would be the most likely outcome of such a war. And yet Khrushchev fears that neither certain West Germans nor certain Chinese have yet been willing to face this near-certainty. Some Germans still think in terms of an initial knock-out blow, while some Chinese think there will always be enough Chinese to survive and conquer the world, without wishing to realize that with 600 million people concentrated in a relatively small area, China is even more immediately vulnerable than some of the others.

INDEX

INDEX

345

350 INDEX